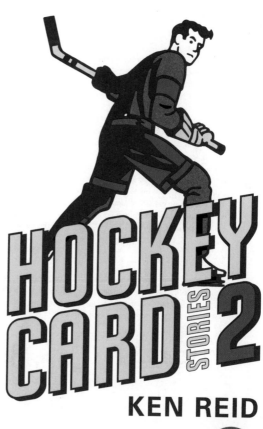

HOCKEY CARD STORIES 2

KEN REID

Published by ECW Press
665 Gerrard St. East
Toronto Ontario, Canada M4M 1Y2
416-694-3348 / info@ecwpress.com

LIBRARY AND ARCHIVES CANADA
CATALOGUING IN PUBLICATION

Reid, Ken, 1974-, author
      Hockey card stories 2 : 59 more true
tales from your favourite players
/ Ken Reid.

Issued in print and electronic formats.
ISBN 978-1-77041-350-4 (softcover).—
ISBN 978-1-77305-226-7 (HTML).—
ISBN 978-1-77305-227-4 (PDF)

      1. Hockey cards. 2. Hockey players--
Anecdotes. I. Title.

GV847.6.R452 2018   796.962075
C2018-902522-0

C2018-902523-9
Editor for the press: Michael Holmes
Cover design: Michel Vrana
Cover images: ©CSA-Archive/iStockPhoto
Interior image: Gum © Georgios Kollidas/
Shutterstock

The publication of *Hockey Card Stories 2* has been generously supported by the Government of
Canada. *Ce livre est financé en partie par le gouvernement du Canada.* We also acknowledge the
contribution of the Government of Ontario through the Ontario Book Publishing Tax Credit and the
Ontario Media Development Corporation.

Ontario
Ontario Media Development
Corporation

Canada

PRINTED AND BOUND IN CANADA

PRINTING: NORECOB   5 4 3 2 1

MIX
Paper from
responsible sources
FSC
www.fsc.org   FSC® C103560

To Jacoby and Langdon.
Thanks for the endless smiles.

KEN REID   TOC

HOCKEY CARD STORIES 2

When I was a kid, my dad had a binder full of old Pro Set hockey cards. I found it and started turning the pages. That's my first memory of hockey cards. My dad would tell me stories about when he played and who he played with. Then I would specifically look for his old teammates' cards. It was kind of a cool way for me to learn about the

Sidney Crosby   FOREWORD

game. It wasn't easy to get a lot of stats and information about players when I was a kid, but you could find out a little bit about a player on the back of his card.

I remember going to flea markets in Cole Harbour, the Penhorn mall in Dartmouth, and the big one at the Civic Centre in Halifax. As kids, we'd barter with the card dealers at the markets. Sometimes, we'd make trades with each other. True story, I once had a Mario Lemieux rookie card. I'm not sure if I ever told Mario this — I might have when I first got to Pittsburgh — but I traded his rookie card and it didn't go well. To put it mildly, I got fleeced. I traded my Lemieux rookie for the Pro Set Stanley Cup card and all the other trophy cards. It was not a great trade. I like to think today I would make better trades.

My favourite cards were the ones you got at McDonald's and the ones from Upper Deck. They showed the players out of their uniforms and were somewhat random photos but that's why I remember them. I remember one of Felix Potvin and his black lab, and Doug Gilmour in his Harley jacket, which has a story in the pages to come. I remember looking at those cards and thinking I'd never seen pictures of hockey players like that before. Until then, I had only seen pictures of players in action, never out of their gear. So that sticks out from when I was a young kid.

I remember when my rookie card came out, the card company gave me a huge stack of them. I looked at my card and thought, *this is cool.* I had collected cards for all those years and was fortunate to now have my own.

Of course, it's been a few years since my rookie card hit the shelves. In a few years, I'm sure people will look at it, like they do the cards in this book, and have a different take on it than when they first saw it. What will people think of my rookie card in 25 or 30 years? They may question if I was really 18, because I looked like I was 12. They likely won't even recognize that Pittsburgh jersey. It had a Vegas gold — kind of a different look back then. People will notice the equipment too. A kid looking at my stick might ask, "Why does he have a two-piece stick?" I had a wooden blade when I was a rookie. They probably would not have even seen that type of stick before. Guys I play with now don't even really recognize that stick.

I enjoyed the cards I had as a kid. They were one of my links to the far-off world of the NHL. There wasn't an NHL team in my hometown. You could not watch games or practices in person. I depended on hockey cards and the *Hockey News* and half-hour sport shows to keep me in touch with the NHL. That's really how the story and stats of the game were told to us, through the cards. As a kid, Toronto and Montreal seemed like they were on a different planet, so I had to watch hockey on TV or check stats on the back of a card. Checking your phone or going online to get the information you wanted wasn't an option. For someone like me, hockey cards provided what I considered important information about the game and the players I loved. They brought the game closer to me.

Enjoy the following pages.

— Sidney Crosby

Never meet your heroes. It's something you have probably heard before, and often you will find it to be true.

I remember a public autograph signing I was involved in for Upper Deck. The young basketball player showed up over an hour late with no explanation or apology. Fans were genuinely excited to see him and get his autograph,

Chris Carlin   FOREWORD

but he had nothing to say to them. He didn't smile for photographs. He would not shake the outstretched hands of fans coming through. It was awkward.

I experienced more and more of that behaviour over my early years of doing events and it caused my love for most professional athletes to wane. I wasn't dealing much with hockey, though. To be honest, I was not much of a hockey fan when I came to work for Upper Deck in late 1997. Growing up in Southern California, my passion was baseball, football, and basketball, so those are the athletes I wanted to meet.

An employee I worked with kept telling me, "Chris, you've got to do the NHL All-Star event." I had never gone because it's around the same time as other big sports events I liked going to. Finally, I acquiesced and booked my trip to the 2008 NHL All-Star weekend in Atlanta.

At the All-Star fan fair, I was surprised to see big-name players walking around with their families and friends. When we went to the parties, they were there and happy to talk with fans. When I was introduced to them, they weren't just cordial, they were downright friendly. I'm just an ordinary guy, but now I'm cracking jokes with millionaire superstar athletes. During the weekend, we ended up at an after-party in a sponsored suite. We were playing Guitar Hero with players like Brandon Dubinsky and Corey Perry. It was totally surreal.

Then I saw what they were doing on the ice, and I was blown away. They were exceptionally talented. They were incredibly tough. I was hooked and I had a new favourite sport with plenty of great players (both on and off the ice) to cheer for.

It wasn't too long after that when I met Ken Reid at the Sport Card & Memorabilia Expo in Mississauga, Ontario. After my first interaction with Ken, I remember thinking that he was a super nice guy who desperately needed some time in the sun. Now, understand, I'm pigmentally challenged as well, so I feel Ken's pain.

I was impressed with his remarkable hockey knowledge and genuine appreciation for the glory days of hockey cards. When Upper Deck came on the hockey-card scene, it was a game-changer. Over time, though, the collecting base grew more interested in exciting insert cards that contained pieces of game-used jerseys or authentic autographs from players instead of traditional "base" cards, even if they featured great photography.

Many purists like Ken still carry a flame for great photography on hockey cards, and card photography remains a huge priority for the Upper Deck company. You'd be surprised to know how hotly contested some topics are; raised voices can be heard outside conference rooms and offices as the decisions are made on which photographs will make their way into different card sets.

Upper Deck is almost fanatical about using the best photography available for trading card sets, especially the flagship Upper Deck Series 1 and Series 2 NHL sets. I love watching the image-selection process before the cards go to press and looking at the uncut sheets of those products coming through.

It is a thrill seeing collectors' reactions to the cards when they hit the market in shops or at events. What's even more interesting is when players get to see their cards and hearing their reactions to them. It's not something fans get to see or hear about, until Ken got involved.

In *Hockey Card Stories 2*, Ken will take you behind the curtain to ask hockey players what they think about some of their most iconic cards. Their responses are comical, enlightening, and, in some cases, surprising.

If you've read any of Ken's books before, you'll enjoy the easily consumable way he shapes the players' accounts of their trading cards. Each chapter feels like a mini novel, and Ken has a great way of pulling incredible stories out of all of them.

Remember when I told you to never meet your heroes? Forget about that. Grab your favourite player's card, wait outside after a game, and get it autographed. Ask the player what they think about the card and you'll be amazed by their responses. Not every player is fond of their cards, while other players adore them. Each card really does tell a story.

Ken Reid has been good enough to share several of these stories in this book, but I encourage you to make your own. My personal experiences with hockey players have all been great. Should you find a player who is not a pleasure to speak to, well, they are called trading cards for a reason. Go ahead and trade him!

— Chris Carlin, Upper Deck

BOB McGILL   1991–92
UPPER DECK #62

"I hate that friggin' card." Those are Bob McGill's first words to me when I get him on the phone. I'd left him a voicemail about five minutes earlier, mentioning that I wanted to chat about his 1991–92 Upper Deck card. Apparently, I didn't have to leave such a detailed message: "I knew which one you wanted to talk about as soon as you called."

Chapter One — STRIKE A POSE

I first met McGill in the summer of 1985, and I'll never forget it. When I was a kid, the NHL seemed like a far-off place, but on one glorious day a real-life NHLer appeared right in front of me. It was a typical summer day. As per usual, I was at the Pictou Golf Club, a little nine-hole overlooking the harbour. My brother and I were sitting in the clubhouse when our friend Kris Cooper ran in. He was holding a Maple Leafs postcard in his hand and screaming frantically. We calmed him down enough for him to tell us that Bob McGill, a Toronto Maple Leaf, was on the first tee. Kris had just gotten McGill's autograph. We sprinted out of the clubhouse. It was true. A large man with a Toronto Maple Leafs golf bag was about to tee off.

After McGill crushed the ball, we all headed his way. He was as friendly as he was big. He reached into his golf bag and pulled out a few more of his Maple Leafs postcards and signed them for us. McGill was married to a woman from our area. That postcard was soon tacked onto my bedroom wall. I still have it. From that day on, I was a Bob McGill fan.

I got my hands on his Maple Leafs rookie card but soon discovered a problem. That was the only Bob McGill card out there. Throughout his days with the Leafs, Bob McGill was in hockey-card purgatory: "I played seven years in the Leafs' organization, over 300 games, and I have one card as a Maple Leaf. You got your rookie card, but if you weren't one of the top seven or eight players on a team, you never got another card."

But McGill's patience finally paid off. When the card boom hit, his cards were everywhere. He's quite fond of his 1990–91 Pro Set: "It looks like I've got the puck on my stick and I'm coming around the net. I've got the head up; it's a nice shot." But as we both know, that's not what I really want to talk about.

I need to know about the pure beauty that is the No. 62 card in Upper Deck's 1991–92 offering. We're talking hockey hair, a half grin, and a high school photo half-turn pose. For some reason, the lighting even made Bob's hair look orange. So, yes, this card is wonderful — to me at least. The photo was taken at a hotel while McGill and several of his new teammates were in San Jose for a press conference promoting the NHL's newest team. "They were taking all kinds of different shots. From that same day, I think I got two or three other cards that are regular, straight-on shots. There were a couple of different background colours. It's kind of weird that my hair looks orange on the Upper Deck and on other cards it doesn't. I always get grief whenever anybody sees that card. I hate that card."

Grief? How could anyone give McGill grief over this gem?

"Someone will bring it out and go, 'Oh my God! You had orange hair! Did you dye your hair? Oh my God — you had hair!' Whatever."

So let's do a deep dive here. For the record, McGill's hair was never orange. The mullet — or as my brother and cousin Brandon and I used to call it, the Number 7 haircut — was all Bob. He wasn't alone. Circa 1990, this look was pretty much a basic requirement for an elite hockey player. "That's pretty tame right there. I had way longer hair than that before and it was shorter on the top . . . I had the whale tail going. It was hockey hair. Everybody had it, especially if you were a tough guy. To have the hair flowing was always kind of cool."

Now on to the pose: once again, McGill is not alone. A quick look at my high school yearbook reminds me that the pose was common at the time. The back turned, the head tilted — it happened. A very professional photographer had to be working with McGill in that San Jose hotel room, right? "They had guys doing all different kinds of poses. Guys were turning or standing with the stick held in front of them. They had guys with their stick up over their shoulder and their arms up over the top. It was one of those things where you get led into a room and they start taking all kinds of different shots.

"Craig Coxe had a stick over his head, with his wristwatch on. They had a pair of shoulder pads for us and a Sharks jersey for us to wear with number 91, because that was the first year. So that's what that was all about. I have a shirt and tie on underneath. So it's kind of weird."

Weird but fantastic — kind of like hockey in San Jose in the fall of 1991. I asked Bob how wild that first Sharks training camp was. San Jose loaded up with a lot of tough guys for their expansion season: guys like Bob, Craig Coxe, a young Jeff Odgers, and, of course, Link Gaetz. I thought it must have been a gong show. Wrong. "There wasn't really any fighting in camp. The coaches came in and said we don't really want any fighting going on. Some of the guys got pissed because that's how they thought they were going to make the team . . . We had some toughness, though, that's for damn sure."

Like most expansion teams, McGill's Sharks struggled. McGill had spent his previous four seasons in Chicago. The Blackhawks were a good team — they won the Presidents' Trophy under Mike Keenan in 1990–91. A few short months later, Bob McGill was a Shark, and it was so long, Chicago Stadium, hello, Cow Palace; so long, Iron Mike, hello, George Kingston. "I just finished playing for Mike Keenan for three years, and the first words that came out of Mike Keenan's mouth on day one of training camp were 'You think you know what hard work is? You have no idea what hard work is.' And he was right. I went to San Jose and it was a country club; it was a joke. Was Keenan an asshole sometimes? Sure, he was. But the bottom line was I wanted to win a Stanley Cup. And there was a lot of winning when I played for Mike Keenan. He was the best coach I ever played for. And then you go to San Jose, and the coach never got mad. He never swore. He used to come in and say, 'I don't get mad. I just want to get better.' He never yelled at anybody."

The guy who did get mad in San Jose was Bob McGill. It seems he took a little bit of that Mike Keenan fire to Northern California. One night in Toronto, Bob let loose. "Suddenly, you're 30 games in and it's the same guy making the same mistake over and over, and Kingston never got mad, never benched the guy. I snapped on the coaches. We were playing the Leafs, and the Leafs were shitty. And, remember, we were playing my old team. Well, we had a screw-around practice the day of the game. We used to do this thing where if you shoot right and I shoot left, we switch sticks, and you have a little game, where everyone is really awkward, to warm up. We did it at the morning skate the day of the game! What? Anyway, we lose and the coach came in and it was the same old thing. We'd just lost something like 11 in a row and it's 'Okay guys, we tried.'"

The guy with the grin on his 1991–92 Upper Deck wasn't smiling anymore. The San Jose honeymoon was about to come to an end. "I just had it. I still had all my gear on and I stood up and I threw my helmet on the ground, and I said, 'This is f@#$ing bullshit. We lose to that f@#$ing horseshit Leafs team?! We have a f@#$-around practice and so we f@#$ around in the game!' I went on for about a minute and a half, and then I just sat down."

The coaches left the room in silence. McGill had to apologize to the coaching staff: "I didn't want to apologize because what I said was the truth."

McGill was scratched for the next game. He was traded at the deadline a few months later. His tenure in San Jose lasted 62 games. "Needless to say, it was a great experience, to see what being part of an expansion team was like. The owner, George Gund, was unbelievable. He treated us great. At Christmas, he took the whole team — wives, girlfriends, and your kids if you wanted — to Sun Valley, Idaho, for New Year's. Gund chartered a plane and flew everybody there. We were there for three nights. We practiced every day, we partied. He treated us great. But they had the wrong people in place to start that franchise. You had a coach who never coached in the NHL before. It was a big mistake."

The San Jose Sharks have come a long way since Bob McGill and a few other players posed for those cheesy photos in the summer of 1991. The Sharks won 17 games as an expansion team. They are now one of the premier franchises in the National Hockey League, proof that hockey can work almost anywhere.

As for McGill, he makes his living as a broadcaster at Leafs TV in Toronto. The mullet is gone — in fact, all of his hair is gone — but the card lives on. Not that long ago, someone gave him a case of that particular San Jose card. McGill just shrugs it off. He ends our conversation with the familiar refrain of more than a few NHLers: "I wish I could find them all and burn them."

Here's hoping he doesn't.

TREVOR & JAMIE LINDEN

38

TREVOR & JAMIE LINDEN

Brothers Trevor and Jamie Linden both earned reputations as tough competitors in the rinks of the Western Hockey League. Trevor spent two seasons with the Medicine Hat Tigers of the Western Hockey League and was a member of a Memorial Cup-winning team each year. As the second overall pick in the '88 NHL Entry Draft, Trevor came to the NHL with high expectations and fulfilled his promise, scoring 30 goals and adding 29 assists while playing all 80 games in his rookie season. Though his production dropped in his sophomore campaign, Trevor rebounded with outstanding seasons in '90-91 and '91-92, setting career highs in goals (33 in '90-91), assists (44 in '91-92) and points (75 in '91-92). Trevor's leadership was recognized by the Canucks when he was named a co-captain of the team in '90. Younger brother Jamie matches his brother in size and strength, but has yet to prove himself as a scorer at the junior level. In '91-92, while splitting the season between Prince Albert and Spokane of the WHL, Jamie had nine goals and 11 assists in 64 games. The 20-year-old right winger is a physical player who, with time, will be a solid addition to any team.

Upper Deck and the card/hologram combination are trademarks of The Upper Deck Company. © 1992 The Upper Deck Company. All Rights Reserved. Printed in the U.S.A.

NHLPA

BLOODLINES

TREVOR AND JAMIE LINDEN

1992–93 UPPER DECK BLOODLINES #38

"That was at Kits Beach in Vancouver in the summertime," says Jamie Linden. "We had a bunch of different stuff on. We had Rollerblades. We had pictures taken where we were on Harleys. We did a whole bunch. Trev and I were like, 'We're not really Harley guys. We don't own Harleys so maybe that's not really appropriate.' We ended up picking that picture. It's a really great picture of my ass."

Big ass and all, Jamie Linden hit the NHL card market before he ever earned a spot on an NHL roster. A lot of people think he's wearing a Montreal Canadiens sweater when they see the card, but it's his Spokane jersey. "They had to block out the junior hockey crest because of their licensing agreement," he explains.

"I'm no card expert but Upper Deck was *it* at the time. They sent us Upper Deck jackets that were kind of cool. They got into doing deals with junior hockey players. Guys were getting some pretty good money on card deals. When you're 17 or 18 years old, it's a big deal."

When his card hit the market, Jamie Linden was trying to cut it in junior while his brother was a star in the NHL. Jamie was a high-ranked prospect but a bout of mono knocked him out for a large part of his draft season. No one picked him and he ended up playing as an overager in the WHL. He got an invite to the expansion Florida Panthers training camp in 1993. "I picked the Panthers because they were an expansion team. I thought that would be a better opportunity. I had a really good training camp and signed a three-year contract. I went to the minors and spent that whole year there."

That was year one of the deal; year two was something the kid on the card never envisioned. The NHL locked out its players, but Roger Neilson, the Panthers head coach, made Linden a promise. "I got called in. They said, 'We don't want to lock you out.' I was 22; they wanted me to play. They said, 'You're going to go down and play. And when the season resumes, we'll call you up.' And they did."

On February 9, 1995, Jamie Linden played his first NHL game at the

Spectrum, but it was not the dream he envisioned. "It was just brutal," he says.

"I was skating around and they were playing 'Welcome to the Jungle' for warm-up . . . great. Dave Brown was skating by and his ass was like four feet wide. I'm thinking, *Oh my God. This is the biggest thing I have ever seen on skates — the ice is breaking!* And Philadelphia had a good team — Lindros and LeClair."

So if the Panthers and Linden were going to run away with a win at the Spectrum, they'd likely need a big night from their goaltender, John Vanbiesbrouck. "So I go in and take an easy slap shot from between the blue line and the top of the circle, and I hit John Vanbiesbrouck right in the nuts. And he spent the whole warm-up bent over in the corner. I hit him right in the balls. I felt so bad."

That groin shot to Vanbiesbrouck was foreshadowing. Pain would be the theme of the night for Jamie, and for the first three games of his NHL career. "My first shift in the Spectrum, I got all my bottom teeth knocked out. I spent a period and a half getting stitched up. My bottom lip was hacked to pieces.

"I ended up in the dressing room and I'm thinking, *This is going to be easy. This is the NHL.*" But that Spokane jersey Jamie is wearing on the card would have fit right in with the medical room that night in Philly. Jamie Linden may have been in the NHL, but he was in for the junior treatment. "I'm in the Spectrum in a little room. There's a light hanging from a wire, and the doctor comes in with a suture kit, the portable ones like in junior hockey. There's no assistant. There's no nothing. The doctor is making the loops and I'm holding his forceps while he's clipping off the strings. I'm thinking, *This is the NHL? This is bizarre.* I thought they'd have a really fancy medical room. It's changed now, but back then it was just like junior hockey."

That was game one. Next up, game number two, two nights later, at home against Hartford. "I got hit and I ripped open my top lip. In two games, I had 130 stitches in my mouth."

Game three was the very next night. The New Jersey Devils were in Florida to take on the Panthers. The Panthers were kind enough to outfit Linden with a football face shield to protect his mouth. It didn't protect the rest of his face however. "I was on a line with Billy Lindsay and Rob Niedermayer. We hit a guy behind the net, my own guy's elbow came up and cut me over the eye. In three games, I had my bottom teeth knocked out, my lips looked like footballs, and I got cut over the eye."

This may be the toughest three game stretch to start an NHL career ever. Jamie was on the trainer's table for the third game in a row. "Roger Neilson had seen enough. I was sitting in the dressing room, and I could look down and see my lips. That's how massively swollen they were. Roger looks at me and says, 'You're going to take some time off.'"

Linden took some time off but eventually came back and played. After his return to the lineup, the Panthers told Linden he was staying with the team for the rest of the season. All he had to do was go back to Cincinnati, where the minor-league team was, pack his stuff, and return to Miami. But before he was able to return to Miami, he got a call. "They said, 'Look we're going to call up David Tomlinson for Stu Barnes,' because Stu had a bad eye injury. They wanted me to play that night in Tomlinson's place and go to Miami the next day. So I played . . . and I blew my knee out." Jamie's knee was dangling from his leg. He had to have reconstructive surgery and spent months rehabbing.

He never played in the NHL again.

"This is where Trev and I are polar opposites. My brother was the current NHL ironman at that time. The crazy part about it was when I blew my knee out, Trev got hurt the same night. The whole thing was really challenging. I was 22. I came back when I was 23. I struggled with the knee reconstruction. I was also in the last year of my contract. And by the next year, the team's new draft picks were starting to mature. I'm sure management was sitting there, going, 'Well, we're not going to invest time in a 24-year-old when we got 19- and 20-year-olds.' You become an old man pretty quickly."

Jamie Linden eventually retired at 27. He now runs a construction company in Vancouver that is responsible for building massive homes. We're talking 30,000 square feet. This card and other old photos are just a reminder of a life that was. "Trev and I went to a Florida Georgia Line concert at GM Place, and we were walking through the building and there are so many old photos. I see the ones of Trev, and they look old now. I remember as a kid going in there when Trev was playing and you would see old photos and now that's us.

"I have some friends that say, 'Hey, I came across your hockey card. You're standing backwards with your ass in the air.' I always say, 'Well, you know who picked that photo? Trev.' And when people ask me, 'How long did you play in the NHL?' I say, 'Long enough to get a hockey card.'"

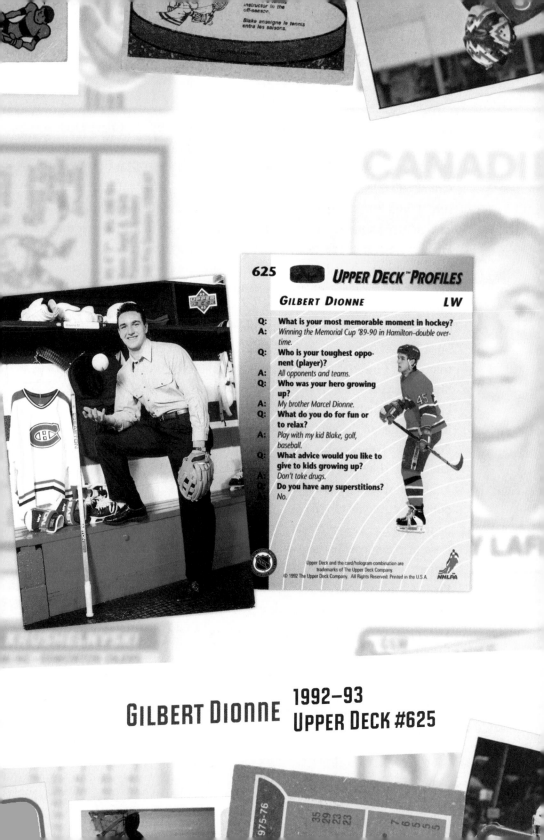

625 UPPER DECK™ PROFILES

GILBERT DIONNE — LW

Q: What is your most memorable moment in hockey?
A: *Winning the Memorial Cup '89-90 in Hamilton–double over-time.*

Q: Who is your toughest opponent (player)?
A: *All opponents and teams.*

Q: Who was your hero growing up?
A: *My brother Marcel Dionne.*

Q: What do you do for fun or to relax?
A: *Play with my kid Blake, golf, baseball.*

Q: What advice would you like to give to kids growing up?
Don't take drugs.

Q: Do you have any superstitions?
No.

NHLPA

GILBERT DIONNE
1992–93 UPPER DECK #625

In the early months of 1992, I dug through my boxes of Upper Deck cards looking for card number 448. When I had ripped open my Upper Deck packs a few months earlier, I had set aside the usual suspects: Gretzky, Lemieux, Selanne. But, like thousands of other collectors, I'm sure, I found myself going back through my cards looking for number 448: Gilbert Dionne's rookie card. It was the hottest thing going at the Highland Square Mall flea market every Sunday morning; his cards were being purchased at a remarkable rate. And why wouldn't they be? Dionne came out of nowhere and was a scoring machine for the Montreal Canadiens.

"You got Burnsy [Pat Burns] behind the bench, and it just keeps you on your toes. I think I just kept it really simple," says Dionne. "Thanks to injuries, I mean, Mike McPhee — Spuds — would tell me I cost him his job because I came up and scored 20 goals, and Spuds couldn't get back in the lineup. I was playing with guys who told me, 'Hey, just keep it simple. Get to the net, put your stick on the ice.' So I did. Things were flowing. Shayne Corson and Mike Keane just couldn't believe it. They said, 'Holy shit. Everything you touch goes in!'"

If you scored goals for the Montreal Canadiens, it meant immediate popularity. And that, of course, meant the following season, a card company would try to jam as many of your cards into their packs as possible. Case in point, this particular Dionne card. Much to my surprise, this picture was not taken in the Canadiens' dressing room. It was taken in Fredericton, New Brunswick. "I had just been sent down. I was a hot item at that point. I had 20 goals in 30 games. I got sent down for a few games and the reporter says, 'Hey, we need to do something different than hockey.'"

Upper Deck wanted to know a little more about the players off the ice. Wayne Gretzky wore a Toronto Argonauts jacket for his "Profiles" card. Back then, he was a part owner of the CFL team. Ray Bourque posed with a set of golf clubs. "The photographer asked me what other sports I like.' I said, 'Well, when I was a kid, I liked baseball and golf.' So he brought out a frickin' ball and glove and that was it. I just had to toss it up and down."

So there's a reason Dionne's wardrobe doesn't exactly scream baseball. "Which is terrible. I've got an ugly shirt on — it didn't even fit me."

The back of the card features a quick Q&A. Gilbert was asked, "Who was your hero growing up?" His answer? "My brother Marcel Dionne." Back when my buddies and I were scooping up Dionne rookies the previous winter, we all wondered if Gilbert was related to Marcel. In the pre-internet days, you got a lot of info from your cards. At first, we didn't think so — there is a huge age difference between Marcel and Gilbert — but his rookie card bio confirmed that Gilbert was indeed the brother of Marcel. "In junior, I slipped under the radar. I was 14 years old and I moved from Quebec to Niagara Falls to play some Junior B hockey. People thought maybe I was a cousin or he was an uncle. It didn't hurt me. There was a lot of pressure, of course, following in his footsteps. But like Marcel would always say, 'Hey, he's scoring the goals. I'm not out there to score goals for Gilbert.'"

The back of his "Profiles" card lists Gilbert's most memorable hockey moment as winning the Memorial Cup. Just a few months after this card was released, Dionne added some more hardware to his resume. In 1993, he and the Montreal Canadiens won the Stanley Cup. It was a magical run that featured an incredible 10 straight overtime wins. My buddy Sandy MacKay and a few other guys did the 13-hour drive from my hometown of Pictou, Nova Scotia, to Montreal for Game 1 of the Final against L.A. I was just a kid. There was another kid too, down on the ice, playing a huge part in that magical Montreal run to the Cup against the L.A. Kings. "When I raised that Cup, I was exhausted. And I pointed to Marcel in the stands to show him we did it as a family and with the Dionne name. I was in the room and everyone is overwhelmed and they want to take pictures. And I'm like, 'I'll win this again. No big deal, I'm only 21.'"

That's how quickly things came for Gilbert Dionne. He was a hockey card hero and a Stanley Cup champ almost immediately. And like a lot of other players on that Cup-winning team, he was an overtime hero. As I mentioned, 10 of the 16 games the Canadiens won that spring were won in OT. It was almost like they were trying to go to overtime. "I tried to tell people that we weren't playing to go to overtime, but when you have the best goalie in the world [Patrick Roy] who's not going to allow more than one or two goals a game, the odds were very good that it would be a tie game. But the confidence we had, the fun we had in the dressing room, the great leadership of Mike Keane, Brian Bellows, Kirk Muller, and Vincent Damphousse saying, 'Who's got the winner, guys?' And one guy would say, 'I've got a feeling. I've got a feeling this line is going to get a goal.' That's how I prepared myself. And then our line, Paul DiPietro and Gary Leeman and I, would say, 'Guys, should we go get that winner?' That's how much fun we had. We were relaxed."

Dionne scored the OT clincher in Game 3 of the second round against Buffalo. It gave the Habs a 3–0 series lead. But it did not come without controversy. Patrice Brisebois took a shot. Dionne, who was in front of Grant Fuhr, pointed to own his jersey to indicate that he had scored the winner. "I scored a goal and I kind of pointed to myself — I was caught up in the emotion, the excitement of the playoffs. That caused a lot of commotion at that time. But we stayed focused. We just carried on to the next game and so on."

Remember, all of this — the goal scoring, the attention, the Cup run — was happening when Gilbert was barely 20. He was a fourth-round pick who was suddenly a star on hockey's brightest stage. "Maybe it all came too fast. It didn't feel right that there was a Patrick Roy jersey and a Kirk Muller jersey and then a Dionne next to it. You're like, 'Wow, I just got here.'

"You can't go to school to learn how to deal with the media. You have to learn so fast. So I did say a few things I shouldn't have. Things just snowballed. It's Montreal, so everything you say is noticed, and it's not just one reporter per dressing room. There are 30 newspapers . . ."

Dionne figures a few things got lost in translation with the media over the years. One thing that didn't get lost in translation was that Cup win. But as fast as all the success came, it ended almost as quickly. Dionne was shipped to Philly in a four-player deal in February 1995. "You can play 18 years, like my brother did, and never come close to winning it. For me, it's all good memories. It's all good fun.

"Some guys struggle with life after hockey, but I just moved on. I don't need hockey in my life to make a living. But it's fun to talk about."

I recently spent time with Dionne at a Hockey Heroes event in Halifax, Nova Scotia. A horde of collectors was waiting for him to sign his old cards. Thanks to playing in the boom era, his cards are not in short supply. "I had 34 out there," he says, jokingly adding, "I was the extra card with bubble gum. You could end up on the bicycle wheel or get tossed on the wall at school."

But no one was tossing away Gilbert Dionne cards in the winter of 1992. I know, I was one of the guys paying anywhere from two to four bucks apiece for them. I still have 20 or so. I was a great collector, not always a great investor . . .

"I sometimes look on eBay at how much my card is worth, and it's funny. It's 25 cents, 50 cents. It's all good."

It's all good for the guy on the card, not so much for the guy who spent all of his high school allowance on them.

Todd Hartje — Center — Winnipeg Jets

568

Todd Hartje

Height: 6'1"
Weight: 180 lbs.
Born: Feb. 27, 1968
Anoka, Minnesota
Shoots: Left

YEAR	TEAM	GP	G	A	PTS	PIM	+/-
89-90	Harvard U.	28	6	10	16	29	
90-91	Sokol Kiev	32	4	6	1	16	
90-91	Fort Wayne	1	1		1	2	

NO NHL STATISTICS

Hartje became the first North American to play in the Soviet
Elite League when he started up for Sokol Kiev in '90-91.

TOD HARTJE 1991–92 UPPER DECK #568

"That picture was taken in Moncton. Upper Deck contracted the photographer. I don't know if he was from Moncton, but he was from somewhere in the vicinity. He came over to the rink after practice. I had been sent down from Winnipeg and he came and took the picture," says Tod Hartje.

I was always under the impression that his photo was from the old Winnipeg Arena. If I looked a little closer, though, I would have noticed the multi-coloured seats of the Moncton Coliseum. One of the first pro-hockey games I ever saw was a Moncton Alpines AHL tilt. In his AHL stint, Tod Hartje suited up with the Moncton Hawks.

The photo shoot started off like most, with Hartje skating towards the photographer, stopping, and snowing the lens. But then the photographer had an idea. In a shot perhaps inspired by Garry Unger's 1973–74 O-Pee-Chee classic, the photographer laid down on the ice and Hartje went to work. "He said, 'I want to try to take some from below here, with a slapper. He took a few and he goes, 'I think I like this.' I can still remember him talking about that shot."

A few months later, a large package from Upper Deck arrived at Hartje's house. It was a four-foot-tall version of his rookie card. As we all know by now, Upper Deck went with the low angle shot. "When you're a younger kid like that, that kind of stuff is cool."

The four-foot version of that card is currently missing in action. But it would give you a larger look at something that, to me at least, really stands out in the background. And it is a sign of the times. These days, you'd be hard-pressed to find a cigarette ad anywhere, let alone in a hockey rink. But there it is, right off Hartje's left hip, at the bottom of the scoreboard at the Moncton Coliseum, an ad for Export A Cigarettes. "Oh my God, that's funny. That *is* a sign of the times," says the Harvard grad. "I played in Fort Wayne for a bit my first year. I'll never forget, we had a couple of really good players there: Scott Gruhl, Bruce Boudreau, and a couple of other guys who were at the end of their careers. They literally had a smoking room off the dressing room. In between periods, they'd go in there and smoke. It was great."

Then I ask Hartje if there was more smoking in Fort Wayne or in Kiev. "Definitely Kiev. Oh my God. Our big excursion at night was to walk down the street, stand in a circle, and just smoke and talk. That was a big night out."

Sokil Kiev was the first professional team Tod Hartje ever played for. One of my favourite lines in *Slap Shot* comes from Charlestown Chiefs announcer Jim Carr. When notorious goon Ogie Ogilthorpe takes to the ice for Syracuse, Carr gives a brief bio of the curly haired enforcer. Carr tells his audience about Ogie's tough rookie season: the litigation, the deportation to Canada, that country's refusal to accept him. As Carr concludes, "I guess that's more than most 21-year-olds could handle." Well, Tod Hartje had one hell of an experience in his early 20s as well — likely more than most could handle. In his rookie year, as the bio on the back of the card says, "Hartje became the first North American to play in the Soviet Elite League when he suited up for Sokil Kiev."

As Hartje explains, this all happened at the start of the Russian invasion. Russian stars like Igor Larionov and Slava Fetisov were leaving Russia for the NHL. The NHL wanted to smooth relations with Russia so they figured they should send a player or two to Russia. The league turned to Winnipeg Jets general manager Mike Smith, who had a PhD in Russian studies. Hartje says Smith picked him for a few reasons, but the main one was that Smith figured that Hartje was the adventurous type.

Coming out of high school, Hartje did the unthinkable for any hockey prospect from Minnesota. Hartje turned down a full ride to play for the Minnesota Golden Gophers and instead chose to go to Harvard. Smith figured that any Minnesota kid who turns down the Golden Gophers must be the adventurous type. Right? "They did their due diligence and thought that I was crazy enough to say yes and that I'd be able to pull it off. When Mike Smith said, 'I want to sign you. But first I want to send you to Russia. Are you up for it?' I was like, 'Yes!' I knew it was crazy but of course I had to go."

In the summer of 1990, Tod Hartje headed overseas. He was on the ice for three practices a day in the middle of July and running through the Russian woods for dry-land training. He was taking notes too. Hartje ended up writing a book called *From Behind the Red Line*, about his year in Russia. "Hockey was such a minor piece of being in Russia. I would do it again in a heartbeat. It was tough, but it was the greatest experience I could have had as a 21-year-old kid."

Hartje says two things have stuck with him, almost three decades later, from his season in Russia: "Be thankful for everything we have here. Don't take things for granted. I had great parents who were really good at getting us to just enjoy life, enjoy what you have and all the good fortune that you have. When you go over there, you really see it. When people complain about how bad this is and that is, and how they're not getting their due, I'm like, 'You don't have any idea.' We have so many opportunities, so many avenues. So that's a big one that really has stayed with me.

"The second thing is the people over there were so great. I can't say enough about how good they were to me, accepting me. They had to accept me as a role player on their team and I was coming with the baggage of not speaking their language. But they were all great; the team, the players, the people, the city were just so welcoming and helpful. I took the lesson away to make sure that I always made the effort to welcome the new guy who joined my team. I want to make sure that when I see somebody who looks lost on the street corner, I ask if I can help — we don't do enough of that here."

The next season, Hartje was cut from the Jets and sent down to Moncton. Soon enough he was posing for this card. "When they took that picture, my career was sort of all in front of me. I had achieved everything I had set out to do up to that point in my life. You know, I won this or that, or made this team or that team. It sort of all just kept working out, until finally it didn't."

One month after the picture was taken, Tod Hartje's career came to a standstill. It's the kind of thing that happens to players all the time — it's also something no player is ever ready for: a major injury. "I remember the injury too well. We were killing a penalty near the end of a period. There was a faceoff to the left of our goaltender. I was the inside forward and we won the draw back. Our defenceman tried to shovel the puck around, but he didn't make it. I had to go into the Zamboni corner to chase the puck. The guy never stopped. He ran me from behind and my foot went into the little hole at the Zamboni door. I fell and it snapped.

"The next thing I know I was on all fours at the top of the circle. Apparently I had tried to get up about 10 times and skate back to the bench. I was messed up."

One of Hartje's teammates tried to ease the tension of the situation with a quick one-liner that still makes Hartje chuckle. "He looked down [and said], 'My God, Harts, guys will do anything to go golfing.'"

Hartje's first season in the AHL was done after 38 games, and his recovery lasted for an entire calendar year. He came back halfway through the next season but says he was never the same player. At the time he thought he was playing well, but, in retrospect, he can see how he changed. "There were a lot of indicators. I wasn't a fighter but I was a hard player to play against. I was a pain in the butt. But when I came back, I think I had two penalty minutes in the first 40 games. And usually, I would have 100, 150 minutes in a season. So clearly, in hindsight, I wasn't playing the same game. My aggressiveness, that extra step, was gone. You don't realize it at the time — you think you're back, but you aren't. You're not the same player."

The injury was both a mental and physical hurdle that Hartje says he had to overcome. He missed out on his prime window to make the Jets, when he was new to the organization. By the time he finally got his game back, the NHL was just too far away. "My last couple of years, I was a better player than I ever was before, but by then I was a 26-year-old guy. I didn't have that special step. I didn't have that special shot. I was just a really smart two-way player who could play in any situation, but I wasn't special at anything.

"In the grand scheme of things, it was a great lesson. It helped me be a better dad, and it definitely helped me to be a better coach. Nobody worked harder at practice. And if I was at a workout, I worked my butt off. But I didn't shoot pucks every day. I didn't go find extra ice. I did it within my seasons; I did it within the structure of the team. I didn't work as hard as I needed to; I didn't do extra work on my own."

Hartje's AHL career ended in 1996 with the Providence Bruins. He played a few ECHL games over the next few years. His final game was with the Toledo Storm during the 2002–03 season.

He says his family isn't one to display their athletic achievements around the house. His sons, however, do have binders full of hockey cards. Hartje left the game with a lifetime full of experiences. Life in Russia, life riding the buses in the American League, a devastating injury, his own book, and his very own hockey card (where his first name is misspelled "Todd") — all before he was even 25 years old.

I love this card. It's the great photo that led me to call up Tod Hartje and dig a little deeper. This card is kind of the poster boy for *Hockey Card Stories*. It's not worth much, maybe a nickel, a quarter if a dealer is really sticking it to you. But it has a great story, and to one kid, at least, this thing is pretty much priceless. "I did notice the other day that my youngest son has my card leaning on a puck on his dresser . . . but, of course, it's behind his Sidney Crosby stuff."

KEITH, WAYNE & BRENT GRETZKY

...e backyard rink at Walter and Phyllis Gretzky's ...me in Brantford, Ontario, played a key role in ...ng the hockey careers of their sons, Wayne, ... and Brent. Wayne became a professional at ...ge of 17 with the Indianapolis Racers of the ... Hockey Association in '78-79. A year later he ...n his NHL career with Edmonton. Over the ...ng 13 NHL seasons with the Oilers and the ... Wayne won nine scoring titles and ...ned four Stanley Cup-winning teams. He is a ...time NHL MVP and is the league's career ...ato in the third round of the '85 NHL Entry ...following his second season in the Ontario ...y League. After two additional junior ...gns, Keith began his professional career in ... splitting the season between Rochester of ... and Flint of the IHL. Since that time Keith ... played pro hockey in Finland and Britain ...ost recently, with San Diego of the IHL. ... Brent, the youngest of the three Gretzky brothers, ... had 43 goals and 78 assists for 121 points in 62 ... '92. He was drafted 49th overall in the OHL in '91- ... Entry Draft by the Tampa Bay Lightning.

KEITH, WAYNE & BRENT GRETZKY

BLOODLINES

BRENT GRETZKY

1992–93 UPPER DECK BLOODLINES #37

A question to Brent Gretzky about a simple hockey card takes the conversation in so many different directions. We talk about how close he felt to a career in the NHL when this card hit the market; we talk about his brothers, Keith and Wayne; about his dad; and about the time he faced off against his older brother, the Great One, in a NHL game. And, of course, we talk about my favourite VHS tape of all time. It was called *Hockey My Way* — an instructional video put out by Wayne Gretzky. My brother and I watched it religiously. We couldn't get over how lucky Brent Gretzky was. He was just a couple of years older than us, but he was on the ice with his older brother and Kevin Lowe, being put through the paces. So how did he end up in the video?

"Keith might have declined, I don't know," says Brent. "That took a long time to make. It was fun. It was cold. It was at the local rink. I can't remember times other than playing the one game against Wayne, being on the ice with him. In the backyard, if Wayne came home for a day or two, we'd get out there in boots maybe. Just being on the ice and being able to pass and skate with him are great memories."

It was hockey Wayne's way, but it was hockey Wally's way too. Wayne used a lot of drills in the video that Walter used to put his boys through on their famous backyard rink in Brantford, Ontario. "The passing and the pylons were my favourite drills in the video. Skating with the pylons. That's what Dad emphasized a lot in the backyard: puck handling and the pylons, making your dekes. We were out there all the time trying to perfect that."

Brent perfected his skills enough to be chosen 49th overall in the 1992 Draft. A few weeks later, he got a call. He was wanted for a hockey card. "Upper Deck was coming around and they wanted to do a picture with the three of us. The next thing you know, I was asked to fly to San Diego. I believe Keith lived there. He played with the San Diego Gulls. We ended up doing the picture there."

For Brent, the photo shoot was a great chance to hang out with his older brothers. There's an 11-year age difference with Wayne and five years with Keith. When Brent was going through the paces on the back-yard rink, Wayne and Keith were already deep into their pro careers.

"Keith, from what I hear, was a tremendous hockey player. He just bounced around a little bit in the minors. He put up some good numbers when he played. He worked hard. I think he was a little bit smaller, and back then, when he played in the IHL, that was the federal of all federal leagues. There was no obstruction being called back then, that's for sure.

"And it was a great time just hanging out with Wayne. Whenever I get a chance to hang out with him, it's always a great time. I cherish every second, whether it's golfing or getting the brothers together. I played golf with him once down in Carolina. He taught me a punch shot from under a tree. He was the Great One, but he was a big brother too, and those are the times that I think about. I have such respect for him, not because he's somebody, but because he's a big brother."

Being on a real NHL card with his brothers was also a dose of reality for Brent. He was one step closer to playing in the NHL. The photo shoot for the card made it all seem quite real. "Absolutely. That comes next: it's the draft, and then your hockey card. To be on a hockey card, it's going to be around forever. To get a card, you feel like you're a part of that sport."

A few months after this picture was taken, Brent Gretzky played in his first NHL game. Eleven days later, he played his second. The second is the one that sticks with him. The Tampa Bay Lightning played the Los Angeles Kings. It was little brother versus big brother; Gretzky versus Gretzky. "It was the best thing in the world to play against my brother."

There were only two things missing: Gretzky's parents, Walter and Phyllis. "My dad was going through his aneurism recovery. So, unfor-tunately, he wasn't able to be at the game in Tampa. I know for a fact that they all watched it at the house. But not having our parents at the game, that sucked, for lack of a better word. But, you know, that's the way life is. But they were always there to help us and support us and give us everything that we needed to play. We talked to each other after the game. It was just a great moment."

The Gretzky brothers did not talk much on the ice. "I saw him just at the start of the game, in warm-up. We had made plans earlier to go for dinner after the game." But they did go face to face on the ice. More specifically, right in the dot. Both Wayne and Brent are centres, so they did face off against each other several times.

"I think I lost maybe four in a row. Finally I won one and the crowd cheered."

Brent also got a strong dose of just what it was like to be on the ice playing against the greatest player on the planet. "One time, he had the puck in his own zone and I saw him. I'm forechecking, and I'm thinking, *I got you. You gotta come out the other side.* And just like he did to many other players, suddenly he was in my zone and I was behind his net wondering, *Where the heck did he go?* He's that quick. He's that smart. I was looking for my jock, that's for sure."

Brent has a few copies of this card floating around and, who knows, maybe there are a few in his father's famous Brantford basement. "I'm not sure. He has glass cases downstairs for the three of us and I think it might be buried in there with our sweaters. There might even be Wayne Gretzky rookie cards down there. I don't know."

Before I say so long, there's just one more thing I need to know. One of my great takeaways from *Hockey My Way* was to keep my upper body still when skating backwards. The video showed Brent waving his arms from side to side when he was skating backwards. Number 99 quickly corrected young Brent. The next thing I knew, Brent was skating backwards perfectly. His upper body was super still, and his arms weren't waving around at all. I had to ask Brent, "Did you move your upper body and wave your arms around on purpose for the video?"

"To overemphasize? No!" says Gretzky, laughing. "I played forward."

So there you go. I wasn't the only kid who learned from *Hockey My Way.* Of course, it took me a few years to perfect a very still upper body when skating backwards — it took Brent only a few seconds.

Gino and Paul Cavallini

646 BLOODLINES

Gino and Paul Cavallini

Gino and Paul Cavallini have been teammates with St. Louis since Paul came to the Blues in a trade midway through the '87-88 season. Born in Toronto, both went south to play college hockey in the U.S. Gino, a left wing, played two seasons with the Bowling Green State University Falcons where he was part of a NCAA championship team in '83-84, scoring the winning goal in quadruple overtime against the Minnesota-Duluth Bulldogs. He signed as a free agent with Calgary in May '84 and began his NHL career with the Flames in '84-85 before a six-player trade in February '86 sent him to St. Louis. During his five and a half seasons with the Blues, Gino has established career highs of 20 goals in '88-89, 27 assists in '90-91 and 44 points in '86-87. Paul was drafted 205th overall in the '84 Entry Draft by the Washington Capitals. He played one season on defense for the Providence College Friars and then joined the Canadian National Team for '85-86. He made his pro debut with the AHL's Binghamton Whalers at the end of that season. He played six games with the Capitals in '86-87 before earning a full-time NHL job in '87-88. Washington traded him to St. Louis in December '87. During the '89-90 season, Paul recorded career highs of 39 assists and 47 points. He also led the NHL with a plus/minus rating of plus-38 and appeared in the '90 NHL All-Star Game.

GINO AND PAUL CAVALLINI   1991–92 UPPER DECK BLOODLINES #646

Just like the Cavallini boys, my brother Peter and I are three years apart. And just like the Cavallini boys, we never got to play on the same team as kids. "We never played with each other growing up. It wasn't until he was 16 or 17, playing at Henry Carr, and I'd come back from college, and we'd play summer hockey. That's really the only time we ever really played together in an organized setting," says Gino Cavallini.

Peter and I didn't play together until we hit the beer leagues. We were in a tournament once when we convinced our mother to come check out a game. "I will," she said, "but no stupid stuff." As soon as she said that, Peter and I looked at each other and smiled.

During the game, with Mom in the stands, there was a bit of a ruckus near the other team's goalie. When the whistle went, I knew what was going down. Peter got a jab in, their defenceman got a jab in, then in I went. It was nothing more than face washing, but Peter and I broke out laughing the moment we heard our mom losing it in the stands: "I told you guys, no fighting!"

No matter what level you play at, you gotta stand up for your brother. "Once the puck dropped, he was my teammate. He wasn't my brother anymore," says Cavallini. "I mean, obviously there were a few times when I had to come to the aid of my brother. But, you know, we would have done the same for anybody on the team. We were all in the trenches together. Someone showed me some highlights a couple of years ago where the two of us were squared off against everyone."

Of course, unlike the Reid brothers, the Cavallinis made it to a league where hockey actually *counts*. And Gino and Paul were the guys on the hockey cards that my brother and I were trying to collect back in the early 1990s. "Paul and I are both involved in youth hockey coaching. Every once in a while, a kid will come in and say he just bought a pack of cards and one of these was in it. Kids get a kick out of them more than anything. It's not like we have them hanging in our basements or anything like that."

The Cavallini brothers ended up on two cards together, this one and one produced by Score. "Our heads look a little disproportioned to our bodies on that one."

Paul and Gino Cavallini became teammates on December 11, 1987. You've heard the saying, *when one door closes, another opens*. Well, in this scenario, Gino says it was more a case of when one door slams, another opens. "Paul had a meeting with [Capitals GM] David Poile. They were going to send Paul to the International League. Paul walked out, slammed the door, and said, 'I'm not going.'"

Paul's tactic worked: soon enough, Gino Cavallini got a call from his younger brother. "Five hours later, he's like, 'Hey, you gotta pick me up at the airport. The Caps just traded me to St. Louis.'" Turns out slamming a door can be very effective.

The two kids from Toronto were now living the dream in the NHL — on the same team. "It was pretty cool to play together in St. Louis. You know, come on, we are first generation Canadians. As far as we were concerned, the second we were still playing hockey in our 20s, we were blessed."

In the late 1980s and early 1990s, if young kids wanted to see the Cavallini brothers side by side, they could do it when they opened up a pack of Upper Deck. But a hockey card wasn't good enough for the brothers' biggest fan. Their father, back in Toronto, had to figure out a way to watch his boys in action. At the time, there was no such thing as the NHL Centre Ice package. Mr. Cavallini had only one option, and it was a large one. "Dad got a satellite dish. It was one of those dishes that was about 12 feet in diameter. Somehow, he convinced one of the neighbours to cut a tree down because he wasn't getting good reception. When there was a hockey game on, there was no disturbing him. My parents were both in front of the TV. Nothing was going to pull Dad away. Even if the house was on fire, he wasn't leaving."

Mr. Cavallini's boys spent parts of five seasons together in St. Louis. This card is just another reminder of the days when their dad used to tune in on satellite, and Gino used to take care of his brother (his words, not mine) for the St. Louis Blues. As for how long it took to get that classic pose on the front of the card — with snow flying, brakes on, and the smiling faces of the Cavallini boys — who knows? "Honestly, I can't even remember. It was so long ago. We're talking almost 30 years."

Darren Rumble
Defense

Although he has not yet had the opportunity to prove himself in the NHL, Darren Rumble has enjoyed considerable success in the AHL, prompting the Ottawa Senators to draft the six-foot one-inch, 200-pound defenseman off the roster of the Philadelphia Flyers during the '92 NHL Expansion Draft. A product of the OHL's Kitchener Rangers, Rumble was the Flyers' first choice in the '87 NHL Entry Draft. He has spent the majority of the past three campaigns with the AHL's Hershey Bears, where he has increased his offensive totals in each of his three seasons. After compiling 15 points as a rookie, Rumble had his finest season in '91-92, registering 12 goals and 54 assists to lead all Hershey defensemen in scoring.

DARREN RUMBLE

DARREN RUMBLE   1992–93 UPPER DECK #110

"It felt like it was a big deal. They were bringing us in to do a card, and there were only a couple of us doing the shoot," says Darren Rumble.

In the summer of 1992, Rumble, now the head coach of the Moncton Wildcats, and a couple of other soon-to-be Ottawa Senators put on a smile for the cameras at an Upper Deck photo shoot. Rumble, who had three seasons of pro hockey under his belt, was picked up by the Senators in the June expansion draft. "It was my first time putting on a Senators uniform. I had put on the Flyers jersey a few times; I had played a handful of games. It was a weird feeling because I still hadn't technically made the team, but they were giving me the red-carpet treatment, and they brought me in for a big photo shoot. So it was a weird feeling, having rode the bus for three years.

"They had the lights set up and the cameras. We did it several times. They'd look at the picture and ask you to do it again and again and again. They'd say, 'Try to make yourself look mean. Give me an angry look when you come in and put on the brakes.' Now when I look at the card, I laugh at myself. *That's what I look like when I'm mean?* No wonder I didn't scare anybody."

Winding up in a Senators uniform came as a bit of a shock for Rumble. He was on the Flyers protected list until the night before the expansion draft on June 18, 1992. The Sens and their expansion cousins, the Tampa Bay Lightning, were looking to fill their rosters. Rumble, a 23-year-old former first-round pick, didn't think he was going anywhere. He had spent three years in the Flyers organization and was Hershey's top-scoring defenceman in 1991–92. "I was ready to join the Flyers — an established team — and get insulated as the young guy and be brought along slowly. So I often wonder where my career would have gone had that happened. The Flyers had gotten me a personal trainer that summer, so I was rocking as far as conditioning goes, and then, boom, I was in a new organization. I was not sure what that meant. Obviously it was going to be a change. I went from one mindset to another."

Rumble showed up at Sens camp with about 72 other hopefuls

looking for a full-time NHL job. If the fact that he was one of only a couple of Sens selected for a photo shoot didn't convince him he had a spot in the NHL, the words of his new head coach, Rick Bowness, soon did. "I had an individual meeting with Rick. I said, 'Where do I stand?' He said, 'Well, we didn't take you for you not to be on the team.' So that helped my confidence. I felt like I had a spot to lose."

The Senators opened their season on October 8, 1992. It was the high point of Rumble's tenure in Ottawa. "We came out and got a 12-minute standing ovation. I can still remember the hair on my back standing up. Then we listened to the best rendition of the national anthem I have ever heard in my life by Alanis Morissette." The Senators beat the eventual Stanley Cup champions, the Montreal Canadiens, 5–3. Rumble assisted on the game-winning goal scored by Sylvain Turgeon. "We were all jacked up. The Canadiens were probably thinking, *Who the heck are these guys?* They probably didn't have their best game, and we did. One thousand percent that was the high: the standing ovation, the appreciation from the fans, that rendition of the anthem."

But with an expansion team, there are bound to be more lows than highs. The opening night win was followed by Rumble's lowest moment, or moments, as a Senator. The team went winless in the next 21 games. The team won just 10 times in its expansion year and just 14 the next season. "I almost quit hockey after my second year," Rumble says, semi-seriously. "I was certainly not enjoying myself after that much losing. For two years, that is really tough to take. And you know how the Canadian media is. We got a lot more coverage than they did in Tampa, so it was difficult. I was still one of the young guys. I wasn't established, so I took it pretty hard. It was tough, mentally, to stay positive and confident. You're questioning whether you belong. That was probably the biggest hurdle."

Rumble's NHL career eventually took him back to the Flyers. He ended up playing in 193 NHL regular-season games between Ottawa, Philly, St. Louis, and Tampa. This is the hockey card that started his NHL

journey. That summer day in 1992 made him believe that he was a legit-
imate NHLer, and it's what this card represents to him. That, and pain.
"I had to do so many takes. It felt like it was a bloody conditioning skate.
'Do it again. Do it again. Do it again.' I love the way the card turned out.
I'm glad I have it."

ProCards®

CAM RUSSELL
Defense
Indianapolis Ice

CAM RUSSELL ● Defense
Indianapolis Ice ● International Hockey Lg.
Ht: 6'4" Wt: 175 lbs. Shoots: L
Born: 1-12-1969 Halifax, N.S.
How Acq: Chicago's 3rd choice 1987 Entry Draft

Season	Club	Lea	GP	G	A	PTS	PIM
1985-86	Hull	QMJ	56	3	4	7	24
1986-87	Hull	QMJ	66	3	16	19	119
1987-88	Hull	QMJ	53	9	18	27	141
1988-89	Hull	QMJ	66	8	32	40	109

71

© 1989 ProCards, Inc.

Cam Russell 1989–90
PROCARDS #71

Full disclosure: this is not the card I wanted to write about. It turned out, however, it is the card I needed to write about. I ran into Cam Russell, like I always do, at my favourite charity golf tournament: the Danny Gallivan Cystic Fibrosis Golf Tournament in Halifax, Nova Scotia. I told Cam I wanted to chat with him about his 1990 Score

Chapter Two

MAKING IT LOOK MEAN

rookie card for this book. He had no problem doing an interview. "But," he said, pulling out his iPhone, "check this out."

Mary Mother of all that is holy! I immediately bent over laughing. So much for my plans to talk about Cam's Score rookie. This ProCards minor-league card is unlike anything I've ever seen. This is the card I have to interview Cam about. A few weeks later, we have our official chat.

Broken nose: check. Black eye: check. Moustache: check. Feathered hair: check. Menacing grin: check. Seventy-five-pound Koho hockey stick: check. Where to begin? Cam Russell, the floor is yours. "It was during my first year in the minors. I'd just taken a severe beating. I can't even remember who it was from. That's how bad a beating it must have been. I had my nose fixed. I had it packed. I was sent down to the minors." Now that sounds glamorous.

It was during one of Cam's many stints in Chicago in his first pro season when his nose was rearranged. There were no plastic surgeons waiting to fix your nose in the late '80s, just an eager team physician. "In those days, if you broke your nose, the team doctors were looking at upgrading their BMWs. So they were always fixing your nose. I think I probably had my nose fixed three or four times."

Well, in Indianapolis, the day after his unfortunate mishap, he arrived at practice for Darryl Sutter's Indianapolis Ice to discover that it was picture day. *"This is really bad timing* was my first thought," says the now Memorial Cup–winning general manager of the Halifax Mooseheads.

Luckily for Cam, the Ice had a top-notch photographer working that day. He took one look at his mangled subject and made a quick suggestion: "'Let's turn this into a good picture.' He told me to go with it and I thought, Hey why not."

The world's toughest-looking six-foot-four, 175-pounder complied. No one else was on the ice — just Cam and the photog. He lifted his 75-pound Koho and delivered a cross-check to the camera. Almost three decades later, this card is likely in binders and cardboard boxes everywhere. And why wouldn't Cam have it on his phone? It is one hell of a conversation piece. In 1989, a broken nose and a black eye sure as hell weren't going to keep you out of a game, so why would it be an excuse to pass on picture day? "There was no taking any time off. A broken nose was just like having a black eye. You just played with it. The odd time you'd throw a visor on, but you just played through it."

Was there any mercy from opponents? "Guys didn't care," Cam says. "If you had a black eye, if you had stitches on your face, if you had a broken nose, they didn't care. You're in the minors. You're slugging away every day. You're living with two or three other guys. Your dream is to make the NHL. So if you got a black eye or a broken nose and you get a chance to drop the gloves, you drop the gloves."

Cam didn't spend that entire first season in Indianapolis; he played in 19 games with the big club in Chicago after being called up 12 times. "Mike Keenan was coaching, so any time things would go bad, he'd call a player up from the minors just to put a little scare into the guys. I can remember getting called up; he'd fly me in that morning. You'd show up for morning skate at 10 a.m. The players would be nervous, thinking I was there to take their job. Keenan would skate the crap out of me for an hour and then send me back home. Sometimes, I wouldn't even play. If you were lucky, you'd get to sit in the organ loft and watch the game."

This picture was taken during one of Cam's many Indy demotions. Take one more look: it's the kind of pose he likely struck a lot out on the ice, that big Koho digging into a forward's back. "It's amazing when you think back to the abuse the forwards used to take in front of the net. If you were standing beside a forward in front of your net, you had to cross-check him. Otherwise, you'd get back to the bench and your coach would give you heck because you were just standing there watching the game. You'd cross-check guys, you'd hold them up, slash them. I remember holding guys' sticks in front of the net and the referee is telling you to let go. It was tough for the forwards. They took a lot of abuse. That Koho was great for that."

And when you play that way for a guy like Darryl Sutter, you're going to hit it off with the now-legendary coach. Sutter was just cutting his chops behind the bench in 1988–89. "Oh yeah, he loved me. I was his kind of player. He liked the guys that played hard and the guys that played through pain."

As far as I can tell, Cam doesn't have any stitches on his face in this picture, but if he did, he would have been the guy taking them out himself, no fancy doctor required. "I had my own stitch-removal kit in my shaving kit. I remember our equipment manager took my stitches out with toenail clippers and pliers."

Any tips for readers if they ever need to remove their own sutures? "Well, with toenail clippers, snap the centre of the stitch. Then take the pliers and just yank on the biggest piece of the string. Pull it, but make sure you don't pull the knot through the skin. Pull it the other way." Thanks, Cam.

Life in the minors was not glamorous. Nobody got rich. But when you're 21 or 22 years old, it seems like a pretty good gig. Cam Russell

spent parts of three seasons in Indianapolis, before he finally made it to the NHL on a full-time basis in the fall of 1992. "I can remember coming up to Chicago and putting A535 on my legs. Steve Larmer looked at me and said, 'Right up from the minors, eh?' He was smiling. In the NHL, you just sat on a table and they took care of you. In the minors, you fixed your own sticks, you taped your own ankles. You did all that stuff yourself. It was a grind, but we loved it. It's not like you felt hard done by. It was a great living. The three years I spent in the minors were some of the best times I ever had: you felt alive, you played hard, you played hurt. We won the Turner Cup my first year. We had a really good team. Darryl Sutter was a great coach. You're playing hockey, and you're getting paid to do it. I can't think of anything better."

When Cam shows this card around at the Gallivan golf tournament, it gets a lot of laughs. To be honest, I'm basically making him show it off. It's damn funny, but when you really dig deep, you'll find there's more to it. It's the philosophy Cam Russell lived by when he patrolled the Chicago Blackhawks blue line for almost a decade. "You have to be able to look at yourself in the mirror at the end of the day and know that you didn't cut corners. If you had to play hurt, you played through it. If you were injured, well, that's a different story. When I was younger, my dad said, 'The days of feeling great every time you step on the ice are probably over. There's always going to be a little booboo or a little pain somewhere.' It's the Wally Pipp story. I always thought that if I was out with an injury, or for some other reason, I might never get back in. I had a high-ankle sprain one time, and I didn't miss a game because I was too afraid that if I came out of the lineup, I'd never get a chance to come back in. That was the fear I always had."

So, no, a broken nose was not going to keep Cam Russell off the ice, whether it was for a game or for a picture that lives on his phone almost three decades later.

Willi Plett

RW 17

Height: 6'3"   Weight: 205   Shoots: Right
1st Pro Season: 1975-76   Acquired: 1975 Amateur
Draft   Born: 6-7-55, Paraguay, South America
Home: Atlanta, Georgia

MINOR LEAGUE AND NHL RECORD

YEAR	TEAM	GP	G	A	PTS	PIM
1975-76	FLAMES	4	0	0	0	2
1975-76	TULSA	73	30	20	50	163
1976-77	FLAMES	64	33	23	56	123
1976-77	TULSA	14	8	4	12	68
NHL TOTALS		.68	33	23	56	125

● One of the NHL's outstanding rookies of the 1976-77 campaign, he palyed 14 games at Tulsa during the season and was superb. Possessed with a strong wrist shot and fine scoring ability, he's acknowledged as one of the Flames' aggressive players.

● Une des meilleures recrues de la saison 1976-77, il joua aussi 14 matches pour Tulsa où il brilla. Willi a un bon lancer du poignet et on le considère comme un joueur agressif.

WILLI PLETT • R. WING
FLAMES

1977 O-PEE-CHEE PRINTED IN CANADA

WILLI PLETT   1977–78
O-PEE-CHEE #17

Every beer leaguer has been there. The penalty box can be a lonely place. And in the words of Denis Lemieux, "You feel shame." But then again, life's what you make it: if the world gives you lemons, make lemonade. And if a ref gives you a penalty, make new friends. "You do get to know the guys working in the box," says Willi Plett. "I only had 123 minutes my first year. Later on in my career, I had a 300-minute season. You do get comfy with the guys working in the box, you sure do. I was kind of an easy-going guy. I'd be in there, laughing and joking. I was not one to sit there all serious. You talk about how the game is going or someone on the other team. 'Can you believe this; can you believe that?' Some crazy stuff."

Plett's rookie card came on the heels of an absolutely incredible season. He scored 33 goals and had 23 assists in 64 games for the Atlanta Flames. If he had gotten his way in the penalty box, he would have gotten a few more helpers. "I'd go, 'Hey. What do you have on the score sheet for our second goal? I think I got an assist.' They'd go, 'You weren't even on the ice!'"

The fact that Willi Plett is sitting in a penalty box on this card is astonishing. These days, parents are rushing out to sign up their five-year-old for minor hockey. Some kids are playing year-round. Ten years before this picture was taken, Willi Plett wasn't even playing organized hockey. "I actually signed myself up for hockey in the little town that I grew up in, Niagara-on-the-Lake. They built an arena in 1967. So I got my brother, who is a couple of years older than I am, and I said, 'Let's go sign us up for hockey.' At school I got the name of the guy to go talk to. I went to his house and signed myself up when I was 12 or 13."

Plett's parents came to Canada from Paraguay a year after Willi was born. "My dad was a brick mason. He wouldn't have known what a puck was."

But he learned what it was and more when young Willi started to take to the game. It's really an incredible journey, almost unthinkable today. Just five years after he signed up, Willi was playing junior hockey with the Niagara Falls Flyers. "I don't try to live in the past, but I do think of how crazy my path was. I wasn't much of a junior player, either. I was a fifth-round draft pick who just showed up to training camp. All the stars were aligned for me, I guess."

And soon enough, he was an NHL rookie sitting in a penalty box on a hockey card. When you mention the name Willi Plett to old-time hockey fans, most will usually talk about how tough he was. When I look at Willi Plett's numbers, I think *power forward*. He scored 33 goals as a rookie, so let's start there. "It's no secret. If I played with a good centreman, I could score. Tom Lysiak was my centre and he was a heck of a player. If it weren't for him, there was no way I would have scored 33 goals. With my style, I needed someone to do all the stickhandling. I'd do the mucking and I'd get myself in front of the net like a Dino Ciccarelli. He scored 500 to 600 goals and all he did was hang around the front of the net. And he couldn't stickhandle either. I was kind of like that. Now Dino's in the Hall of Fame. He was tough in front of the net. He knew where to go. That's kind of what I did."

A few years later, things really took off for Plett. Look at these numbers and try not to think about what kind of contract he'd get today. Thirty-eight goals and 239 penalty minutes for the Calgary Flames in 1980–81. Willi gives all the credit to the man the hockey world knew as the Magic Man, Kent Nilsson. "Talk about a guy who could control and pass the puck around. There are only a handful of players who could do what he could. Gretzky was one of them and Mario Lemieux. There were not that many more who were that good with the puck. He gave me a lot of easy goals. He used to laugh at me. 'Willi,' he'd say, 'just put your stick there. You won't even have to move it. I'll just bank it off your stick and you can score.' It was crazy. And he was right. He'd say, 'You just wait. It's coming. If you can hang in there, it's coming.' Next thing you know — bop — it's off your stick and into an open net."

Willi scored so many goals like this that Nilsson came up with a name for Willi's tallies. "He used to call them *yayers*." *Yayers?* I ask. What's a *yayer?* "You'd score and you'd just put your hands up. *YAY!*" That makes sense. But it was also a two-way street. When you're a skill guy playing with one of the toughest players of the late '70s and early '80s, you get a little something out of the relationship as well. "Kent would say, 'I don't mind playing with you, Willi. The guys don't check as hard.' He liked playing with me because he got a little more room."

Creating room for a guy like Kent Nilsson meant standing up for him. Players knew that if you touched the Magic Man, Willi would soon be on his way. And that often meant an opponent's tough guy would have to answer the call and stand up to Plett. Believe it or not, though, Plett picked up only nine fighting majors in 1980–81. Sometimes the threat of a tilt or a player's reputation is enough to keep everyone's gloves on. But when they do come off, that's when you have to make things count. "The only thing you had to be careful of is losing real bad. If you can kind of have a tie, each guy carries on. When you're a tough guy, you don't want to be losing a lot of fights.

"A win is always good, but if you have four or five losses in a row, you're in trouble. You lose your respect. The last thing your teammates want to see is one of their tough guys get the crap kicked out of him. I knew some guys that were trying to be tough guys in the league — I'm not going to mention names — but they got the crap kicked out of them early in their careers. And they were done. There's a fine line there."

No respect, no gig. It's a tough way to live. That style of play put Plett in the position we see him in on this card, sitting in the box, for 2,572 minutes in his NHL career. When you're not chatting it up with the guys working in the box, there's a lot to think about. And sometimes there's nothing to do at all. "The best part is you get some rest. You get to chill out. The bad part is if the other team scores, then you kind of feel bad. Of course, that depends on what kind of penalty it is. If it's a fight, that's fine. You get a good five-minute rest. But if it's a silly hooking or tripping or roughing call and they score, it's not good. But a fight is fine."

The kind of hockey Willi Plett played was a young man's game.

Grinding it out in front of the net, mucking it up in the corners, dishing out the body, dropping the gloves — it's not an easy style. There's a reason why teams honour players who have suited up for 1,000 games. Now, try playing like Willi Plett and lasting that long. It's twice as tough. "When I was young, I could recover fairly quickly. But when I was older, if you got in one of those long fights, oh my goodness it would take you 10 or 20 minutes to recover. I had a fight with someone late in the second period once, I went right to the dressing room. And I was so tired, I wasn't able to go out for the third. When you're young, though, it's not a problem.

"You tried to keep that edge but it got more and more difficult as you got older because your heart's not in it. That's why I retired. I probably could have played another year or two, but my heart wasn't in it anymore. When I got to that point, it was time to retire."

Plett hung up his skates at the end of the 1988 season, after playing the hard way for 834 regular-season games. In addition to spending the equivalent of almost two days in the penalty box, he scored 222 goals and added 215 assists for 437 career points. He added another 46 points and 466 PIMs in 83 playoff games. Plett's 1988 Boston Bruins lost to the Edmonton Oilers in Game 5 of the Stanley Cup Final. A week later, Willi Plett turned 33, and he knew it was time to say goodbye to his NHL career. "You don't want to be 33, 34 and not playing as much as you'd like. Nothing good comes out of it."

The very-easy-to-talk-to Plett still lives in Atlanta. "At my age, you don't work very hard. My life is good. It's all good." He's a long way from that penalty box. When you look at his hockey card, it's easy to forget that Willi Plett was more than just a tough guy. But he's cool with the card. He looks pretty relaxed after all: getting ready to towel off and then maybe start a chat with the timekeeper or even the photographer. "I'm fine with the card. I had a mullet — '70s hair. I don't have the mullet anymore, but it's still blond . . . with just a little bit of grey on the temples."

Maybe they should have given Plett an extra two minutes for looking so good.

48

Height:	6-2	Birthdate:	4/9/71
Weight:	212	Hometown:	Paddockwood, SK
Position:	Defense	Shoots:	Right

YEAR	TEAM	GP	G	A	PTS	PIM
89-90	Spokane	65	01	13	14	384
90-91	Spokane	65	11	16	27	505
TOTALS		130	12	29	41	889

Kerry Toporowski SET A MEMORIAL CUP RECORD LAST SEASON WITH 63 PENALTY MINUTES AND WAS THE THIRD PLAYER IN WESTERN HOCKEY LEAGUE HISTORY TO RACK UP MORE THAN 500 PENALTY MINUTES IN ONE SEASON. HIS EXTREMELY PHYSICAL DEFENSE STYLE MADE HIM ONE OF THE MOST FEARED PLAYERS IN THE LEAGUE. TOPOROWSKI WAS DRAFTED 67TH OVERALL BY SAN JOSE.

© 1991 • ALL RIGHTS RESERVED

Kerry Toporowski
S · A · N · J · O · S · E
D

KERRY TOPOROWSKI

1991–92
ULTIMATE DRAFT PICKS #48

The money game is risky. Buy low and sell high, that's what we've always been told. A good financial advisor, though, will often tell you that slow and steady wins the race.

In the early 1990s, a lot of people suddenly saw hockey cards as an investment. If you could cash in on the next hot rookie, surely you would be set for life. In addition to new collectors, new card makers started to show up on the scene too. And they were looking to cash in as well.

Now, what could be better than a rookie card? How about the pre-rookie card of the next best thing! In the summer of 1991, a card company going by the name of Ultimate brought together a number of top draft picks, outfitted them in cheesy uniforms with the word Smokey's on the front, got them on the ice, and started snapping pictures. The end result was a legendarily awful 90-card set called Ultimate. The set was stacked with players who went on to superstardom, with names like Scott Niedermayer, Peter Forsberg, and Markus Naslund. But it was also full of 1991 draft picks who never made the NHL at all. One of those players was future minor-league legend Kerry Toporowski.

Now, while Forsberg was shown flying on the ice and Pat Falloon was pictured off-ice with a towel around his neck, it's this Toporowski card that really stands out. Why? Because you can't see his eyes. You can't see his face. All you can see is the back of his head and half of his left ear.

"I totally remember that card because that picture isn't me. I wasn't at the shoot."

Okay. That sums it up. In fact, Toporowski wasn't even aware the shoot was taking place. It didn't stop Ultimate from making up a uniform and slapping it on a player and making a card of the 67th overall pick in the 1991 Draft. "I believe it is Brent Bilodeau on the card."

Toporowski got his agent to do some digging, and a few of his Spokane teammates confirmed that there was a Toporowski jersey at the shoot. Ultimate, it seems, found a way around airbrushing and came up with a new way to produce a card: just take a shot of someone's back.

Regardless, it was a payday for the then 20-year-old. "I think I got $1,500. I didn't care at the time, and I still don't. It's kind of a joke and it was good cash for doing nothing."

Toporowski's photo isn't on the back of the card either. But his stats are, and his bio is correct — although, it's a bio that you won't likely see on another draft pick card anytime soon. Today, I chuckle when a younger fan says, "Did you see that brawl in the game last night?" My usual answer is "No. I didn't." Actually, chances are I did see it, but the truth is, it wasn't a brawl. Ten guys standing around hugging each other after a hit is not a brawl. In Kerry Toporowski's WHL days, however, brawls were *brawls*. Here's part of his bio from the Ultimate card: "Kerry Toporowski set a Memorial Cup record last season with 63 penalty minutes and was the third player in Western Hockey League history to rack up more than 500 penalty minutes in one season."

Let's start with the 1991 Memorial Cup. Toporowski's Spokane Chiefs took out Drummondville 5–1 in the final to win the championship. They did not do it the easy way. "We had two line brawls and I was involved in both. One was against Chicoutimi and the other was against Drummondville."

The brawl with Chicoutimi started when Toporowski took a late hit on an icing call. For about two minutes, his teammates did most of the work, with scraps breaking out all over the ice. Two minutes into the ruckus, Toporowski dropped the gloves with Chicoutimi's Eric Duchesne. "Toporowski did not lose a fight all year in the Western Hockey League!" the announcer says. He didn't lose this one either.

As for the brawl against Drummondville, Toporowski had a go with Guy Lehoux. Seven players got kicked out of that game. Now remember, this all happened during the Memorial Cup tournament. This did not take place in a late September exhibition game or in the middle of a December write-off game. These scraps happened in the annual springtime CHL championship tournament. "Hockey in general has changed drastically," says Toporwoski. "I think it needed to change a little. It's gotten away from some of the hard hitting and fights that were exciting for the fans and exciting for the players. But I do think it had to change."

Oh, and as for his 505 regular-season PIMs in his last year of junior, you have to consider this as well: "The penalty minutes back then didn't include 10-minute misconducts or game misconducts. So if you look at it now, I think my last year would be 800 and some." The WHL record for penalty minutes was 511, set by Brent Gogol in 1977–78. "Looking back, I wish I would have gotten the record, but then I didn't really care."

Shortly after this picture of Brent Bilodeau was taken, Kerry Toporowski was at his first NHL training camp. It was with a physically loaded San Jose expansion team. Gaetz, Odgers, Coxe, and Toporowski. Well, not really Toporowski. He was traded on the first morning of camp. "The GM [Jack Ferreira] called me first thing in the morning and woke me up. He asked me to come up to his hotel room. He was on the top floor. I went up to this room. He told me I was traded to Chicago."

Training camps and exhibition games were the closest Kerry Toporowski would ever get to life in the NHL. During his first year of pro, he played in 18 games for the IHL's Indianapolis Ice. He had 206 penalty minutes. To put that PIM total in perspective, it would have won him the NHL PIM total in 2015–16. And Toporowski did it in only 18 games. He slugged it out anywhere and with anyone for the rest of his 12-season minor-league career. "During my career, I battled through major injuries. I just kept coming back. I was told a couple of times by the doctors that I should really stop playing, but I wanted to keep going, and I did. As the years went on, I had more fun."

Toporowski believes he had more fun because the stress went away. As the years went by, he was no longer trying to make the NHL. "It actually got easier. Your reputation follows you. At the time, I was playing and having fun."

And fun was easier to have because hockey wasn't the only way that Toporowski was paying the bills. Towards the end of his career, the man who was once upon a time featured in a set that cardboard

investors jumped at was now calling the financial shots himself. Kerry Toporowski, tough guy, became Kerry Toporowski, financial advisor. He stepped away from the game, moved back to Spokane, and entered the financial world. But hockey kept calling. "The Quad City Mallards continued to call me and say, 'Come back and play.' I stopped playing in '98, but they got me to come back in 2000 to finish the year and go through the playoffs."

Toporowski was either moonlighting as a hockey player or moonlighting as a financial advisor — it depends on how you look at it. He put up a staggering 478 PIMs in 80 regular-season and playoff games in 2000–01. And his Mallards won the UHL title. He did some good business as well. "I picked up several clients."

Toporowski is now a full-time financial advisor and hockey dad. He has two sons who followed in his footsteps and played for the Spokane Chiefs in the WHL. I can guarantee very few, if any, card collectors out there made any cash on Ultimate Hockey if they invested in that product in 1991. To me, it seems the guy who cashed in the most on that set is Kerry Toporowski. He made $1,500, and unlike Forsberg, Niedermayer, or Falloon, he didn't even have to show up for the photo shoot. That's a good day for any investor.

What would Toporowski say to the 20-year-old version of himself who pocketed $1,500 off that hockey card?

"Save your money. It doesn't last forever. A hockey career can be short and you have a lot of years ahead of you."

TROY MALLETTE 1991–92
UPPER DECK #326

"I don't know why, but I ran with it. They asked to come into the locker room. I had no idea what they were going to do. Then they asked me to take my shirt off . . . and that's how it became a card," says Troy Mallette, who posed for this card almost three decades ago.

Mallette was just 21 years when he went *sun's out, guns out* on this Upper Deck card. Just a kid on top of the world, performing on one of the biggest stages in sport, Madison Square Garden. "I've never been able to duplicate it [the feeling of playing at MSG]. I was so naïve my first three or four months with the Rangers . . . basically right out of the sticks. I'm from a town of about 1,200 people. My big move was to Sault Ste. Marie to play for the Greyhounds. That was a big city. I spent three years in the Soo, kind of building up a little bit of character, and then at 19, I'm in New York City."

Mallette was a kid, but he soon became a fan favourite at MSG. A look at his PIM totals will tell you why. He spent 305 minutes in the box as a rookie and another 252 in his second year with the Rangers. The fans, he says, made embracing the role of tough guy a lot easier. "Being 19 or 20, I could go out there and get beat up and it didn't really matter," says Mallette, who fought 21 times in his first regular season. "I was sticking up for myself or sticking up for a teammate. So win or lose, I was getting pretty good applause. I was in a good position at the time."

For most teenagers, going away to college can be tough. But try to imagine being the young man on the front of this card. Like Mallette said, he was from the sticks, but suddenly he was in one of the most electric cities in the world. Chris Nilan was a big help. He set Mallette up to live with a family out by the Rangers practice facility in Rye for the first few months of his rookie season. Later, Mallette and the Rangers' trainer rented a place together. "I was just in awe. I went to the practice rink; I did my thing. We had a few rookies that year, with Mark Janssens and Darren Turcotte. Even Mike Richter was just kind of breaking in. There were five or six of us who would hang out, have our lunch . . . it was low key. The first year, I just kind of stayed on the straight and narrow. The rule was if half the team went out, then I would go out. If less than half went out, then I'd stay in. We had a good team, we had pretty good chemistry, so we did hang out in bunches. It was a very memorable year."

And here's the thing, if Mallette goes looking for memories of his time with the Rangers, he can look at this card, which always gets a laugh. He can also go online — but when he goes to the internet, the only thing he seems to find are the scraps. As I said, Mallette got in his fair share of tilts, but he could also score. He had 13 goals as a rookie and another 12 in his sophomore year. "[The feeling of scoring a goal at MSG was] better than fighting. There's nothing better than scoring. And that's one thing that gets lost. I've got a son who just finished playing four years in the OHL. He goes on YouTube once in a while and he sees my fights. I say, 'Trent, I scored a couple of nice goals too. But I can't find them on the internet.' Scoring goals in Madison Square Garden was second to none. I just wish I could have scored more of them."

As you can see from the size of him on the front of this card, Mallette was not a man to be messed with. He basically takes up his entire stall in the Rangers room at MSG. It was an interesting time to be a young guy in the NHL. In the early '90s, salaries were starting to climb. When the money got big, the training got more serious. Big salaries meant conditioning was starting to consume the life of several NHLers, but a few of the old guard were still around. Some of them were literally hacking away in the bowels of MSG. "We were going through a transitional era where you'd have five or six guys smoking in the room. And then four or five years later, you've got all the guys working right through the summer, working out hard. So there was a transition taking place on how people were preparing for a hockey season."

The game was changing. The darts disappeared and the uniforms stayed on, at least Mallette's did. Just a few years after this card hit the market, when Mallette was an Ottawa Senator, a photographer tried to recreate this moment. "They mimicked this card, but I was wearing a

shirt in that photo. It was a little bit more of a headshot than a body shot, but they used the same pose again."

Mallette spends his days now as a firefighter in Sudbury, Ontario. And, yes, they produce a firefighter calendar every year. Mallette even dabbled in a bit of firefighter modelling early in his firefighting career, just as he struck a pose early in his hockey career. For now, though, his modelling days have been extinguished.

"I did the first two calendars. I haven't made the cut the last six years. I've been letting the younger guys claim their fame."

Fame is what Mallette found when he was a young New York Ranger. He was an entertainer in the city that never sleeps. And, as he said, being a New York Ranger was a feeling he could never duplicate. But it's that feeling that this card captures: a young guy confident enough to say, sure, *I'll strike a pose.*

"It's just one of those cards that when a buddy comes across it, he makes sure to give you a jab. He'll say, 'I can't believe you posed like that. I dare you to do it now.'"

Ken Sabourin   Defense

CAPITALS

417

Defense

Washington Capitals

YEAR	TEAM	GP	G	A	PTS	PIM	+/-
88-89	Flames	6	0	0	0	26	+3
89-90	Flames	5	0	0	0	10	
90-91	Salt Lake	16	1	3	4	77	+9
90-91	Capitals	28	2	15	17	36	+10
91-92	Capitals	28	2	4	5	81	+9
	3 NHL SEASONS	55	2	8	10	153	+5

Height: 6'3"
Weight: 205 lbs.
Born: Apr. 28, 1966
Scarborough,
Ontario
Shoots: Left

Ken

Ken Sabourin   1991–92 Upper Deck #417

"Come on, ref! Really?"

I'm occasionally guilty of losing it on a poor referee. You'd think I would have mellowed after spending a year as a ref as a 14-year-old. It was torturous. A ref cannot win. No matter what you did, it ticked someone off. That's true at any level, whether it's Peewee or the NHL. "I've

EXPRESS YOURSELF

Chapter Three

taken a lot of heat over the years from this card. From what I recall, I was yelling at the referee about why a penalty wasn't called," says Ken Sabourin.

It must have been something pretty obvious that the guy in stripes missed. It's not a look of anger on Sabourin's face, it's more of a *How in the hell did you not see that?* look. "My mouth is wide open. It's not your typical action card. Guys ask me, 'Why don't they have you skating?' I tell them, 'You know, when you don't skate that well, it's hard for them to get you skating.'"

This is one of Sabourin's six NHL cards. It came out when he was 25 years old, seven years after the Calgary Flames took him 33rd overall in the 1985 Draft. Sabourin took the long road to the NHL, slugging it out in the American and International Leagues while trying to stick with the Flames and later with the Washington Capitals. For some, a hockey card is a sign that you made it. When Ken Sabourin was playing, though, the last thing on his mind was having his very own hockey card. "It really wasn't on my mind. It's pretty neat after the fact. I have the odd one come in the mail. But I never really thought about that stuff when I played. I just wanted to play. I didn't care about any accolades or cards or anything like that. I loved playing the game. To me, that was most important. Should I have enjoyed it all a little more when I played? Probably, yeah."

You can't blame Sabourin for being so focused. When he was with the Flames, he was trying to crack a blue line that featured Al MacInnis, Gary Suter, Jamie Macoun, Brad McCrimmon, Rob Ramage, and Dana Murzyn. "It was tough to really let your hair down. You're on pins and needles. If you make one bad pass, you're back in the minors. One regret I have is I didn't enjoy the moment as much as I should have. Again, it's tough to do when you're young. That was one of the best teams in the NHL. That's a hard defence corps to crack."

Sabourin played in only 27 regular-season games for the Flames. His first was on March 18, 1989. He picked up 15 minutes in penalties. "My first game was against Wayne Gretzky and L.A. I hit him going back for an icing and it started a big five-on-five brawl, and we all got kicked out. Then we went back to Calgary and it was the same thing. It was an eye-opening experience. I didn't hit him to hurt him, but it just kind of happened that way. That's not your ideal way to break into the NHL in your first game, but it is one you will always remember.

"I know [Marty] McSorley was on the ice. I know [Ken] Baumgartner was on the ice. I think maybe even Jay Miller too, because we had Hunts [Tim Hunter], [Gary] Roberts, and myself. So it wasn't like I was by myself. They all came after me, but we all ended up squaring off. I believe, if I remember correctly, McSorley fought me, Hunts, and Roberts in the same little scrum. A lot of guys made a lot of money protecting Wayne.

"Back then, it was team first. If one is in, then 20 are in. That's the way it was. The guys could handle themselves too. It's not like Hakan Loob was out there fighting. That's the way the league was then."

On January 24, 1991, Sabourin finally left the Flames organization. He was sent to Washington for Paul Fenton. Once again, Sabourin had to crack another solid blue line. The Caps had Al Iafrate, Rod Langway,

Calle Johansson, and Mike Lalor. "It's very hard, but it is exciting. You have good mentors. You watch the way guys play and you say, 'Okay, I'm not that type of player, but I can take something from that.' I'm a believer that if you are around good people, good things happen. When you're around bad people, bad things happen. Looking back, could I have had a longer career in the NHL? Probably, if I came in on a different team than Calgary. But I don't regret anything."

Sabourin played in 74 career regular-season NHL games and 12 more in the playoffs. One of those playoff games was for the Flames when they won the Cup in 1989. But in 1993–94, when Sabourin signed with the International League's Milwaukee Admirals, he knew he was saying goodbye to the best league in the world. "I knew that my NHL dreams were done. You went to the 'I' back then because it was good hockey and they were paying the money. Quite frankly, teams wanted their prospects in the American League. The timing was pretty good that way for us too. It was a good time to go to the 'I,' where you could make a pretty good living."

The IHL doesn't get as much respect as it deserves. Players earned a living there in the 1990s, and the level of play was high. Some guys could light up the "I," but it just didn't translate to the NHL. Players like Rob Brown, Kip Miller, and Greg Hawgood all skated in the "I" in those days. "There were a lot of ex-NHLers. There were a lot of guys who could play. It was just a numbers game in the NHL. It was very good hockey, I thought."

And then there were the tough guys. In Sabourin's first year in the league, he put up 271 PIMS. The next year, he came up just three minutes short of 300. If some of the finesse guys in the league were NHL vets, a few of the tough guys in the league were young up-and-comers with nothing to lose and everything to gain by dropping the mitts. During Sabourin's first stint in the IHL, while still with the Flames organization, he crossed paths with a couple of them. "Peoria had Tony Twist and Kelly Chase. Twist and Chase, that was a pretty good one-two punch.

There were a lot of tough guys, but those are the first two who come to my mind. There were positions back then for tough guys."

There are very few spots on most teams for that type of player today. Speed is the name of the game now. "Everyone can play, not just the top six forwards."

Sabourin knows this for a fact. As a colour commentator on Washington Capitals radio broadcasts, he has one of the best seats in the world when it comes to watching the game. On many nights he's right between the benches. "It's the closest you can get to playing without playing. You get the feel for the game.

"You still get the juices going a little bit. There's nothing else you can do to get that feeling if you don't play anymore. I like being that close to the action of the game. I do appreciate the skill of the game now, though. It's incredible the way it is. The skill is just off the charts.

"When you're upstairs in the booth, it doesn't do the speed of the game justice. Everything looks easy. But when you get to ice level, you really do appreciate the skill and the speed. They have no time to make decisions. They are so talented and so well brought up throughout their careers."

You can hear the passion in Ken's voice when he talks. It is a game he truly loves, even though the hockey is very different than it was when he was screaming on this card. Back then he was yelling at refs, doing anything he had to, to earn a spot in an NHL lineup. Now, though, he can sit back a little and smell a rose or two. "Now I appreciate having a few cards. I did end up living my dream out — not as long as I wanted to, but I still played in the NHL. I think my kids get more of a kick out of my cards than I do, but I think back and I say, 'Geez, I had hair back then . . . and I was a lot skinnier too.'"

DOUG ZMOLEK

1992–93
UPPER DECK #509

Pinpointing the moment a photo on a card was taken is not always easy. Some hockey players have had dozens of pictures taken of them over the years. Some have had hundreds taken of them. And others, thousands. "I don't remember the play," says Doug Zmolek, who politely answers my call out of the blue one Friday afternoon.

That kind of sends me for a loop. I figured with the smile and post-goal celebration on the front of the card, it would be easy for him to identify the play.

No problem. Let's go another route. As you can see on the back of the card, Zmolek went right from the University of Minnesota to the NHL. He didn't spend a second in the minors after college. "Playing college was a huge, huge step from high school. And then the next one was just that much bigger. My memory is not the greatest about all those events. To tell you the truth, I think I was just in the moment and wanted to make it. It wasn't like it was nerve-racking or anything like that. The challenge was to make the team."

Once Zmolek made the team, he found himself in the not-so-passive world of the NHL. In college hockey, there was no fighting. There sure as hell was in the NHL — especially if you played on the San Jose Sharks in 1992–93, their second year in the league. "It was definitely a much more intimidating game. San Jose being a new team, we weren't the greatest, and to have pride when the score was 4–1, 5–1 — you just dropped your mitts and fought. I can remember playing Edmonton . . . and good grief Edmonton had probably nine or 10 guys who would fight. It was tough. It was mentally very tough."

Zmolek had 229 PIMs in his rookie season. He dropped his gloves 14 times. "You didn't really think about it. It just happened. I mean, fighting is easy when you're mad and it just happens. Fighting is tough when you're not really mad and you're defending a teammate or you're going in knowing you might have to do it without being angry."

The other big adjustment from the NCAA to the NHL was the schedule. The NHL had an 84-game season in 1992–93. Zmolek played in every game, more than double the number he'd played in Minnesota the year before. "I can't imagine how bad I was in some of those games. You're exhausted. It was one of those years where you're always a little bit beat up. Your skills and everything else basically diminish throughout the year because you can't practice. You can't do anything. You're just trying to survive. It was very, very difficult, playing every other night or every third night. You just gotta try to prepare yourself mentally."

It's funny how a certain word can spark a memory. Once Zmolek finishes telling me just how exhausting that first year was, I say there must have been a few highs. That's when the memory of what was happening on the front of this card comes: "I remember I dumped one in against the Buffalo Sabres. It hit the Plexiglas. The goalie had come out to stop it behind the net. But it went off the glass and in the middle of the net. It looks like we're kind of giggling . . . so that might have been that goal."

That makes sense. Zmolek does have that *Can you believe that just happened* look on his face. For the record, his goal against the Sabres was scored on November 5, 1992, in a 7–5 San Jose win at the Cow Palace. One of the things Zmolek and I talk about are the great arenas he got to play in. He played in classic arenas like the Montreal Forum, Boston Garden, Chicago Stadium, and Maple Leaf Gardens. And he got to play in the Cow Palace as well. It had its own charms. "The crazy thing about that rink — and this is what I've heard, I don't know if it is true — is that the Cow Palace was even smaller than the Boston Garden back when that was a very tiny rink. But it didn't feel like it because the seats didn't start right at the boards. They were out a little bit. It was a crazy little set-up."

It was a crazy little set-up because, as the name of the joint tells you, cows frequented the place — cows, bulls, horses, basically any kind of livestock. The little arena on the edge of San Francisco hosted everything from livestock shows to the Beatles to the San Jose Sharks and, of course, the rodeo.

The rodeo could make for a long road trip. And an awkward return. "There were flies all over once you came back. I think we had a 22-day road trip or something like that. I think we were on the road almost the whole month of January. And the rodeo was the reason. Our locker room was upstairs. I can remember flies all over the place in there."

But it was part of the charm of the Cow Palace that helped contribute to this card. Seamless glass is all the rage now. That wasn't the case at the Cow Palace. It had the old-school glass that could make for a funky bounce once in a while. Over 25 years ago, it made for a bounce that found the back of the net and resulted in Zmolek's rookie card smile. I love goals that are whacked in from an inch away of the goal line or courtesy of a strange bounce off an old sanction. "That's my kind of goal," I tell Doug.

"Mine too," he says.

Hubie McDonough — Center

YEAR	TEAM	GP	G	A	PTS	PIM	+/-
88-89	Kings	4	0	1	0	10	+2
89-90	Kings	22	3	4	7	10	+4
89-90	Islanders	54	18	11	29	26	+10
90-91	Islanders	52	6	6	12	10	-14
	3 NHL SEASONS	132	27	22	49	46	

Hubie McDonough New York Islanders

Height: 5'9"
Weight: 180 lbs.
Born: July 8, 1963
Manchester,
New Hampshire
Shoots: Left

McDonough signed with L.A. as a free agent after a season in the IHL.

138

HUBIE McDONOUGH 1991–92 UPPER DECK #138

"I wish I had my eyes open and I had more of a smile instead of a *Finally* type of face," says Hubie McDonough, one-time New York Islander and now director of hockey operations for the Ontario Reign, the AHL affil-iate of the L.A. Kings.

McDonough has that look on this card because he *finally* scored. The 1990–91 season was not easy for McDonough. Just a year earlier, everything was going right for him as a rookie. He split the season between the Kings and the Islanders and racked up 21 goals. His sophomore season was a different story. He split time between the Islanders and the Capital District in the AHL. When McDonough played in the American Hockey League, scoring wasn't a problem. He found the net nine times in 17 games. Goals didn't come as easily in the NHL, which explains the way he looks on this card. "I hadn't scored in a while. It was such a relief. I remember it was at home, in New York."

I love it when a player can tell me when and where the picture on his card was taken. It doesn't happen all that often, but in McDonough's case, it's easy to understand why he remembers the exact moment this picture was snapped. The goal was a long time coming. McDonough had gone over three months since his last NHL tally. He scored his third goal of the season on November 2 — number four did not come until March 10, against the Penguins. And in his words, it led to "the worst picture ever."

I don't care where or when you score, it always feels good. I used to get a little too pumped up when I sniped in beer league, but when you score in the NHL, you should look as excited or as relieved as you want, as far as I'm concerned. After all, you are scoring in the greatest hockey league in the world. McDonough managed to score 40 regular-season goals in his NHL career. "Scoring any goal at the NHL level is a really great feeling. Guys who do it all the time kind of take it for granted, but I never did. I was fortunate enough to get to that level and then to play a regular shift. Whether you get to score or make a play, if you get a win and you contribute, that's all part of it. I enjoyed my time in the NHL for sure, because it took a long time to get there and a lot of hard work went into it."

McDonough took the road less travelled to the show. Check that — he took a road *never* travelled. McDonough was the first player to make it to the NHL out of St. Anselm College, a U.S. Division II school. McDonough is the son and grandson of New Hampshire sports royalty. His grandfather Hubie was a local legend; his father, Hubie, was a local legend; and now this Hubie had made it all the way to the NHL. He made his debut on October 28, 1988. "I'll never forget getting called up. I was in New Haven, and I got called up for a game in Winnipeg. Being in that room with Dave Taylor, Wayne Gretzky, Larry Robinson, Bernie Nicholls — All-Stars and Hall of Famers — and to look down and see Los Angeles written across my chest for the first time was a tremendous feeling. To be able to go out there and play in the NHL, it was like walking on air."

Players that McDonough watched as a kid and while he was a student at college were suddenly teammates. He played in four games with the Kings that fall, but he spent most of the year in the AHL where he put up an impressive 92 points in 74 games with the Nighthawks. That total was good enough for eighth in the AHL points race. The next year, McDonough started the season with the Kings. He was a full-time NHLer. He scored his first NHL goal in the Kings' first game of the season. "Wayne Gretzky assisted on it. I came around the net and shot it at the net. It went through the legs of Toronto's Allan Bester. We won the game."

McDonough added an assist as well, for two points in just his fifth NHL game. Life was good. Hubie scored three goals with the Kings before he was shipped to the Islanders in a three-player trade on November 29, 1989. He scored another 18 goals with the Islanders that year. Then came 1990–91: an up-and-down year that produced goal number four on the season and this card. It wasn't an easy year, but it was NHL reality. Repeatedly, McDonough was called up and sent down. Now, in his new line of work, he's often the guy who gets to tell a player that he is being called up to the NHL. "As I'm calling guys now to tell them they're getting called up, I say, 'Enjoy it, because it goes by fast.' All of a sudden your career is over and you're in management or you're in another job and you look back and, man, it's gone in the blink of an eye. And that's what I'm trying to do even now in this role — enjoy it. I'm in the hockey world, and you can't beat that." McDonough played his final NHL game with San Jose in the 1992–93 season. He spent the rest of the decade in the IHL. If McDonough's face was pictured on a card after his first NHL goal, it likely would have shown a lot more ecstasy than relief.

But it could always be worse. You could be the guy just *behind* Hubie. It looks like No. 20 of the Pens is doing the old skate-of-shame back to the Pittsburgh bench after picking up a minus, courtesy of Hubie McDonough. "I didn't think about that. That's a good point."

TOM FERGUS

TORONTO
MAPLE
LEAFS

"NOW
WITH
MAPLE
LEAFS"

TOM FERGUS   C

TOM FERGUS

Ht: 6'0"   Born: 6-16-62, Chicago, Illinois   Home: St. George, Ontario
Wt: 200   Last Amateur Club: Peterborough Petes (1980-81)
Shoots: L   Acquired: 3rd Round Choice (60th overall) 1980 Draft

NHL RECORD / FICHE DANS LA LNH

YEAR ANNÉE	TEAM ÉQUIPE	GP	G	A	PTS	PIM
81-82	Bruins	61	15	24	39	12
82-83	Bruins	80	28	35	63	39
83-84	Bruins	69	25	36	61	12
84-85	Bruins	79	30	43	73	75
NHL Totals/Totaux dans la LNH		289	98	138	236	138

PERSONAL: A Boston fan while growing up in Montreal. Tom now wears #28 for the Bruins. Has two dogs, Arrow & Nipper. Partisan de Boston durant sa jeunesse à Montréal, Tom porte maintenant le chandail numéro 28 des Bruins. Il a deux chiens appelés Arrow et Nipper.

© 1985 NHL/NHLPA

PEE CHEE

©1985 O-Pee-Chee
Ptd. in Canada / Imprimé au Canada

113

TOM FERGUS   1985–86
O-PEE-CHEE #113

"I never thought I'd be on a card that had me wearing a Bruins sweater and a Leafs logo at the bottom. That goes to show the times. Today, they would have a new card out in a month, with you on your new team."

Tom Fergus makes an excellent point.

This is Fergus's fourth O-Pee-Chee card, and you better believe it was a big deal to him. "It was great. I don't think any guy would tell you that having your face on a hockey card isn't a great feeling. Most of the guys collected hockey cards as kids. And now you're on one of them? It was definitely good."

If you were to describe Tom Fergus's look on this offering, you might call it a poker face. It's kind of fitting, really, given that his poker face was likely the one he was wearing when the Bruins decided to ship him to the Leafs. Tom Fergus was in contract negotiations with the Bruins, or, at least, he wanted to be, before they sent him to the Leafs for Bill Derlago on October 11, 1985. "The reason behind [the trade] was money. It's so funny today. I was asking for $30,000 more per season. The kids today get a million or two million dollar raise on their second contract without really doing too much. I asked to be traded because the Bruins wouldn't give me a raise.

"I wasn't happy with how the Bruins were trying to negotiate, or, rather, their lack of negotiating. It was more irritating than anything. I wasn't being a diehard trying to get more money. I just thought they were treating me, as they treated a lot of guys, unfairly. They say you have to do something to get a raise, and then when you finally do it, you don't get a raise. And I had already played for four years. The average length of a career back then was 3.7 years. If I wasn't going to get more money then, when was I going to? So it was a catch-22. Yeah, I was mad. I went on TV and asked to be traded. That's why the trade happened so quickly."

Fergus was making around $100,000 a year with the Bruins at the time of the deal. When he got to Toronto, he played out his contract. He suddenly didn't need to renegotiate. His contract was in U.S. dollars.

"Funny part was back in the '80s I got a 40 percent raise just moving to Canada."

You have to wonder if Fergus kept his poker face on when he went to work with the Leafs. In the mid 1980s, he pretty much joined the circus when he moved to Toronto. The ringleader was the man at the very top: Harold Ballard. "Toronto was and always will be a great hockey town. You can always blame the management and the coaches, but the actual reality was Harold stepped in too much and really was too cheap to keep the coach we had. My first year, the head coach was Dan Maloney. I thought he got better as the year went on, as the team improved. But then [Harold had] no extra money for Maloney, so he was gone. And then it became a nightmare."

The following are the Leafs' total wins for Fergus's next five seasons: 32, 21, 28, 38, 23. The coaches were changing, the management was changing. The only constant was Ballard, until he passed away in April 1990. "The players knew to stay out of Harold's way. 'Hello. How ya doing? Nice to see you,' and then move on. Don't get into a conversation with him because you never knew if you'd be the topic of the next TV or newspaper headline. I said hello to him when he was around the dressing room, but to sit and have a conversation with him? No. When he talked, you never knew what the hell he was going to say.

"The best part of hockey is winning. We did a lot of that in Boston. If you look at our team in Toronto, we had some good players. The Leafs just weren't run very well from the top down. It's like any business. You got great products, you got great this, great that, but if you don't have good people running it, how well does it do?"

Fergus still lives in Toronto. I see him quite a bit at hockey fundraisers, and I can attest he still has the hands that helped him snipe the 30 goals this card states he had for the Bruins in 1984–85. Fergus has a chuckle when he talks about what else is on the back of the card. Part of his bio states he "has two dogs, Arrow & Nipper."

"I had two German shepherds. I don't know where they got that information. We did have a laugh when that came out. We were like, 'Where in the hell did they get that?' Back then, I wasn't going around telling people I had two dogs. The idiotic or pointless information on the back of those cards was usually true. Somebody asked somebody a question."

The information may have been a tad off the wall, and sometimes the pictures weren't the best, but Fergus will let you know, those old cards made you legit. "You didn't feel like you'd made the NHL until you had an O-Pee-Chee card. O-Pee-Chee was your second year. You had to have stats to have an O-Pee-Chee card."

It's true: you had to play in the league to earn a card, at least up until the start of the 1990s. The old "NOW WITH" on the front of a card is a thing of the past as well. Fergus started his career when O-Pee-Chee was the only game in Canada. By the end of his career, his cards were everywhere and seemingly produced by everyone. "As it got going, there were so many cards out there. It just wasn't as big a deal."

Garth Butcher — 1991–92 Topps Stadium Club #223

It's my firm belief that hockey cards are small glimpses into history. They can bring you back to a point in time when the game was just a little bit different. Looking at this candid shot of a mulleted Garth Butcher is kind of like going to a museum and seeing the skeletal remains of a long-lost beast. We are travelling through time to

Chapter Four — IT WAS IN AT THE TIME

examine one of the game's toughest players from more than a quarter-century ago.

Let's start with the wood, or in this case the aluminum. For a good five- to 10-year period, the best players didn't terrify goaltenders with wood, instead they terrified them (and opposing forwards) with aluminum. Some of the game's best, such as Wayne Gretzky and Brett Hull, did their damage with a wooden blade jammed into a shaft made of aluminum alloy. "They were so strong compared to the wood," says Butcher. "I used a really stiff, hard one. Hully [Brett Hull] used one that would bow and bend when he shot."

Hull scored a career-high 86 goals with an aluminum stick in 1990–91. Butcher used his for a different purpose — like clearing opposing forwards from in front of his net. Aluminum, it turns out, presents many benefits to big, strong, no-nonsense defenceman. "When I used the wood sticks, it was pretty hard to argue with the referee that you didn't cross-check a guy when you're standing there with your stick in two pieces. It's like standing there with a knife or a gun and saying you didn't do it. The aluminums would just bend and the ref couldn't see that. I feel much shame now for the guys in front of the net. There were some pretty hard cross-checks."

Needless to say, if Butcher was using his aluminum stick as more of a defensive than offensive tool, he didn't spend a ton of time outside the Blues room fiddling with his Easton. This photo was likely snapped while Butcher "was gluing the blade in."

And blades were something that Butcher was just lucky to find. He shared the same blade pattern as Hall of Famer Brendan Shanahan, who Butcher says had some sticky fingers. "I kept running out of my blades, and I kept yelling at our trainers, 'Where are they going? You told me you just got some in.' But Shanny was using them. Though he seemed to be able to score better with them." Butcher scored 48 career regular-season goals — Brendan Shanahan had 656.

The next thing that jumps out on this card is Butcher's upper body gear. This was just around the time that "big gear" was in its infancy. Butcher wore pads that protected. By today's standards, Butcher's elbow and shoulder pads are nothing. Now, some players wear pads that not only protect but also can hurt opponents. In fact, about 25 years ago, Butcher's equipment size was the norm, but guys like Brendan Shanahan were still skating around with shoulder pads that Butcher describes as "the ones that we had in Regina in Peewee."

"The guys who weren't wearing the big pads tended to be the guys who were your really good players — the guys you want to protect. They were the guys who weren't going out to maim someone. They were out to score goals and make plays."

And at times, Butcher was the one being called upon to protect his high-scoring Peewee-equipped teammates. (Shanahan aside, of course.) Butcher's PIM total on the back of this card tells you a lot about him. He had a career-high 289 minutes in the box that season, which was only good enough for sixth in the NHL. That alone is evidence that in the last 25 years, aluminum sticks and regular-sized upper body protection aren't the only things that have changed. What happens out on the ice has changed as well. "No doubt about it. And in some ways it's for the better. I still believe that it's important for the players to . . . I'll call it policing, for lack of a better word. If the players take responsibility for what goes on out on the ice, I think it would save a lot of this marching to New York to find out how long you're suspended for. The suspension used to be: you have to play against these three tough guys because of what you just did to Mr. Gretzky or Mr. Lemieux. And that made 95 percent of the problems go away because the guys just didn't do the cheap stuff — they didn't want to pay that price. They would rather pay 10 grand."

Butcher says a lack of responsibility on the ice has not only changed the way the game is played, but it's also put a lot of pressure on the men handing out the suspensions. "It's hard when you're looking back at the film, and you're saying, 'Oh, the guy shouldn't have done that.' That's really hard. I don't see how you can be a suit and make that decision. Unless you've played in the last couple of years, it's not relevant to what's going on out there."

Perhaps just a few short minutes after his picture was taken, Garth Butcher would have been on the ice for a Norris Division tilt. The "Chuck" Norris was loaded with toughies. Five of the top 10 penalty-minute leaders in the 1990–91 season spent at least part of that year playing in the Norris. If something went a little sideways on the ice, though, a fight didn't always break out. Players did the policing. And it wasn't always in a physical way. "You used to be able to just skate by a guy — say a respectful guy, like Steve Yzerman — and stand in front of the bench and say, 'Did you just see what your guy did to my guy? Now I'm going to do it to you. I'm not going to fight him and break his wrist, I'm going to break yours. So you better have a chat with him.' And Yzerman would look at his bench and say, 'Hey! Take it easy. Don't do that! Now they're going to beat me up.'"

The fear, rather than the fight, often kept things in line a quarter of a century ago. But just like aluminum sticks and foam shoulder pads, it's

a thing of the past. Chances are we won't return to the Wild West days of the Norris, and aluminum won't make a return either. As for foam padding, one can hope. I've maintained for years it will help cut down on concussions, but equipment manufacturing is a big-money business. You can charge a lot more for a hard plastic elbow pad that can knock a guy out on impact as opposed to soft padding.

The only thing I'm positive Butcher could bring back from this card is his standard issue hockey player mullet. Garth owns five restaurants in the Toronto area and looks all-business these days. Sadly, there is no party in the back. But unlike a lot of ex-players, he still has the follicle game to bring back that great hockey hair. "Not that I would," says Butcher, "but I can still grow it."

Mark Napier

Ht: 5'10" Wt: 185 · Shoots: L 1st Pro Season: 1975-76
Acquired: Trade with Canadiens
Born: 1-28-57, Toronto, Ontario
Home: Pointe-Claire, Ontario

105

WHA and NHL record / Fiche dans l'AMH et la LNH

YEAR	TEAM	GP	G	A	PTS	PIM
75-76	Toronto	78	43	50	93	20
76-77	Birmingham	80	60	36	96	24
77-78	Birmingham	79	33	32	65	9
78-79	Canadiens	54	11	20	31	11
79-80	Canadiens	76	16	33	49	7
80-81	Canadiens	79	35	36	71	24
81-82	Canadiens	80	40	41	81	14
82-83	Canadiens	73	40	27	67	6
83-84	North Stars	5	3	2	5	0
83-84		58	13	28	41	17

NHL TOTALS 425 158 187 345 79
WHA TOTALS 237 136 118 254 134

Scored GWG at 6:39 of 3rd period, 10-15-83, vs. Canucks.
Le 15-10-83, contre les Canucks, Mark marqua le but gagnant à 6:39 durant la 3ème période.

NHL NHLPA Ptd. in Canada
Imprimé au Canada
©1984 O-Pee-Chee

Mark Napier
NORTH STARS
RW

MARK NAPIER **1984–85**
O-PEE-CHEE #105

The first time I saw one, I knew I had to have one. It appeared on a full-page ad on the back cover of the Pictou Junior C Mariners Saturday night program. It was one of the coolest looking things I had ever seen. Cooperalls had been introduced a couple of years earlier, and by the mid 1980s, they were a hit — at least, they were in my eyes. So this bucket had to be the next big thing. The XL7 was billed as the future of the hockey helmet. And, for me, the future could not come soon enough.

The first kid in my neighbourhood to get one was my buddy David from across the street. Dave was a year older, and I had gotten his hand-me-down Daoust 301 skates a year or two before. But I was not going to settle for a hand-me-down XL7. I didn't have to. Soon enough I had my very own. As did seemingly every other kid in my town. I remember my dad telling me, "Boy, you'll never have to buy another helmet for the rest of your life." That was the plan. The XL7 could expand or contract to fit a head of any size. I had my helmet for life.

As much as the XL7 was the must-have hockey accessory in rural Nova Scotia, it didn't seem to go over so well in the NHL. In fact, based on my hockey card collection — my window into the hockey world — only two players wore the lid of the future: Craig Ramsay and Mark Napier.

I was a big Napier fan. He was one of the top scorers on my Montreal Canadiens. In the spring of 1984, though, he seemed even cooler to me. Sure, he was a Minnesota North Star by then, but he was wearing the lid of the future. If even the smallest part of me wondered if my XL7 wasn't all that cool, Napier stuffed those fears. He was an NHLer, and he wore one. I have two things to thank for Napier's choice of helmet: his trade, along with Keith Acton and a third-round pick, to the Minnesota North Stars for Bobby Smith; and his larger than average head.

"My head was so big," begins Napier, "that I couldn't get into a CCM helmet. So when I was playing with the Habs, the Cooper was actually the only helmet that fit my noggin. When I got to Minny, they had these new helmets that had just come out. And I tried it on and it was really,

really comfortable. And it didn't need any screws; it just had those flaps. You'd open the flaps and it made the helmet as big or as small as you wanted. I probably had it right to the max on the flaps. It was just very comfortable. It wasn't the prettiest helmet in the world, but it sure was comfortable."

Still, in 1985, I thought this helmet looked pretty attractive. In hindsight, when you were wearing a mask like all of us minor hockey players, it kind of made you look like a human lollipop. The thing was a perfect circle by the time it was decked out with a shield.

However, as Napier points out, its comfort could never be questioned. The lid of an XL7 was stuffed with this great padding; it was almost like being enveloped by a well-worn couch. "I think they were trying to make it similar to a football helmet. So it had a little more padding and it was supposed to have a little more protection for you. But I just got it because it was big and comfortable."

Even though he was one of the few players in the NHL going for the futuristic look, Napier didn't hear a lot from his on-ice adversaries about it. "No more than normal. I wasn't a tough guy or a fighter, but I'm sure if I was, there would have been a little more chirping about how beautiful my helmet was."

Soon enough, though, one of hockey's most feared men would put Napier (and his helmet) in his place. After just 97 regular-season games in Minnesota, Napier was sent to the Edmonton Oilers for Gord Sherven and Terry Martin. Before his trade from Montreal, Napier was a Cup-winning teammate of Guy Lafleur. Now he was a teammate and would soon win a Cup with Wayne Gretzky. Good company. "They were both such great offensive players. Obviously you can argue Wayne is the best of all time and Guy may be in the top ten. Different positions too, so it's a little bit tougher to compare them. We used to joke with both of them. We would tell them, 'Don't think out there.' If Guy or Wayne had a breakaway from the far blue line, very seldom would they score. But if they had two men hanging over them, they'd

score every time. They didn't have time to think; they just reacted. That's how great they were."

Sadly, though, for me at least, that trade to Edmonton would soon mark the end of Mark Napier's XL7 experiment. Within a year or two, you'd be hard-pressed to find any NHLers wearing the helmet of the future. The last time I wore my XL7 was around 1991, right before I traded it in for the much more stylish Cooper SK2000. I got a good six or seven years out of my XL7. Napier traded in his XL7 for the SK2000 as well. He, however, made the switch about six years earlier than I did, and at the urging of one of his new Edmonton teammates. "The last time I wore it was when I got traded to the Oilers. I was going out with a white XL7 — it may have been my first game there — and Dave Semenko was behind me and he says, 'Napier, get rid of that friggin helmet.' I ended up going back to the Cooper after that. When Dave Semenko said something . . . you did it."

But those XL7s were built to last . . . forever. Napier figures he may still have one or two lying around. "I should look to see if I got one in the basement. I'll try to find one for you."

I think I definitely need to have that helmet again.

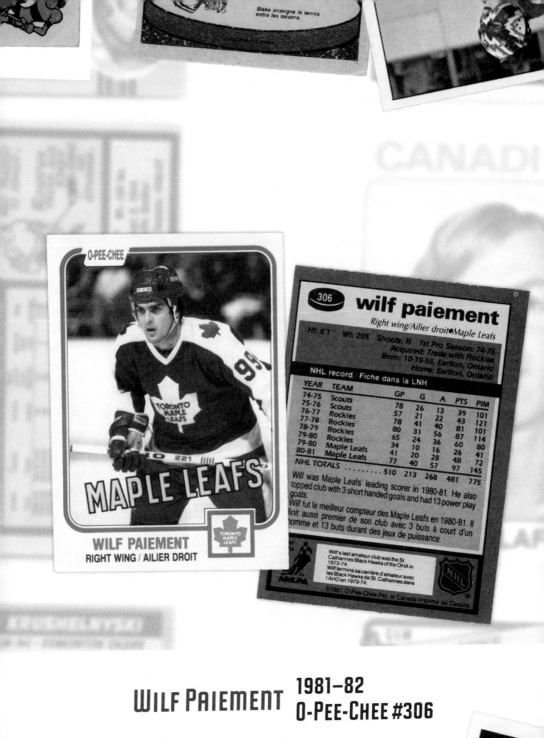

O-PEE-CHEE

WILF PAIEMENT
RIGHT WING / AILIER DROIT

TORONTO MAPLE LEAFS

306 **wilf paiement**
Right wing/Ailier droit•Maple Leafs

Ht: 6'1" Wt: 205 Shoots: R 1st Pro Season: 74-75
Acquired: Trade with Rockies
Born: 10-16-55, Earlton, Ontario
Home: Earlton, Ontario

NHL record / Fiche dans la LNH

YEAR	TEAM	GP	G	A	PTS	PIM
74-75	Scouts					
75-76	Scouts	78	26	13	39	101
76-77	Rockies	57	21	22	43	121
77-78	Rockies	78	41	40	81	101
78-79	Rockies	80	31	56	87	114
79-80	Rockies	65	24	36	60	80
79-80	Maple Leafs	34	10	16	26	41
80-81	Maple Leafs	41	20	28	48	72
NHL TOTALS		510	213	268	481	775

Wilf was Maple Leafs' leading scorer in 1980-81. He also
topped club with 3 short handed goals and had 13 power play
goals.
Wilf fut le meilleur compteur des Maple Leafs en 1980-81. Il
finit aussi premier de son club avec 3 buts à court d'un
homme et 13 buts durant des jeux de puissance.

Wilf's last amateur club was the St.
Catharines Black Hawks of the OHA in
1973-74.
Wilf termina sa carrière d'amateur avec
les Black Hawks de St. Catharines dans
l'AHO en 1973-74.

© 1981 O-Pee-Chee Ptd. in Canada/Imprimé au Canada

NHL

WILF PAIEMENT   1981–82
O-PEE-CHEE #306

You miss things as a kid that, years later, you pick up on and wonder how they ever escaped your 10-year-old eyes. I think it's safe to say that 99 is the most famous number in hockey history. You say "99" and the first thing that comes to mind is Wayne Gretzky. But the Great One wasn't the only player to ever wear the number in the NHL. Back in the 1930s, a few Montreal Canadiens wore it, and circa 1980, Wilf Paiement wore it as well.

Today, it seems sacrilegious to wear number 99 if your last name isn't Gretzky. But when Wilf Paiement was traded to the Toronto Maple Leafs on December 29, 1979, wearing 99 wasn't that big of a deal. "Wayne wasn't as popular then. I mean, he was getting into his fame then, but it was 1979," says Paiement. Gretzky ended up wearing 99 in Sault Ste. Marie because 9 was already taken. The same thing happened to Paiement when he landed in Toronto.

"I always wore number nine. When I was a kid, Gordie Howe was my idol and I played the same position as him, so nine was my number. I wore nine when I played amateur hockey back home. I wore nine in junior. I wore nine in pro the first six years. When I came to Toronto, Dan Maloney had nine. Dan was older than me so [Punch] Imlach suggested that I wear 99. I wasn't going to argue with him."

Three players wore 99 in the 1979–80 season. Paiement, Gretzky, and the Jets' Rick Dudley. And like Gretzky, the Leafs version of 99 was a pretty decent goal-scorer himself: the guy on this card knew how to put the puck in the net. When Paiement landed in Toronto, he had big shoes to fill. Lanny McDonald was gone and No. 99 Wilf Paiement was in town. "Lanny was a favourite in Toronto. Everywhere he played, Lanny was a favourite. He was a hell of a hockey player. I don't know if I felt the pressure. I came in here with an open mind to play as hard as I could — that was all I could do. I played hard and I enjoyed Toronto. I loved it."

Paiement played on a line with Darryl Sittler. In his first full season with the Leafs, Paiement scored 40 goals. Out in Edmonton, number 99 Wayne Gretzky scored 55. When you watch video of games from 1980–81, it looks like a different game. I'd have to say that's because it was. It was wide open. "Teams didn't concentrate on defence like they do now. Our system wasn't as good defensively. We could get closer to the net without being penalized. I remember going through the crease and rubbing into a goalie. I think guys that had good shots like [Rick] Vaive and I, we could make goalies flinch because they didn't have good equipment like today. Today I see the guys wind up and a goalie doesn't even move. He figures, *Hit me anywhere you want, I don't care, it's not going to hurt.*"

It's a great point. Goalies felt more shots in 1981, and players used that to their advantage. "Mickey Redmond was awesome. He was a sharp-shooter. He'd shoot pucks high at goalies and they would duck. And, naturally, the goalie would go up on the next shot and he'd come in and put it on the ice. For sure, it was the equipment that wasn't protecting them."

By the time this hockey card hit the market in the winter of 1981–82, Gretzky was on his way to a 212-point season. But what could Paiement do? He took 99 when he arrived in Toronto in 1979 — he couldn't change his number now, could he?

As any beer leaguer out there knows, you just don't wear 99. If you do, you're going to get chirped. So I'm wondering: did anyone chirp Wilf Paiement of the Toronto Maple Leafs? "No, never. I was playing good hockey then too." Besides, Paiement was pretty tough, as his 145 PIMs during the 1980–81 season can attest, and he was a big six-foot-one, 205 pounds back in the day. "I was pretty mouthy too, so if somebody chirped me, maybe I could have done something about it."

Paiement's days as number 99 ended when he was traded to the Quebec Nordiques in March 1982. By then No. 99 *was* Wayne Gretzky, and Paiement was never going to wear it again. "When I got traded, I said 99 belongs to 99, not me. So when I went to Quebec, I took a different number."

Wilf Paiement was the last player other than the Great One to wear No. 99. This is a pretty cool card because it's shocking to see anyone

other than Gretzky with that number on his jersey. And, of course, we'll never see it again. Ninety-nine is retired for good. I tell Wilf it must be something to know that no one will ever wear *his* number again. He then makes one thing very clear. "It's not my number. It will never be my number. I just happened to wear that number when I played for the Leafs. It's Wayne Gretzky's number."

BLUES

O-Pee-Chee

TOM TILLEY • D

D · St. Louis Blues

498

TOM TILLEY

HEIGHT: 6'0" WEIGHT: 180 SHOOTS: RIGHT
LAST AMATEUR CLUB: MICHIGAN STATE UNIV. (1987-88)
ACQUIRED: 10th ROUND CHOICE (196th OVERALL) 1984 DRAFT
BORN: 3-28-65, TRENTON, ONT. HOME: TRENTON, ONT.

NHL RECORD / FICHE DANS LA LNH

Year Année	Team Équipe	GP	G	A	PTS	PIM
88-89	Blues					
89-90	Blues	70	1	22	23	47
		34	0	5	5	6
NHL Totals/Totaux dans la LNH		104	1	27	28	53

GAME WINNING GOALS/BUTS GAGNANTS 1989-90: 0

Tom has played very consistently ever since breaking into the NHL. He's a good skater and will challenge opposing forwards, forcing hurried passes and giveaways. Led St. Louis in +/- in '89 playoffs. • Tom a fait preuve d'une grande constance depuis son arrivée dans la LNH. C'est un bon patineur qui ne craint pas de défier les attaquants de l'autre équipe pour les forcer à faire des passes à l'aveuglette. Meilleur cote +/- de St-Louis durant les éliminatoires de 1989.

NHL PLAYOFF RECORD FICHE DURANT LES ÉLIMINATOIRES		GP	G	A	PTS	PIM
1990		0	0	0	0	0
CAREER/CARRIÈRE		10	1	2	3	17

NATIONAL HOCKEY LEAGUE LIGUE NATIONALE DE HOCKEY

OFFICIAL LICENSED PRODUCT PRODUIT LICENCIÉ OFFICIEL

©1990 NHLPA

©1990 O-PEE-CHEE CO. LTD.

™ NHLPA

PTD. IN CANADA/ IMPRIMÉ AU CANADA

PEE CHEE

Tom Tilley

1990–91
O-PEE-CHEE #498

"The mullet years," says Tom Tilley. "Look good, feel good, play good, as we used to say."

I remember making the trek from Pictou to Montreal with my dad and brother for my first NHL game. I was in the seventh grade. Walking into the Forum was, as many have said before, pretty much a religious experience. And for me, at least, my sermon began with the warm-up. I was so excited to see players up close and in the flesh. My brother and I got as close to the ice as we could to watch the 20-minute session. Warming up back in the day meant blaring non-dance track tunes and, of course, no lids. "Everybody had their own rituals," begins Tilley. "For me it was during warm-up, before I put my helmet on."

This card, taken during a Blues warm-up, captures Tilley in the perfect pre-game stretch, with the perfect pre-game hair. It looks like he just came out of the salon before he hit the ice. But, as he said, looking good was part of the whole routine. Tilley has his hair greased back and there's not a speck of stubble on his 25-year-old face. "Some guys, like Gordie Roberts, my first defence partner, would shave after morning skate the day of a game. He always wanted to be clean-shaven. Some guys would rather not shave. Part of it was the look and part of it was laziness.

"For me, warm-up was generally just a time to get out there and get comfortable. Are my skates sharpened the right way? Does the curve of my stick have a good feel? Then it was just getting a good-enough work in to get loose. You can't play tense or think about it too much. You've thought about it all throughout the day: *Who are we playing against? Who am I going to be playing against?* Warm-up is just an opportunity to let that all fade away. You think in practice and you react in a game. And I needed to be loose. I don't mean joking around. Everyone had their own way of getting loose. For me, it was just making sure that my legs felt good and that my skates were good and all the tools of the trade were feeling good."

But warm-up can often come with consequences, especially when you take your lid off. Oiler Taylor Hall took a dangerous cut to the face during warm-up. The worst warm-up Tom Tilley had was at Maple

Leaf Gardens. Tilley is from Trenton, Ontario, about two hours east of Toronto. That night he had about 20 family and friends in the stands. Of course, he went out for the pre-game warm-up with his hair slicked back and not a helmet in sight. Not that the lid would have helped on this night. "It was near the end of warm-up. You know, you just skate down the middle and take a shot. A goalie pops in the net, a goalie pops out of the net."

Right away, I'm thinking Tilley drilled Curtis Joseph in the head or something. No. Tilley took his shot and then curled to the left. "And all of a sudden, it was like I got hit by a bullet. I took a Brendan Shanahan snapshot that ricocheted off the crossbar and caught me right in the front teeth. The only good news was that I had lost my four front teeth in Buffalo earlier that year, so this one just blew my lip apart."

That's a positive way to look at things. The bad news at the time was it took the medical staff at the Gardens two periods to put Tilley's lip back together. Yes, looking good in warm-up does come with a price — in this case, about an hour and a half of impromptu lip reconstruction. When the third period began, Tilley had only one thing to do: play. "The guys were like, 'What are you doing on the ice? What are you doing out here?' It was like, 'I bought tickets for my family, so I'm playing.' That was one of my tougher warm-ups: taking Shanny's snapper off the face."

Tilley played with a lot of talent when he was with the Blues. His first season was in 1988–89, and he arrived in St. Louis right at the beginning of Hull and Oates, as in Brett and Adam. The two made up one of the best playmaker-sniper duos in NHL history. "Oates wasn't a very big guy. He was smaller than me — probably 180 pounds. He had pretty good skill, and even though he didn't look that fast, you could never catch him — he always had his head up and made just ridiculous plays. Hully could score from anywhere. My rookie year was his first full year there. He showed up out of shape, and you're like, 'Geez, man. If this guy could just lose a few pounds, he'd be really special.' And to his credit, he did."

Oates was the set-up man, and Hull was the finisher. In 1990–91, Hull had 86 goals. Oates had 90 assists. One thing that always amazed me about Oates was that he played with a sawed-off blade. Take a look at an old Oates hockey card and his blade is sawed off at the end. Tilley says the blade was pretty much straight too. "He didn't really stickhandle a lot. He wasn't trying to beat you one-on-one; he was trying to draw you to one place and open up the ice for other people. He had an uncanny way of ragging the puck. He could make a quick turn or a quick pivot. It wasn't like he was giving you side-to-side stickhandling, quick stick, and stuff like that. That wasn't his style."

A lot of the Hull and Oates magic happened on the power play. Tilley was mainly a penalty killer, so he watched a lot of it from the bench. Practice was also always a treat: "We would do three-on-twos all the time. If it was me or another defenceman, they'd isolate a defenceman. Oates would skate it up the middle and you'd have to go to him, and he would sauce one over your stick and Hully would go in and score and come back laughing. Then the next time you'd shade towards the middle, and Hully would get the puck and drive wide. You'd turn to him, then Oatsie would go to the net and tap in an empty netter."

Tilley played in 174 career NHL regular-season games. He sounds like a guy who appreciated it even back then; he didn't let the moment pass him by. "I was a tenth-round draft pick," Tilley points out. That's something that shaped his understanding of how far he'd come as a player.

And he looked good too, as his rookie card demonstrates. "It's a little bit of nostalgia. For any player who has a hockey card, people think that's pretty cool. They're like, 'Wow, he lasted long enough to get a card.'"

1993
NHL
ALL
STAR

ÉTOILE
1993
DE LA
LNH

Al lafrate

DEFENSE
DÉFENSEUR

Upper Deck and the card/hologram combination are trademarks of The Upper Deck Company.
© 1993 The Upper Deck Company. All rights reserved. Printed in the U.S.A.
Upper Deck et la combinaison carte/hologramme sont des marques de commerce de The Upper Deck Company.
© 1993 The Upper Deck Company. Tous droits observés. Imprimé aux États-Unis.

McD-16

WASHINGTON CAPITALS

Washington Capitals defenseman Al lafrate let a shot rip at 105.2 MPH to claim the Hardest shot in the skills competition of the '93 NHL All-Star game. His participation in last winter's competition marked the third time he has skated at the midseason classic. lafrate, Sylvain Cote and Kevin Hatcher made NHL history last season, becoming the first trio of defensemen on one team to have simultaneous 20-goal seasons. lafrate collected 25 goals and 41 assists last season. He placed second on the Caps in power-play goals with 11 and he added four game-winners. lafrate is a quick skater who is very adept on the power play with either his blast from the point or a deke and a well-placed pass.

CAPITALS^ DE WASHINGTON

Le défenseur Al lafrate a décoché un tir de 105.2 m/h pour gagner le concours d'habileté du tir le plus rapide lors du match des étoiles en 1993. Il en était à sa 3ᵉ participation au match des étoiles. lafrate, Sylvain Côté et Kevin Hatcher ont passé à l'histoire de la LNH en 1992-93 en devenant le premier trio de défenseurs sur une équipe à chacun marquer 20 buts ou plus pendant une saison. lafrate a pour sa part récolté 25 buts et 41 passes. Il s'est classé au 2ᵉ rang chez les Capitals au chapitre des buts marqués en avantage numérique (11) et a marqué 4 buts gagnants. lafrate est un patineur rapide et très habile sur le jeu de puissance avec son tir puissant de la ligne bleue, ses passes précises et ses feintes.

1993 All-Star Game Totals: Totaux - Match des Étoiles 1993:	GP	G	A	PTS	PIM
	PJ	B	A	PTS	MIN
	1	0	0	0	0
Career All-Star Game Totals: Totaux en carrière - Match des Étoiles:	GP	G	A	PTS	PIM
	PJ	B	A	PTS	MIN
	3	0	0	0	2.00

Al Iafrate
1993–94 Upper Deck McDonald's #16

"Hockey hair was everything. Who's the guy who got his hair cut off and then he got weak?" asks Al Iafrate. I don't remember the name off the top of my head, but afterward I recalled the Bible story of Samson and Delilah.

"I had the skullet going. I couldn't let go of my hair. I had that long tail in the back even though I was going bald on top. The hockey hair was important. You had to have a little flow going out of the back of the helmet, especially in the early '90s, when Whitesnake and Poison and all those bands came out. You had to have decent hair."

Maybe the hair, or, more precisely, the skullet, gave Al Iafrate his superpowers. Hockey's version of Samson came to life during the 1993 NHL All-Star Game. This McDonald's Upper Deck card tells the tale of a Skulleted Hockey God who unleashed the power of his KOHO Evolution. "Al Iafrate let a shot rip at 105.2 MPH to claim the hardest shot in the skills competition of the '93 NHL All-Star Game," the card reads. The record stood for the next 16 years, until Zdeno Chara broke the mark in 2009. Chara then set another record in 2012, with a shot clocking in at 108.8 miles per hour. "I was hoping my shot was harder. I felt like it was harder. I had shot hard the year before. It was 102 point something, and this felt a lot harder. I think I was feeling better too. I was a little banged up at the previous All-Star Game, but at this one I felt really healthy, so I got a good head of steam going into it. I thought it was 109. I think it should still be the record today . . . there must have been something wrong with the gun," Iafrate says and laughs.

In 1993, the hardest-shot competition was still in its primitive stages. It was only the fourth time the event was ever held. "I knew I had a hard shot, but I didn't realize it was harder than everyone else's until the All-Star. It's kind of like the slam-dunk contest or the home-run derby; the lights are on and it's the main stage."

In the early years, players had to qualify for the skills competition. Even if you weren't an All-Star, you could still have a chance at the skills. The one thing that always got my attention during the events was the radar gun. In the early years of the skills competition, I swear the thing worked only half the time.

"Believe it or not, it takes a ton of energy to lace one. I've done it at different events or different hockey schools where they have a radar gun. The first shot and the second shot are key; they have to register. You're skating with 35 feet of steam and then you're blasting it and then you gotta line up and do it again and again. The earlier the shot registered, the better chance you had of setting or breaking a record."

Iafrate had a stick that was built for a slapshot. Today, composite sticks can adapt to any type of shot. Back in the day, you set up your stick to cater to your biggest strength. For Iafrate, that was the slapper. So, of course, I have to ask: how would he fare with today's stick technology? "I get asked that question a lot. I think incrementally I could shoot a little harder. I think I'd be in the mix with Chara and Weber if you could preserve me cryogenically. They froze this fish for five days, and then when it thawed it was alive again. So we can do it . . . I'll do a test." So if anyone out there has a time machine, and you want to go back to 1993, pick up Al Iafrate, and freeze him for a few years, he's willing to give the new technology a shot.

If you haven't picked up on it yet, Al Iafrate is more than a guy with just a shot. Sure, he's known for that and the skullet, but he was a dynamic player and a big personality who picked up 463 points in 799 career regular-season games. He was a four-time All-Star, and he makes up one-third of a record that may never be broken. It's noted on the back of this card: "Iafrate, Sylvain Cote, and Kevin Hatcher made NHL history last season, becoming the first trio of defencemen on one team to have simultaneous 20-goal seasons."

"What's the adage? Sometimes your best attributes are your biggest weaknesses. We were a team that relied heavily on us from the blue line; whether it was the power play or five-on-five, we were active. Every set of defencemen — [Kevin] Hatcher and [Calle] Johansson, me and Sylvain [Cote] — had at least one guy who was offensive and another guy who was *really* offensive. We had four guys who were very offensive-minded. It was always kind of a battle as to which guy would stay back with each pairing. Me and Hatchy were never partners, but we were probably the two most offensive guys. It was kind of our Achilles heel, because when it came time to try to beat Pittsburgh, we just couldn't get past them. When you are relying that heavily on offence from your blue line, you're kind of playing cutthroat hockey. The opposition are banking on the defenceman they are playing against trying to score, and they're going to be up ice, and then we've got these high-powered boys with one less defenceman in our zone."

The Caps, with all their talent, never could get by Mario Lemieux's Penguins. The Pens eliminated the Caps in '91 and '92. They went on to win the Cup in both of those seasons. Still, the record established by the three Caps D-men still stands. "I think that's an interesting record: three defencemen with 20 goals on one team. Now I don't think there are even three in the whole league who score 20. Three in a year who score 20? That's a lot. I'm not going to lie, the goalies are better now, with the technology and advances in the way they train. It's going to be harder for defencemen to get 20 goals."

Iafrate was more than just a shot and a hairdo. But still, he has a good sense of humour about the two things that people associate with him the most. After all, if he is hockey's version of Samson, the hair and the power do go hand in hand. Aside from the shot, one of my earliest memories of Al Iafrate came courtesy of *Don Cherry's Rock'em Sock'em Hockey*. My brother and I were stunned when we watched the tape and saw Tom Laidlaw propel Iafrate into the stanchion. But it wasn't the hit that shocked us, it was when Iafrate's lid came off. His hair was flying everywhere. "It was always kind of tough when the helmet got knocked off during a game. It was kind of an anxious moment . . . maybe someone would notice I was balding. Before that, no one could tell.

"Big Daddy Bob McGill tells that Laidlaw story all the time: when I got helicoptered, I cracked my ribs and went down. On the bench, everyone looked at each other. They were like, 'Is Al going to get up? Is he going to go for the helmet or is he going to stay down?' Bob said, 'He's going for the helmet for sure.'" McGill was right. Iafrate went for the helmet.

When this card came out, it was a salute to the man with the hardest shot on the planet. If Michael Jordan was the slam-dunk king, then Al Iafrate was the slapshot king. And to this day, it's his shot, not his overall game, not even the skullet, that fans remember. "I guess it's kind of cool to be acknowledged as the best in the world at something. But for the record I'm the best in the world at four things — most people are lucky to be at one — but I'm not going to tell you the other three. It's funny, that's all people talk about: the shot, the shot, the shot. It's what I'm synonymous with. Every once in a while, I'll say, 'You know, I thought I was a pretty good player too.'"

Jamie Matthews · Center

Jamie Matthews

76

BLACKHAWKS

JAMIE MATTHEWS

A strong skater with a good slap-shot and wrist shot, center Jamie Matthews was selected 44th overall by the Chicago Blackhawks in the second round of the '91 Entry Draft. A two-year veteran of major junior hockey with the Sudbury Wolves of the OHL, Matthews is a talented two-way forward possessing great play-making and offensive skills. He is a deft passer on both the forehand and backhand, stickhandles well, and has excellent anticipation and hockey sense. He adjusts quickly to changes in the flow of a game and works hard on every shift.

Jamie Matthews · Chicago Blackhawks · Center

YEAR	TEAM	GP	G	A	PTS	PIM	+/-
89-90	Sudbury	60	16	17	33	25	
90-91	Sudbury	66	14	38	52	41	

NO NHL STATISTICS

Height: 6'1"
Weight: 180 lbs.
Born: May 26, 1973
       Amherst,
       Nova Scotia
Shoots: Right

BLACKHAWKS

JAMIE MATTHEWS
1991–92
UPPER DECK #76

When we were growing up, it felt like my buddy Mark was some sort of regional hockey scout. We would go down to the Hector Arena and watch the Pictou Junior C Mariners on Saturday night. If the Mariners were on the road, we'd pack into Mark's dad's car and catch a road game.

And every so often, when his family would make the

Chapter Five — YEAH, I HAD A CARD

trek up to Springhill to visit his father's relatives, Mark would head straight to Amherst Stadium to check out the Ramblers, the local Junior A team. One night in Amherst, Mark spotted an up-and-coming Nova Scotia hockey star. When he got back to Pictou, he told me all about 15-year-old Jamie Matthews, a hometown boy who was suiting up in the then–Metro Valley Junior Hockey League for the rough-and-tumble Ramblers.

"Back then, the game was a lot different. I don't want to say violent, but the game has changed a lot," says Matthews, who didn't really have any options other than Junior A in his hometown. "There were two 15-year-olds on our team. Back then there was no AAA Midget in this area. Kids today from my area go play for Pictou. But back then, you just didn't do that — you played in your area and that was it."

Soon enough, other hockey scouts, aside from Mark, made the trek to Amherst to check out a 15-year-old who was outplaying 19- and 20-year-old men. "I was proud. Being from Amherst, I always watched the Ramblers play.

I had a great experience playing as a 15-year-old. There were some ups and downs, and obviously I was playing with bigger, stronger guys. But it was kind of exciting and kind of a thrill."

Back before the QMJHL claimed Atlantic Canada as its exclusive territory, East Coast kids got to choose where they would play Major Junior. Matthews chose the OHL. The kid from Nova Scotia went second overall in the 1989 OHL Draft, behind another big deal. Let's rephrase that: behind a Very Big Deal. Eric Lindros went number one. "It was a big thing to get drafted high. At the time I hadn't really heard about Lindros. I just heard he was good and he was a big player, but being on the East Coast you didn't really hear much about him."

Matthews did just fine playing against players like Eric Lindros and the rest of the young men in the OHL. He did so well that within a few years, I was on a mission to collect all the Jamie Matthews cards I could. His smiling face was stuffed into packs of 1991–92 Upper Deck, and if I was lucky, I could get a card of a kid who grew up in a town just 90 minutes up the Sunrise Trail from me. Matthews is all smiles on his Upper Deck, striking a pose on draft day 1991 when Chicago took him 44th overall.

"At that time, you're excited that you're going to get the opportunity to take the next step. There are not many people you actually know who have hockey cards. We all know that there's a million hockey cards out there, a million baseball cards out there, but it's not like you're buddies with the guys on them. It was kind of a thrill, and it's something that I will cherish forever."

Once the buzz of draft day and his very own hockey card wore off, it was back to the OHL for Matthews. He had two years to work out a deal with Chicago. He attended a couple of their camps, but the two sides could not get a deal done. "It was sort of a mutual thing. They weren't interested and that was fine." Matthews re-entered the draft. By this time my Matthews cards were stuffed away in boxes as I moved on to college. Matthews went 262nd to San Jose in the 1993 Draft. This time there were no hockey cards to mark the occasion. But he and the Sharks had a future together, or so it seemed.

"I had a contract worked out with them before I went back and played my last year in Sudbury. I went to a training facility the Sharks had in Minnesota for their prospects," says Matthews. And that's when it all went wrong for Matthews. In a scrimmage one day, Matthews took a skate right to the face.

"I had reconstructive surgery on part of my nasal passage. It was quite a long recovery from that. And it just sort of, I don't want to say went downhill, but it wasn't great after that." By the time Matthews got set to rejoin the Sudbury Wolves, the offer from the Sharks was off the table. If he could recover from the injury and put together a decent season with the Wolves, maybe he could earn a deal. He missed the first third of the season but he turned it on when he finally hit the ice. Jamie Matthews scored 97 points in 46 regular-season games. Once again, the future was bright. But when Matthews returned to Amherst, he had to deal with something that would make getting kicked in the face with a skate feel like a paper cut. "I wasn't home for a week and my dad passed away, unexpectedly. He was just as healthy as you and me. He had a stroke."

Matthews had come home with the intention of carrying on with his hockey career, hoping to sign a NHL deal. When his dad died, those plans didn't just go on the backburner, they went totally off the rails.

"It's quite a thing. I'm not trying to make excuses. There are days that I get up and I kick myself in the ass, but it was just sort of downhill after that. It was an emotional time, kind of a blur for quite a while.

"I don't know if it affected my love of the game. At the time, there were bigger issues than the game. It's nice to make lots of money and be famous and all that, but sometimes you've gotta put your family first. I'm not saying that was totally the issue, but at the time, San Jose and I had a contract and my agent had called me, and we had talked about some numbers. Don't get me wrong, it wasn't really a negotiation. They held all the cards because I was coming back from an injury. I basically had a decision to make: 'This is what they're offering you. Will you take it or not?'"

Matthews, the kid who was all smiles on his rookie card, spent a summer in turmoil. He didn't take the deal. "I don't know if I made the right decision or not, but that's just the way it goes. You look forward one day at a time. You know what I'm saying?'"

There isn't a 21-year-old on the planet who's ready for what Jamie Matthews had to deal with that summer. Cardboard hero or not, Matthews was just a kid. Hockey slowly went away for Matthews. He dabbled in some senior hockey in Nova Scotia and New Brunswick. "I was playing in Miramichi and I got a stick right under the eye. I thought I lost my eye. I said, 'Nope, that's it. I'm done. I gotta get up for work the same as everybody else the next day. I can't be doing this.' I missed a few games, let the stitches clear up, finished the season, but I said, 'No, I can't be doing this.'"

This Upper Deck card shows the smiling face of a kid who didn't have an easy road to the pros. He represents the last era of Atlantic Canadians who didn't have the option of joining a Major Junior league in their own neck of the woods. Until the mid '90s, East Coast kids, like the kid on this card, had to leave home to pursue their big-league dreams. "People don't realize that with no Quebec League [in the Maritimes] there weren't a lot of people playing Major Junior; there was just a handful. Now there's all kinds of guys; they're getting more of an opportunity. I'm not saying it's easier now, but there are better opportunities and they're getting better training too."

Kids growing up in Amherst now can head down the road to play AAA Midget. If they're lucky enough, they may suit up for the Ramblers, where Matthews was an assistant coach a few years back. Up the road in Moncton and down the road in Halifax, there are teams in the Q. It's a different hockey world than the one Matthews grew up in. "There are a few of the cards at the house here. There are a few at my mom's house," says Matthews. "It's probably more than a little piece of cardboard.

It's kind of nice. My kids are getting older, and they look at the card. Although I wish I would have played a little longer and I never did play in the NHL, there's a little bit of a legacy there."

BRENT TULLY D

WORLD JUNIOR CHAMPIONSHIPS
SWEDEN '93

592

NHLPA

BRENT TULLY   **CANADA**

Strong skating is just one of the outstanding skills
that earned Brent Tully a berth on the First All-Star
Team at the '93 IIHF World Junior Championships.
Selected by Vancouver in the '92 NHL Entry Draft,
Tully led the Canadian National Junior Team in
plus/minus, with an impressive plus-eight rating.
Tully registered one goal and two assists in seven
games at the '93 junior tournament.

BRENT TULLY 1992–93
UPPER DECK #592

I swear that about 95 percent of the people who watch the World Junior tournament think that every player in the tournament is going to make the NHL. Every holiday season, Canadians by the millions gather around the tube and watch the future of the NHL play in the World Juniors tournament. And, sure, there are future stars on display . . . but nothing is ever guaranteed.

In 1993, Paul Kariya and Chris Pronger were on the Canadian roster that won gold. They were billed as future NHL Stars — and they were. But there was also another guaranteed future NHL star on that team: Brent Tully. He was a First Team All-Star defenceman on Team Canada and ended up with his own Upper Deck hockey card. The NHL was his for the taking . . .

"Obviously you have the ambition: you are going to have a career in the NHL — a long one, you hope," he says, almost a quarter of a century later. "I was one of those guys who didn't have it quite work out that way."

The gold medal he won in '93 was his first of two in the tournament. He came back in '94 and won again, this time as the captain of Team Canada. Tully was at the peak of his hockey career. Everyone expected that he would only get better with time, and the outcome would be a spot in the best league in the world.

"Some guys are 10 years old, some are 19, and some are 30 when they peak. And, of course, it's circumstance and everything else when you get to that level. I've always said, I can be a spokesperson for the 19-year-old can't-miss prospects, for guys who never play a game [in the NHL]. It's a lesson. And 24 years later, the expectations and pressure on kids have only gotten worse."

When Tully was on this hockey card, he wanted to win gold. "It's a little surreal when you watch the tournament now. It was starting to get big when we played, but certainly not how it is today."

It seems like the weight of the world is being put on the shoulders of 17-, 18-, and 19-year-olds. "I think it is too much pressure," says Tully.

"Some people would say it prepares them for the future because regardless of who they play for in the National Hockey League — if that's what they are fortunate enough to do — they are going to have a ton of pressure on them from day one. So there's something to be said for that. I think there's enough pressure at their club or college level. I can't say what the kids feel now, but I guess it's their norm, and they expect it and, to some extent, are used to it. That's reality. That's the way it is. We're not going to change that."

Tully should know. He is the former general manager of the Cobourg Cougars of the Ontario Junior Hockey League. So what did the one-time World Junior star, the can't-miss guy, say to his young players? "I tell kids this is a life experience, not just a hockey experience. You can't forget that. I've always maintained that whether you win a championship in Atom or you win the World Junior championship or you win the Stanley Cup, it's the same feeling. You're winning a championship, and you don't forget that. So take time to smell the roses, but at the same time, work your hardest and never give up, because you never know when that next opportunity is going to come."

Brent Tully played pro hockey until he was 28. The Vancouver Canucks took him 93rd overall in the 1992 NHL Draft, but the closest he ever got to the NHL was the American League. Like a lot of future stars, his cards hit the market when he was still only a kid. But unlike his World Junior teammates Kariya and Pronger, he never had a card showing him in an NHL uniform. "My draft year was '92 and cards were really getting popular. Upper Deck was at the forefront of that. It was extremely exciting to get a card. I ended up with a few different ones. But the one from the '93 World Juniors was cool. The next year I was on the checklist card for our team. I know they did an alumni set years later. It is humbling to have a card. It's an honour to have cards as memories and for kids to understand that you were a part of something so many years ago. It's absolutely amazing, really."

When I look at the back of this card, I can't help but think how Brent

Tully would look in today's NHL. "Strong skating is just one of his out-standing skills," his bio says. While today's game is all about speed, it wasn't nearly as fast in the mid 1990s. "It's amazing to see the kids who succeed today who wouldn't have had a chance in the mid '90s. Back then, a smaller skilled player was a real rarity. They could maybe squeeze by, but now they can flourish. I think the game is great and the improvements to it have been fantastic. But on some levels, I do question them. I'm a big advocate of player safety, but I don't like the idea of going too far with rule changes. It kind of takes away, in some instances, the creativity and the character of the game."

So yeah, you have to think that today's game would have suited the strong skating Tully, who was on the First All-Star Team in the '93 World Juniors, along with this list of future stars: Peter Forsberg, Markus Naslund, Kenny Jonsson, Paul Kariya, and Manny Legace. "I get that comment on a pretty frequent basis: 'You would have flourished in today's game.' But you know what, hindsight is 20/20."

DAVE GAGNON

RED WINGS

SCORE 91

TOP PROSPECT

TOP PROSPECT

DAVE
GAGNON

RED WINGS

G

Ht: 6'0''   Wt: 185   Catches: Left
Born: October 31, 1967
Windsor, Ontario
Acquired: Signed as Free Agent
(6/11/90)

Dave played for three teams in '90-91, but enjoyed his
greatest success with Hampton Roads. He was
named co-MVP of the ECHL playoffs after leading the
Admirals to the championship. Dave lost only one of
11 post-season starts and stopped 52 shots in a
pivotal game. He began the year with Adirondack
(AHL) before going to Hampton Roads for the stretch
drive. Dave also appeared in two games for Detroit.

SCORE

277

©1991 SCORE, PRINTED IN U.S.A.

Dave Gagnon   1991–92
SCORE #277

You never know when or where you'll run into a fellow collector. Let's face it, once you're past the age of 12 or 13, few of us advertise that we like to hoard tiny pieces of cardboard. But when you do find someone who also collects cards, an interesting chat will usually follow.

When I gave Dave Gagnon a call, it was to talk to him about having his very own hockey card. Turns out Dave had, and still has, a lot of them. He collected as a kid and when he got a little older. "Once I turned pro, I started collecting cards. I probably have thousands of them now. I have a Gretzky rookie card and a Bobby Hull, Yzerman, Lemieux, Patrick Roy. I've got quite a few good cards now.

"Some of the guys I was playing with at the time, in Norfolk, Virginia, were collecting cards and they got me into it. It was kind of fun. And then over the summers, I'd do some autograph signings of my own cards."

Gagnon's favourite cards in his collection? Ones a lot of collectors wish they had. "The Gretzky rookie card. That means a lot, and the Bobby Hull rookie card. That's probably the first rookie card that I ever bought, and it was in pretty good shape. I bought it for $200. I thought it was a great deal. I don't know what it's worth now, $1,000 or $800, but it's appreciated quite a bit. I didn't get it for that — it was to have one of the greats."

Gagnon's card came out in the fall of 1991. The Colgate University product had one year of pro and two NHL games on his resume. "It was kind of exciting to get a card. It means that you're on people's radar. I think my dad was the one who told me I had a card — he saw it before I did."

Along with future stars like Dominik Hasek, Doug Weight, and Tony Amonte, Dave Gagnon was listed as a top prospect by Score. "I look back at some of the other guys who had rookie cards that year, or the top prospect cards, and I'm honoured just to be in the same kind of class as those players. I don't think rookie cards from years prior got the kind of attention they got in the '90s."

So as a card aficionado, I have to get Gagnon's take on his one and only NHL card. "I thought it was cool. The picture was good, though I don't remember it being taken. There's one thing — on the back it says I'm from Windsor, but actually I'm from Essex. That's the one thing my dad always wanted me to correct. Nothing against Windsor but I'm from Essex, Ontario. Dad always wanted me to clarify that.

"That's where I grew up. That's where I played all my minor hockey. That's where all my friends and family were. That's probably the only thing I didn't like about the card: it said Windsor."

Gagnon had a small role in helping to produce another card in the 1991–92 Score set. Brett Hull has a card that commemorates his 50 goals in 50 games. According to Dave Gagnon, it was 50 goals in 49 games for the Golden Brett. "My first NHL game was against St. Louis. I went into the third in relief of Tim Cheveldae, and Brett Hull scored his 50th goal on me in his 49th game. I was sitting in a bar the other night after work and they were doing a special on Brett Hull. It showed that goal, so that was kind of cool. The game was in Joe Louis Arena, and when he scored everybody started clapping and cheering. I didn't realize it at the time. I was like, 'What's going on?' I heard about it afterwards."

As a young guy in the Wings system, Gagnon ended up with a number of his teammates' cards. And just like collectors never quite know who will be the next great thing, the players don't necessarily know either. "When I started my first year, it was Nicklas Lidström's first year. I probably have 30 or 40 of his rookie cards, but back then I didn't know they were going to be special. It takes years and years for the cards to become special. And I don't just mean monetarily. I got to play with a Hall of Famer. Lidström was very quiet and humble. I really didn't know much about him. He was a solid player, obviously, but then he matured into a fantastic player."

Dave Gagnon doubled down on the card boom. His Hampton Roads teammate Dennis McEwen got him into collecting early in his pro career. "He probably had the best collection. When you play, whether you're in the minors or the NHL, you have a lot of downtime. And if you don't fill up the downtime, you can find a lot of other things to do that aren't necessarily in your best interests. So collecting was a lot of fun — on the bus, in hotel rooms, in your apartment. I mean on a normal day you could be out of the rink by one o'clock and your day is done. So instead of just going to the mall or sleeping all day, it gives you something to do."

Gagnon, who owns a Michigan publishing company, says he's no longer an active collector. He got out once the market got flooded, but he still has his old collection. And who knows, maybe this little conversation is enough to get Gagnon back into the hobby. "Now is a good time too. There are some very exciting players emerging, like McDavid and Matthews and Larkin. There are all kinds of exciting young players out now," says Gagnon.

Gagnon didn't hoard his Score rookie cards, at least not enough to see him through two decades. If you're online and you find that the price of Dave Gagnon rookie card is inflated, there's a reason. There is still someone out there who is buying up his rookie cards: "Believe it or not, I had to order some of mine online because I always have people tell me they want a copy. I ordered 20 at one point. I definitely thought I overpaid."

DEAN KOLSTAD

1991–92
O-PEE-CHEE 4S

In the fall of 1990, Dean Kolstad's mom knew that if her son wanted a promotion at work, he needed to look his best. "That was a bad picture because my mom made me cut my hair before I went to training camp in Minnesota. My hair was a lot longer. Before it was cut, it was big-time 1990s hockey hair," Kolstad says about his only hockey card.

Dean was off to Russia in search of a promotion. He had 25 NHL games on his resume but had spent most of his first two professional seasons in the IHL with the Kalamazoo Wings. Looking to land a full-time gig in the NHL, he was heading to Russia with the rest of the North Stars for training camp. "Mom said if you're going to go to Russia and you're going to do all this stuff, you better look presentable."

On September 11, 1990, the North Stars flew out for what was called the Friendship Tour. They played four games in eight days on their Russian odyssey, and there was nothing friendly about it. The Montreal Canadiens were also in Russia that September. The Habs finished off their four-game series with a bench-clearing brawl against CSKA Moscow. One day later, the North Stars did their part to take the "Friend" out of Friendship Tour when they got on a bus and headed out for their fourth and final game of the series. "It was kind of scary. We stayed in Moscow and we took a bus trip a good two hours to get to wherever it was. We had guys like Basil McRae, Shane Churla, Mark Tinordi, Link Gaetz — I mean, we had a pretty tough team playing that night."

The North Stars were in Kiev to face off against Sokol Kiev. As Kolstad says, there was a lot of toughness in the Stars lineup — the kind that would step in when one of the team's finesse players was messed with. That's exactly what happened. "Dave Gagner got hooked, a fish-hook, right on the corner of his mouth. Gags probably got 20 stitches out of it."

The North Stars toughies were ready to dole out some swift justice against the player that hooked Gagner. "When that happened, it started. The poor kid had to fight about five guys to get off the ice. Fans were throwing bread and food and fruit . . . all kinds of stuff. Mark Tinordi was my partner, and we left the bench. There were some other guys out there — Churla, Basil McRae — it was bad.

"When we went over there, we were told not to try to sneak anything out of the country. Montreal was a few days ahead of us, and they got caught trying to take some paintings and stuff like that when leaving. So they wanted to make sure we didn't get in any trouble, and here we go and play this game. I thought we'd never get out of there."

Kiev eventually won 5–0. And once the North Stars got off the ice, they not only had to worry about getting back to Moscow but also getting out of the parking lot. "The fans tried to tip the bus over when we left. It was pretty bad."

Back in North America, Kolstad played only five NHL games that season. Once again he was relegated to minor-league duty with Kalamazoo. The next year the NHL expanded into San Jose. In the fall of '91, the picture that Kolstad posed for during North Stars training camp ended up on his first hockey card. He was a San Jose Shark by then, claimed by the Sharks from Minnesota. With a shot at a new NHL roster, Kolstad's NHL future looked a bit brighter, but he never really cracked the NHL full-time. He played the final 10 games of his NHL career for the Sharks in 1992–93. Kolstad is a big guy: six-foot six and 230 pounds. I ask him if his coaches wanted the big guy on the hockey card to drop the gloves. It was a style that was perhaps more in line with what coaches of that era expected of a guy of his size. "I heard that in Minnesota and I heard that from different general managers in San Jose. That was pretty much the exact statement. It was 'We can find defencemen who can get us 30 or 40 points a year, but we need guys who are six-foot-six and can fight.' If you look at the guys I fought over the years, they're all tough guys. There weren't any cupcakes, that's for sure."

Kolstad dropped the mitts with Mike Peluso and Joey Kocur in the NHL — *really* tough guys. But fighting, despite what he kept hearing, was not his game. "I'd never say it to disrespect anybody, but I could play for 15 years today the way I played. I was a physical player who kept

YEAH, I HAD A CARD • DEAN KOLSTAD

the puck moving. I could skate fairly well for my size. I was smart. I averaged, from my first year of junior until my last year pro, around 35 points a year."

Kolstad had pretty soft hands off the ice too. While he was playing hockey, he was also thinking of his future. He was a good enough golfer to become a PGA golf professional. When I caught up with him on the phone, he was just wrapping up a golf lesson. He's a club pro in Michigan. But he still takes time to trade in his golf spikes for the blades every winter. "I play 10 games a year with the Detroit Red Wings alumni. I have an absolute ball."

His two kids are both college athletes. They get a kick out of the fact that their golfing dad has a hockey card; they keep a video of his fight with Joey Kocur on their phones. And like good teammates in any hockey dressing room, Kolstad's buddies at the golf course like to give him the gears about his one and only piece of cardboard history. "Without a lie, I probably get one card a month in the mail. I take it in to show the guys at work because they give me a hard time. They say, 'Your dad probably sends them to you and just puts different addresses on them.' It's a conversation piece, and I'm really lucky to have a hockey card."

Mark LaForest   Goaltender

81

Goaltender

Toronto Maple Leafs

Mark LaForest

YEAR	TEAM	GP	W	L	T	GA	SO	AVG.
85-86	Red Wings	28	4	21	0	114	1	4.95
86-87	Red Wings	5	2	2	0	12	0	3.29
87-88	Flyers	21	5	9	2	60	1	3.70
88-89	Flyers	17	5	7	2	64	0	4.12
89-90	Ontario	27	9	14	0	87	0	3.89
	NHL TOTALS	98	25	52	4	337	2	4.17

Height: 5'11"
Weight: 190 lbs.
Born: July 10, 1962
Welland,
Ontario
Catches: Left

TORONTO MAPLE LEAFS

MARK LAFOREST   1990–91 UPPER DECK #81

"The dasher boards are green, so it was Minnesota."

Mark Laforest, better known as "Trees," is telling me where the picture for his one and only hockey card was taken. "There was only one building in the '80s and '90s that was green, and that was Minnesota."

Laforest suited up for the Leafs in all four of their visits to Minnesota in the 1989–90 season. The Leafs won one of those games. That year's edition of the Leafs was not a defensive juggernaut. On November 22, 1989, the Leafs lost 6–3 in Minny, even though Laforest made 48 saves, and perhaps this photo was taken on that occasion. It makes sense — Laforest sure does look like he's working hard. "I think the puck might have been going up and over the net and I might have reached up and grabbed it, a deflection or something. One of those pop-up flies . . ."

It looks like a goalmouth scramble. High-scoring Leafs centre Eddie Olczyk even makes a cameo. You can see him on the blocker side of his desperate 'tender. "And he says he never backchecked in front of the net," Trees says, laughing. "He might have been lost."

Like a lot of NHL veterans, Laforest waited a long time for his first card. The kid who collected Tony Esposito cards growing up had to wait until his eighth year of pro hockey before he finally got his first big-league card. "I turned pro in '83. I played 28 games with Detroit in 1985–86, and then I played a couple years backup to Ron Hextall, 21 games one year and then 17 the next. I figured I'd earned a card, for God's sake. I guess they showed up at certain rinks at certain times and I either wasn't dressed or wasn't playing, so I didn't get one.

"It was fun to finally have one. Pretty damn cool to a kid from Welland, Ontario. It doesn't really happen very often."

Laforest clearly knows his card well, front and back: "You look at the back of the card and I have my stick in the air. There was an extra attacker, and I fed the D. I was open and I was calling for it, and he wouldn't pass it to me. The prick."

Laforest started the 1989–90 season in the AHL, with the Newmarket Saints. It was his first season in the Leafs organization. Before he knew it, he got the call to join the big club. The Leafs crease starred four goalies that year: Laforest, Jeff Reese, Allan Bester, and Peter Ing. They all faced a lot of rubber on a team that gave up a league high 2,798 shots against. "It was fun. I went through a stretch where I was only giving up two or three goals a game, but we weren't scoring. It was nice when we were winning 5–2, 4–2, 4–3, 8–5, but then I'd give up two goals and we'd lose 2–1 or I'd give up three goals and we'd lose 3–1. I thought, *Are you kidding me? You guys are killing me.*"

Laforest played in 27 games for the Leafs — and he won only nine. On one of those nights, he had his most memorable (or it is infamous?) Leafs moment. It, of course, lives on, courtesy of YouTube. On October 23, 1989, Laforest took to the crease for the Leafs for the second time ever. At the 17:14 mark of the second period, a skirmish broke out in front of the New Jersey net. A few seconds in, Devils goalie Sean Burke grabbed hold of Dan Daoust and put him in a headlock. Remember, this was 1989 — Mark Laforest had one thing to do: he skated the length of the ice to even things out with Burke.

"Burke didn't look that big from 200 feet away." Laforest gave up six inches and 28 pounds to the six-foot-four Devil. "I'd never met the man. I knew he was a big guy. He said, 'Who do you think you are? Ron Hextall?'"

Laforest could think of only one thing to say: "I'm way tougher than he is."

After the quick get-to-know-you session, it was go time. The first thing Burke did was rip off Laforest's mask. "He grabbed my mask, and oh my God, my neck was killing me. So I unclipped my mask and I stepped on his stick. The linesman grabbed me."

Just like that — it was over. For the time being at least.

For a good two minutes, most of the players were on the ice just holding on to one another. Nothing overly nasty went down. Laforest eventually made his way back to his own end of the rink. And then, just when things looked to have settled, Leaf Brad Marsh and Devil David

Maley started swinging. That — and perhaps the fact that he had time to catch his breath — seemed to be enough to inspire Laforest to give Burke another go. Laforest motioned to Burke, once again 200 feet away, to remove his mask. Burke looked more than willing. It was time for Laforest to go for another skate, and Burke met him at the top of the faceoff circle in the Jersey zone. "Look out — the goalies are going to go at it. Laforest and Burke are going to square off!" announced play-by-play man Jim Hughson.

The two started trading shots. Each connected on a few. "We went and then we hung on for a while. I was tired. He was probably tired from all the shots he was throwing at me."

The scrap lasted 30 seconds. Referee Terry Gregson, who was right beside the goalies, and utter exhaustion seemed to calm down the well-padded gladiators. Suddenly, things started to escalate at the penalty box area, and Gregson had to leave the two 'tenders alone — it seemed like a pretty safe move. A minute or so passed with the two goalies just hanging on to one another. "Everything was kind of calming down. And then I kind of turned Burke away from the ref who was coming at us, so I could get one more shot in. Just as I go to give him a left, the freakin' linesman turns around and goes back to the penalty box!"

Seventy-five seconds after their last punch, Laforest and his hockey hair and Burke and his hockey hair were going at it again. This round lasted another 25 seconds. "I can never remember witnessing two goaltenders go at it like this," said colourman Gary Green. And that's high praise from a man who coached in the Ontario Junior ranks, the AHL, and the NHL in the late '70s and early '80s.

"The Gardens was going haywire. It was awesome," says Laforest. "I get more press over that fight than the hundred games I played in net."

Five minutes after he first skated the length of the ice to challenge Burke, Mark Laforest finally left the ice to the cheers of the Toronto faithful. The crowd was going wild, his teammates were patting him on the head, a fan even chimed in with "Way to go, big guy," as one of

the newest Leafs headed for the dressing room. With all his remaining energy, Laforest took off his chest protector, tossed it to the floor, and disappeared into the Toronto dressing room. He was completely and totally exhausted. "I don't know how the tough guys do it. I was so tired after that fight that I didn't have a cigarette for three hours," he says and laughs.

"I couldn't open my hands because I was hanging on to Burke's jersey for so long. I couldn't even lift my arms up to wash my hair in the shower. It was ridiculous. My brother was at the game. It was awesome. He was with his wife. They shed a tear. They thought I was going to die," says Trees.

Almost three decades after the brawl, Laforest is still trying to comprehend just how drained, how physically exhausted he was that night and the next day. "Your hands cramp up, you're dehydrated. My hands were like that for hours. They hurt. I was so drained. I used to room with Bobby Probert. I was friends with Dave Brown, John Kordic, Craig Berube, and all the tough guys; I don't know how they did it. They must have been calm. My adrenaline was through the roof. And when you crash on that shit, oh my God. The next day was horrible."

However, there was a silver lining: "I got an interview with Dave Hodge on TV the next game. So that was pretty cool.

"I got on kind of a role [with Toronto], but then I hurt my ankle and didn't get the number one job back." After his one year with the Leafs, he signed on with the Rangers. He never made it back to the NHL until the 1993–94 season when he played five games with the Ottawa Senators. His pro career ended following the 1996–97 season. Mark Laforest played in 103 NHL games, was a two-time AHL goalie of the year, and had one NHL hockey card. "It's pretty damn cool. It's not one of those expensive cards. I remember a kid came up to me one time and asked me to sign it, and I said, 'Of course. Where did you get this?' He said, 'I bought it at a card show.' I said, 'What did you spend, 50 cents?' He goes, 'No, no, no. Twenty-eight cents. And the plastic cover cost me a buck.'"

BLUES

GARRY UNGER   center

Home: St. Louis, Mo.
Born: Dec. 7, 1947
Shoots: Left
Height: 5'11"
Weight: 170
1st Pro Season: 1966-67

Centre/St. Louis Blues

GARRY UNGER

Currently the NHL's "Iron Man" Garry has played in over 400 straight league games. He scored 13 goals on the power play last season. Garry once scored seven points in one game, three goals and four assists to tie a team record.

Garry, "l'Homme de Fer" de la Ligue Nationale, a participé à plus de 400 parties régulières consécutives. La saison dernière, il marqua 13 buts sur des jeux de puissance. Garry a déjà produit sept points en une partie (trois buts et quatre assistances) pour égaler un record du club.

Garry lives on a large ranch outside of St. Louis.

Garry vit sur un grand ranch près de St-Louis.

1972-73 SEASON RECORD
FICHE POUR 1972-73

GAMES PLAYED	GOALS	ASSISTS	TOTAL POINTS	PENALTY MIN.
78	41	39	80	119

© O.P.C.   PRINTED IN CANADA

GARRY UNGER   1973–74 O-Pee-Chee #15

I love the 1973–74 O-Pee-Chee set. Not for the multi-coloured borders that have driven collectors nuts for years, but for the photography. I don't know what was in the water the previous season, but the guys taking the pictures for the 1973–74 cards were trying something new. The set experiments with a ton of action shots. In the previous few

THE 1970S Chapter Six

seasons, most cards featured a player in a classic hockey pose on the front. The 1973–74 set could not be more different. Some of the cards in the set didn't work, like the *Where's Waldo* version of Dave Keon's card. But some were great, like this striking, mid-slapshot image of the Blues star Garry Unger. "The photographer was a guy named Lew Portnoy. He worked for *Sports Illustrated* and lived in St. Louis. So you will see a lot of the *Sports Illustrated* pictures from that era with the Blues in white, our home colour."

Unger and Portnoy met when Portnoy was working on a story for *Goal Magazine*. The story was about the contrast of playing in New York versus St. Louis. The magazine got shots of Rod Gilbert in his New York high-rise apartment. Now they needed a juxtaposition. Enter Garry Unger. The magazine wanted to talk to Unger about life on his farm outside St. Louis. Portnoy was the photographer for the piece. "He brought his family to the farm, and I really got to know him."

Unger had Lew's kids riding horses and playing around his farm. The two hit it off. "Lew said, 'Listen, I got this new lens coming. It's a 360-degree lens. I'd like to take some shots of you.'"

Soon enough, Portnoy and Unger got together after a Blues practice. Unger did his thing as Portnoy experimented with the newest in 1970s technology. "He was lying on the ice, and I was shooting pucks. He got all sorts of different angles. They used one photo for the card, but around 1975, they used another picture for a *Sports Illustrated* poster.

"This card was really different. He was always getting me in my white uniform. But I changed after practice and he put me in a blue jersey so he could have some different photos.

"Lew passed away not too long ago. If you wanted a picture of somebody, you would call up Lew and he'd have it in his basement. He had all sorts of negatives. He actually sold his negatives out of his basement for $100,000. That's more than I made when I played."

Unger played in the NHL in three different decades. His rookie card came out in 1968–69 and he had a card every year until his final season in 1982–83. Right before we did this interview at a Hockey to Conquer Cancer event, he signed about 20 different cards for a collector. This 1973–74 is one of his favorites. "That particular card is really different. It's a neat card."

The one thing you can't get Unger (who once upon a time held the NHL ironman record for consecutive games played, with 914) to do is recreate the image on the card. Gary and I are chatting about the image just seconds after we wrapped up a charity road-hockey game and you get the sense he was a very generous player. He gave me a lot of nice passes. He never hauled back and tried to rip a slapshot like the one you see on this card, and there's good reason. "Look at the angle of the stick on that card. When you do a slapshot, you line yourself up. I used to be really bow-legged. I never fell down. I could run into a train and I never fell down. I never got hit blindsided. I drive my motorcycle on the road like everyone is trying to hit me — the same as when I played in a hockey game. I had really good balance on my bow legs. But I've had both my

knees and both my hips replaced. So now, when I go to take a slapshot, I can't last on that one leg."

So the photo would be impossible to recreate, but Unger has a solution: "I couldn't do that shot. I'd have to get someone like you to take it, and then they'd stick my head on it."

Ahh, classic airbrush.

RON PLUMB • D

HARTFORD WHALERS

"NOW WITH WHALERS"

Ron made The Hockey News WHA All-Star Team in 1977-78. Membre de l'équipe d'étoiles "Hockey News" de l'A.M.H. pour 1977-78.

Look for NHL Products Recherchez les produits de la LNH

HEIGHT: 5'10" WEIGHT: 175
SHOOTS: Right
1st PRO SEASON: 1970-71
ACQ: Trade with Cincinnati
BORN: 7-17-50, Kingston, Ontario
HOME: Kingston, Ontario

Playing Record • Fiche comme joueur

	GP	G	A	PTS	PIM
1978-79	78	4	16	20	33
Lifetime • Carrière	549	65	264	329	341

Ron had 9 power-play Goals for the Whalers in 1977-78. • Ron, qui a un lancer très précis, marqua 9 buts sur des jeux de puissance pour les Whalers durant 1977-78.

© 1979 O-PEE-CHEE PRINTED IN CANADA

RON PLUMB D WHALERS

Ron Plumb   1979–80
O-Pee-Chee #328

In case you haven't noticed, I *really, really* like the movie *Slap Shot*. I referenced it many times in *Hockey Card Stories*, and it keeps popping up as I write this sequel. The reason I love the movie so much is because it was so authentic. The more I talk to players from the '70s, the more I realize that *Slap Shot* got every little bit right. Sure some of the fight scenes were over the top (though not by much, apparently), but that was about it.

One of my favourite scenes in the movie is when Chiefs captain Reg Dunlop wants to get teammate Dave Carlson to up his goon factor. He decides to talk a little trash with his opponent Barclay Donaldson just before a faceoff. Dunlop's trash talk works: Carlson eventually ends up in a scrap. The exchange more than the fight, though, is what I love. Reggie Dunlop simply skates up to the faceoff dot, looks at Barclay Donaldson, and says, "Tough news, Barclay. Sorry."

Barclay's confused.

Then Reg delivers the killer line, "Minnesota dropped you. Yeah, it's in *Hockey News*. I'll save it for you."

Was the *Hockey News* really the be-all and end-all for players in the 1970s? On the back of Ron Plumb's 1979–80 O-Pee-Chee, there's a cartoon figure of Ron reading the *Hockey News*. It says, "Ron made the *Hockey News* WHA All-Star Team in 1977–78." Surely Ron would be able to tell me if *Slap Shot* captured, as Dickie Dunn would say, the spirit of the thing once again. "Oh, yes, we read the *Hockey News*," Plumb says, almost shocked at the question. "It was like the bible to us. Especially in the World Hockey Association. I played there for the full seven years, and the *Hockey News* was a tabloid that everybody read. We read it on buses, we picked it up on airplanes, and it was in the dressing rooms. It gave you a lot of information on what was going on. Maybe not everything was right up-to-date, but it was as good as we had at that time."

Ron Plumb was a 29-year-old veteran when he got his first and only NHL card in the fall of 1979. He was a WHA lifer up until then. He had been featured in three WHA sets, but now he was an NHLer. For some reason, though, this card shows him in a San Diego Mariners uniform. The "NOW WITH WHALERS" on the front of the card gives the impression that he just joined the Whalers. Truth is Plum played 78 games for the Whalers the previous season. And he hadn't played for San Diego since 1975! In fact, the WHA Mariners went out of business in 1977. So how in the hell does a four-year-old picture of Plumb end up on a card in 1979? "They took pictures only once in a blue moon. The card companies try to get your picture, and in the meantime, players are switching teams and getting traded. If I can remember, back then they took one photo and that was it. You'd get with a new team and if you missed a picture day, it was like you were never there."

O-Pee-Chee had plenty of pictures of Plumb in a Cincinnati uniform, but they chose to go with San Diego for this set. That's fine with Plumb; he loved the uniforms and his one winter in San Diego. Plumb played for five teams in seven years during his WHA tenure; no wonder the guys making the cards just went with an old picture. In the WHA, it was tough enough to keep track of where the teams were, let alone the players. "There were a lot of changes. It was the Wild West at times.

"We had a skilled team in San Diego," Plumb continues. "Andy Lacroix was there. And we had a tough team. Kevin Morrison, Teddy Scharf, Norm Ferguson, and I did a commercial." This is what I love about the WHA: the stories.

"One of the public relations guys came to us at Christmas. He said, 'We're going to make a Christmas card.' He got all the guys on the ice, and he said, 'Now pretend that you've had an all-out brawl with another team in front of the net.' So off come the helmets, gloves, sticks you name it. Then he says, 'Everybody freeze. Do not move.' So we didn't move. Then he says, 'Now go sit on the bench, but don't touch a thing on the ice.' So 18 of us all left, and there's a mess on the ice.

"A photographer moved in and snapped a photo of what seemed like the aftermath of a nasty brawl. He built a Christmas card of the scene, and it said something like 'Merry Christmas and Happy New Year from the mad, mean, menacing major league San Diego Mariners,' and we all signed it."

Even in the rather politically incorrect world of 1974, this was too much. Soon enough the Mariners and their Yuletide greeting were making big news. "We got West to East Coast coverage because the *Toronto Star* picked it up and criticized it as a professional hockey team that is emphasizing brutality and violence. We were front-row centre on everything. It was unreal. I still have that poster somewhere."

(For the record, I would love to get my hands on a copy of this Christmas card. If anyone has a copy, please send it to my publisher.)

"The WHA tried to pizzazz the game up a bit. They did some crazy commercials. At times, they had to compete to sell the game. When I played in Cincinnati, we used to go into the Procter and Gamble manufacturing plant and talk to employees and explain hockey to them. You weren't just a professional hockey player, you were a professional PR man too."

This card came out when four WHA teams — the Whalers, Oilers, Jets, and Nordiques — joined the NHL. It was known as the merger. For a WHA lifer like Plumb, it made the summer of '79 pretty stressful. "Nobody knew how things were going to settle. The teams that ended up going on to the NHL went through a lot of changes. And you were caught up in it. You were with a team, but basically there were a number of teams folding, which means there were other players available. It was a real crapshoot for a while."

Plumb stuck with the Whalers in the NHL. He got to see two of the greats during his time in the NHL and the WHA: he played with Gordie Howe and against a young Wayne Gretzky. He used to drive to the rink with Mr. Hockey as well. "I got to know him pretty well. I got to play defence with Marty and Mark. I travelled to and from the rink with those guys many, many times because we lived pretty close together. And Gordie, whenever you were around the boys, he was never too far away.

"I can still remember skating at the end of practice, when you line up at the end boards to do your sprints. It's down and back, down and back, down and back. I mean, we were a professional hockey team at the peak of our strength and ability, and here's Gordie who's turning 50 years old. He might have been near the end of the pack, but you still had to go because he was going hard all the time. I appreciated what he was doing later on, when I reached 50 myself.

"Gretzky was young when I played against him. He hadn't established all those records yet, he hadn't won a Stanley Cup yet, but he was extra special. It was back in the day of intimidating hockey. He had Dave Semenko and two or three other players around him who would basically keep an eye out for him. There was no mickey mousing around. They would protect that guy. It was kind of an unwritten rule that you had to be careful you didn't run Gretzky. I know I had Semenko after me one night in Edmonton because I hit Gretzky three times. I knew that he was the type of player that if you let him get inside the blue line and have that puck on a string, he was very dangerous, and I would stand up to him. Semenko gave me the warning from the bench; he took a swing at me and said, 'Leave him alone, Plumb.' If Glen Sather had put him out on the ice, I would've been chopped meat. Semenko was doing what he had to do: he was protecting the best asset in the league."

Ron Plumb retired from pro hockey in 1986. As we chatted about this card, he seemed to be having a good time discussing his old life. When Plumb retired, it didn't take long for him to realize that life for the guy on the hockey card was going to be very different than the life for the guy going to the office. "What I found out in the early years, once I got into regular work, is your average person seems to work a lot longer and harder and for a lot less pay than what I was used to . . ."

Yup, that pretty much captures the spirit of the thing.

1978-79 NHL Assist Leaders Meneurs pour les assistances

2	Player, Team Joueur, Equipe	No Nbre
	Bryan Trottier, NY Islanders	87
	Guy Lafleur, Montreal	77
	Marcel Dionne, Los Angeles	71
	Bob MacMillan, Atlanta	71
	Denis Potvin, NY Islanders	70
	Bernie Federko, St Louis	64
	Dennis Maruk,	
	Gil Perreault, Bu	
	Mike Bossy, NY	
	Guy Chouinard,	
	Bobby Clarke, P	

Look for NHL Products • Re
©1979 O-P

1978-79 Assists Leaders Meneurs pour les assistances en 1978-79

1 BRIAN TROTTIER NEW YORK ISLANDERS

2 GUY LAFLEUR MONTREAL CANADIENS

3 MARCEL DIONNE LOS ANGELES KINGS

3 BOB MacMILLAN ATLANTA FLAMES

1978–79 Assists Leaders 1979–80 O-Pee-Chee #2

The cards of the '70s were so much simpler than the high-tech offerings of today, and one of the staples was league-leader cards. They were often easy to overlook because they generally featured the usual suspects. Guys like Orr, Lafleur, Trottier, Dionne, and Bossy dominated the fronts of these cards. But when you take the time to really check them out, every once in a while, a name or face may surprise you.

Take the number two card in O-Pee-Chee's 1979–80 set. The card shows the assists leaders from the previous season. There are three future Hall of Famers: Brian [misspelled] Trottier, Guy Lafleur, Marcel Dionne, and Bob MacMillan. On this occasion, MacMillan, a well-known hockey figure in his native P.E.I. and around the Maritimes, was hanging with a trio of superstars. "I don't know if I'd put myself in the same company as those boys. Obviously, they're Hall of Famers. I think everybody has a magical year in their life. It was just one of those years that everything went right," says MacMillan, now a scout for the Calgary Flames.

MacMillan had the season of a lifetime when he led the Atlanta Flames with 108 points in 1978–79, and the total is still a record for Prince Edward Island–born players. I know what you're thinking. Brad Richards must have had more points in a single season, but no. Richards topped out at 91 points on two occasions. In fact, when MacMillan racked up 108 points, he had established the highest total ever for a Maritimer. Of course, Sidney Crosby broke that record.

With the Flames in 1978–79, MacMillan played on a line with Guy Chouinard and Eric Vail. Chouinard had 107 points. Vail had 83. "We gelled, and we bonded and everything worked out great. Guy Chouinard had magical hands. He'd put me in for a couple of breakaways every game. We just kind of learned that if I got a hole, he was going to get me the puck. It was awesome.

"I think it just kind of happened. I wouldn't say we worked at it. It just got to the point where Guy knew where I was. Eric was one of the shooters on that line. He had a big shot.

"It's just a nice thing to know that one year I was able to keep up with the big boys. I guess I was always near the top in team scoring during my career. I think I led three or four teams, but not at the NHL level."

MacMillan did indeed keep up with the big boys. Of the 11 assists leaders listed on the back of the card, eight are in the Hall of Fame. As MacMillan said, it was just one of those seasons where everything went right. And when everything goes right, you have more than just your linemates to thank. Remember, this was 1978–79, so each team had a bit of muscle. It was the job of the muscle to make sure the top guns got to play. MacMillan joined the Atlanta Flames during the '77–78 season. In 52 games with Flames, he got 52 points. The next season was magical, partly because he had a lot of room to work on the ice. And the guys who helped give him that room also helped him end up on this card. "I remember Willi Plett and Harold Phillipoff, two of our tougher players, came up to me shortly after I got to Atlanta and said, 'Don't worry about a thing. If anybody goes near you, we'll be there. You just make sure you get our names in the newspapers.' So every time I got two goals and was interviewed, I always said, 'Oh, you know, Willi Plett was great tonight.' I was happy and they were happy."

MacMillan made the NHL out of the hockey wilderness that was P.E.I. Three players from his junior team, the 1969–70 Charlottetown Islanders — MacMillan, Hilliard Graves, and Al MacAdam — went on to have significant NHL careers. Scouts weren't plentiful on P.E.I., but making the NHL was something MacMillan always thought was in his future. "Maybe naively, I never really thought that I wasn't going to make it. I just thought, *I'm going to make it.* I must have been pretty naive to think that, but I never doubted it."

Like most Maritime kids, MacMillan had to venture far away from home to pursue his dream. He ended up in Toronto on a tryout with the Marlies. He was cut from a team that was stacked with NHL first-rounders, such as Steve Shutt and Dave Gardner. Told he was being let go, MacMillan hoped on a bus to St. Catharines. The next day he was in a St. Catharines Blackhawks uniform, playing against the Marlies

— the team that had cut him 24 hours earlier. "I scored three goals." Bob MacMillan had found his new hockey home. He finished third on the Blackhawks in points, with 103; his 19-year-old teammate Marcel Dionne led the team with 143.

"Being a Maritimer and a small-town kid, I think St. Catharines was a much better fit for me than a big city like Toronto. I would have been lost."

MacMillan's career was off and running. He spent his first two years as a pro with the WHA's Minnesota Fighting Saints, then he joined the New York Rangers, St. Louis Blues, and Atlanta Flames, where the kid from P.E.I. won a Lady Byng and hung with hockey's best on this card.

"When I get to sign one of my cards, it's always nice to sign that one. It brings a smile to my face every time. The biggest thing is thinking, *I hope this doesn't get lost in the mail*, when the other guys have already signed it and I'm sending it back. It's one of the few cards that I put a return address on, just in case it does get lost."

1975-76 TEAM LEADERS
•WASHINGTON CAPITALS

Goals
Nelson Pyatt, 26

Assists
Gerry Meehan, 35

Penalty Minutes
Yvon Labre, 146

Power Play Goals
Tony White, 7

WASHINGTON CAPITALS — **MENEURS DE L'EQUIPE** 1975-76

TEAM LEADERS

Goals / Buts
1. Nelson Pyatt — 26
2. Tony White — 25
3. Gerry Meehan — 23
4. Hartland Monahan — 17

Assists / Assistances
1. Gerry Meehan — 35
2. Hartland Monahan — 29
3. Nelson Pyatt — 23
4. Jean Lemieux — 23

Penalty Minutes / Min. de punition
1. Yvon Labre — 146
2. Blair Stewart — 113
3. Harvey Bennett — 92
4. Jack Lynch — 78

Power Play Goals / Buts jeux de puissance
1. Tony White — 7
2. Jean Lemieux — 6
3. Gerry Meehan — 5
4. Nelson Pyatt — 5
5. Jack Lynch — 5

396

1975–76 Team Leaders
Washington Capitals

1976–77
O-Pee-Chee #396

"That was the '70s," says Tony White. "Helmets were a maybe — you didn't have to wear one if you didn't want to — long hair and moustaches and sideburns were the way. Of course, we were all young kids, trying to fit in."

Tony White was trying to fit in with the best players on the planet. If you've flipped past this old card while going through a pile of '70s commons, it's more than understandable. In truth, the card isn't worth much. After all, it's a team leaders card for a Washington squad that rarely found itself on the winning side of a scoreline. That year, the Caps won a league-low 11 games. That's no misprint: just 11 wins. Tony White had 25 goals as rookie and a team high seven on the power play, which is what got him a spot on this card. "As a young kid playing in the National Hockey League, it didn't matter what team I was with, just as long as I was there. It was a rough ride, but I was having a good year. So you try to ride that and blank out the negativity of all the losing. We had some good guys on the team, like Nelson Pyatt, who made it a little more bearable. But mostly you just focused on the next game and tried to do your thing to stay in the league. When you have a team that's not doing as well as you'd like, there's a lot of turnover. You have to try to do the best you can to make yourself an asset rather than a liability."

When you grew up where Tony White did, just getting the chance to play was special. He came from a place that was the absolute hinterland of hockey: 1970s Newfoundland. When White suited up in his first NHL game in 1974–75, he was one of the first Newfoundlanders to ever play in the NHL. Fellow Newfoundlander Alex Faulkner inspired him. Faulkner debuted with the Leafs in 1961–62 but really made a name for himself the next season in Detroit. "Oh, yeah, I knew Alex, and his brothers George and Jack. The three of them were really good players. And Alex just happened to catch on for some reason. Alex had get up and go. He wasn't a big guy, but he could skate. He could really move the puck as a centre. That's what caught Detroit's eye."

White impressed a Kitchener Rangers scout when his Newfoundland senior team, the Grand Falls Cataracts, made a trip to Barrie, Ontario, for the Eastern Canadian Championships in 1972. At the time, he says, senior hockey in Newfoundland "was extremely good. Because the top players in Newfoundland weren't leaving the island. They were playing in that league." But no one, he says, was watching him in Newfoundland — at least no one was serious about him until his team made that trip to Ontario. "If I didn't play Senior A, the scout for the Kitchener Rangers never would have seen me play . . . No one would even have known I existed."

White was invited to the Rangers camp the following fall and made the team. He spent two seasons in Kitchener. The Washington Capitals took a shot at him and drafted him 161st overall in 1974. A couple of years later, he found himself on a hockey card as one of the Caps offensive leaders. "I was doing things that people wouldn't have expected of someone who wasn't drafted very high. When you get into the league, first you get a position and then you start to score some goals. Well, then you get a little more confidence. And you start to believe that it's possible that maybe you can do something in the NHL. Then you get power-play time and if you get power-play time, you get a little extra time to score. Fortunately, that's the way it worked out my rookie year."

White is quick to give credit to his centre for his 25-goal campaign. He played with Bill Clement, who went to the Caps after winning two consecutive Cups with the Philadelphia Flyers. "Billy was quite a centreman for moving the puck. He was aggressive and a great forechecker. And he played very strong defensively, so playing with him, you got a few more opportunities than you probably would have playing with other people. He had a lot to do with my success. I had a tendency to sniff out the holes, and he was able to get the puck to me. We had Hartland Monahan on the other wing, and Hartland was a pretty good skater who could shoot too. So between the three of us, we chipped away and chipped away, and I didn't have a bad year."

But then the story takes a turn that is not all that unusual when you play for a struggling team. The Caps got rid of their GM, Milt Schmidt, on December 29, 1975. The next day, they hired Max McNab. On January 22, 1976, McNabb sent White's centre, Bill Clement, to the Atlanta Flames. And, of course, the coaches kept changing as well. "It's hard to understand what really happens when things go south. You come back with the intention of doing the same thing that you did the year before. And you get off to a slow start and your ice time is cut back."

White followed up his rookie year with a 12-goal season in 1976–77, and that was pretty much it for his NHL career. At the start of the next season, he was sent down to the Hershey Bears of the American Hockey League. It was 1977 — so no explanation was provided. Whatever White was doing, it was not enough to impress the new management in Washington. "What new management sees makes a big impact on how they want to build their team. If you're playing well at the time [of management change], you'll probably get the benefit of the doubt. But if you're just so-so, they start to find faults. And when they find faults, they start to think about your capabilities and how you can contribute, and they analyze everything to death. It's a different world now, when you look at the way they deal with players. Now they talk to the players and use psychologists and sports analytics. They try to figure out what your problem is. In those days, you were analyzed for skating, shooting, tenacity, work ethic, and all that stuff, but it was never looked at through a statistical or analytical point of view. They didn't say, 'Okay, you had 25 goals and then you had 12. What happened here? What part of your game dropped off?' They work on that now. But back then they would just bring in someone else."

The only message White got when he was sent to Hershey was "work on your game." He scored 24 goals in Hershey but appeared in only one game with the Caps. "Then I hurt my knee, and the rest is history. You find yourself floundering around, trying to find your identity again, and looking for someone to believe in you. And that was pretty much it."

White played in six games with Minnesota in 1979–80 before wrapping up his NHL career. He played in Germany, and 13 years after he won his first Newfoundland senior championship with Grand Falls in 1972, he won another Herder Cup with Corner Brook in 1985. You may not know it by looking at this card, but White was a trailblazer. As a kid from the Rock who made it to the NHL, though, he's quick to point out that he wasn't alone. When I ask him about what this old hockey card means to him, his answer is "Not much."

Instead, he talks about where he comes from and the journey he and other Newfoundlanders took in the '70s. "It's just a card. For me, I went through that whole process and I really, really enjoyed it. To get to play in the NHL, the top league, it's quite something when you're coming out of Grand Falls, a small town of 6,000 people."

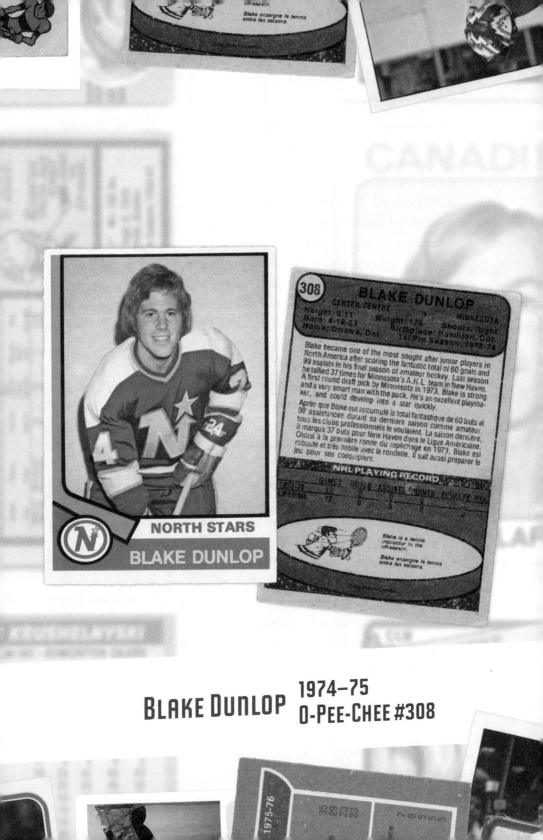

NORTH STARS

BLAKE DUNLOP

308 BLAKE DUNLOP
CENTER/CENTRE
Height: 5'11" Weight: 175 Shoots: Right MINNESOTA
Born: 4-18-53 Birthplace: Hamilton, Ont.
Home: Ottawa, Ont. 1st Pro Season: 1973-74

Blake became one of the most sought after junior players in North America after scoring the fantastic total of 60 goals and 99 assists in his final season of amateur hockey. Last season he tallied 37 times for Minnesota's A.H.L. team in New Haven. A first round draft pick by Minnesota in 1973, Blake is strong and a very smart man with the puck. He's an excellent playmaker, and could develop into a star quickly.

Après que Blake eut accumulé le total fantastique de 60 buts et 99 assistances durant sa dernière saison comme amateur, tous les clubs professionnels le voulaient. La saison dernière, il marqua 37 buts pour New Haven dans le Ligue Américaine. Choisi à la première ronde du repêchage en 1973, Blake est robuste et très habile avec la rondelle. Il sait aussi préparer le jeu pour ses coéquipiers.

NHL PLAYING RECORD

	GAMES	GOALS	ASSISTS	POINTS	PENALTY MIN.
1973-74	12	0	0	0	2
LIFETIME	12	0	0	0	2

Blake is a tennis instructor in the off-season.

Blake enseigne le tennis entre les saisons.

BLAKE DUNLOP   1974–75
O-PEE-CHEE #308

I just love these old poses. Here, Blake Dunlop is all smiles in what my old Highland Hockey School instructor Dave Wiesner used to call "hockey position": stick on the ice (or in Dunlop's case, the floor), body a little bent over, and head up. When you're in hockey position, you're ready for anything. In Dunlop's case, it was a hockey card. Dunlop looks quintessentially '70s in his No. 24 North Stars jersey, but it's a number he never wore for the team except on this day. "It was my rookie year at training camp, and I think they just handed me a random sweater."

Blake Dunlop arrived in Minnesota as a hotshot offensive prospect — maybe that's why he got a card after playing in only 12 NHL games. Back in the day, you used to have to put in at least a season, in some cases quite a few, before you ended up on cardboard. Things were different for the former Ottawa 67. "At the time, I didn't think that much about having a card. Hockey cards were always something special, but I wasn't a huge collector back when I was a kid. To be honest, it didn't really stand out at the time. It's more memorable now. When I look back and see the different cards from different teams I played for, it's something I appreciate more in hindsight."

Unlike a lot of contemporary cards, the back of this one is just loaded with information. You couldn't google Blake Dunlop in 1974, but thanks to this card, that didn't matter. His bio gets right down to business: "Blake became one of the most sought after junior players in North America after scoring the fantastic total of 60 goals and 99 assists in his final season of amateur hockey." Dunlop's 159 points in 1972–73 set an OHL record for most points in a season, and it was a great way to cap off his four years in Ottawa. He left the 67's with 365 points in 231 regular-season games. "It was a combination of having a good team and maturing a little bit at my level, in my fourth year of junior. I had played as a 16-year-old, which not too many guys did back then. Denis Potvin was a teammate of mine, Ian Turnbull too. So we had some good players and we had a good team. It just kind of escalated as things went on. Then I was at the top of the league in scoring."

Dunlop says his stats improved because his Ottawa teammates caught on to what was happening with their fourth-year centre and they wanted in on the fun. He explains that he was always more of a playmaker but as the season wore on, the puck kept coming back to him. "I scored a lot of goals near the end of the season because everyone was cognizant of the fact that I had a chance to win the scoring title. I got a lot more goals towards the end of the season than I normally would have."

After his record-setting campaign, Dunlop embarked upon his pro career. The points came easily in the American League. He scored 37 goals and 41 assists in 59 games with the New Haven Nighthawks. The offence did not come in the NHL, however; Dunlop did not register a single point with the North Stars in 12 games in 1973–74. The following year, he had 27 points in 52 games. "To me, the big difference was just the speed of the game. It was much quicker in the NHL. It was certainly more physical. Everyone was just better across the board. I think where I struggled early on was I had a couple injuries. I had a knee injury and then a hamstring injury. And I also went to a team that was very old and going downhill. I think I got caught in a couple of things and I couldn't get myself established. Most of the players were 30, 35 years old and had had a good run, but they had to rebuild. When I was in Minnesota, we had some teams that unfortunately weren't that great."

The pattern from his rookie year continued for his first few years as a pro, and Dunlop found himself bouncing between the minors and the NHL. He put up huge numbers in the American Hockey League but could not replicate that success in the NHL. He was eventually traded to the Philadelphia Flyers, and in 1977–78 again had a huge season for the Maine Mariners. He finished in a tie for second in scoring on the team and helped lead a very talented and very tough Maine team to a Calder Cup. Ask anyone that was around in the '70s and they will tell you the Philadelphia Flyers were tough, sure, but you should have seen the Mariners. "That is a very accurate statement," begins Dunlop, who won the Les Cunningham Award as the AHL's MVP in 1977–78. "It was probably the first year that I played hockey that I never got a bruise because my teammates wouldn't let anybody touch me. We had two lines that could play and we had two lines that were as tough as anyone in the league."

The following season, Dunlop put up 48 points in 66 games with the Flyers. But it was a trade to St. Louis that summer that finally got his NHL career in gear. "When I played in Philly, I led the team in plus minus. I got to play and scored some goals. I matured and got some confidence. I think other people had confidence in me when I came to St. Louis. Emile Francis [the Blues GM] brought in a lot of guys like me. They were high draft picks that had never gotten over the hump. He put us on a team, and we all pulled together. We had a great goalie in Mike Liut. He allowed us to hang in a lot of games."

After being traded this time, Dunlop never played another game in the minors. The kid on the card in that Minnesota training camp all those years ago was finally a full-time NHLer. The promise he showed in junior finally came to fruition. In 1980–81, he had his most productive NHL season when he scored 87 points in 80 regular-season games. "The Blues gave me the chance to be a number one or number two centre — I got to play in offensive situations, and I think that's what I needed."

Dunlop was piling pucks into the net instead of trying to hit a tennis ball over it — and yes, that was an option once upon a time. I love that the cartoon on the back of this card gives us a glimpse of an alternate past: a hockey player with a tennis racquet. It's captioned: "Blake is a tennis instructor in the off-season." Dunlop's family was always involved with tennis. His parents played. He has a brother who is now a tennis instructor in North Carolina. Another brother has been involved with Tennis Canada over the years. "I was always ranked in the top three in Canada — top three or four for junior tennis all the way through. I played until I was 18 and had some opportunities to go and play college tennis and hockey. But I got to the 67's at an early age, so that kind of negated that option."

Dunlop still lives in St. Louis, where he is a successful businessman who better understands his career trajectory. "If I could do anything different? I don't know, maturity isn't the right word, but being more prepared and understanding what that opportunity was . . . I look back and I know I accomplished a lot. I'm very proud of what I accomplished on and off the ice. But I think there were certain things — if I had paid a bit more attention and realized how valuable that time was — that maybe I could have done a little bit differently. I certainly have no regrets. I had fun. I had a great career. I've been fortunate to be successful as an athlete and now as a businessperson. I wouldn't trade anything. I feel blessed to have had those opportunities."

DOUG GRANT   1974–75
O-PEE-CHEE #347

You may not know it at first glance, but when you look at this card you are looking at hockey history — Newfoundland hockey history, to be more precise. The young man on this card, Doug Grant, was the first Newfoundlander to ever play goalie in the National Hockey League. "My first game was in Madison Square Garden — you talk about being dumbfounded," begins Grant. "I walk into Madison Square Garden, which is a big, big rink, and I'm looking up at the lights and I'm saying, 'What am I doing here? Really. Where am I?' It was really something. It was our first game of the season, and Teddy Garvin, for some reason, started me instead of Roy Edwards, who was a great goaltender. We lost to the Rangers 4–1. Vic Hadfield scored on me for the first goal."

That first game was on October 10, 1973. About 45 years later, Doug and I are having lunch in his hometown of Corner Brook, Newfoundland chatting about this old card and his hockey career. We are here for Hockey Day in Canada, where Doug is getting the treatment as a hometown hockey hero. Doug was a kid from the west coast of Newfoundland, who made the improbable climb to the NHL. "This week has been really special," says Doug, one of the most likeable guys you'll ever come across.

Imagine working in your local mill and playing senior hockey. Then after a few years, you decide to go away to university, only to somehow end up on a hockey card with the Detroit Red Wings. That's Doug story. It is unusual, but very true. Along the way, Doug got a little help from one of the greatest hockey play-by-play men in history, who just happened to be a fellow Newfoundlander. "I was in Victoriaville playing in the Allan Cup, and Bob Cole was there — I think he was covering it for CBC Radio — and I guess he mentioned to Sid Abel to keep an eye on me."

Sid Abel was the head coach of the Detroit Red Wings. The seed was planted, but nothing happened, at least not right away. Doug continued to play in the Newfoundland Senior League. Eventually he made the move to St. John's and enrolled in Memorial University of Newfoundland, where he played for the university team. "When I went to MUN, I thought I would get a law degree and get on with my life. I never expected hockey to become a career that way. It's funny how it ends and how it starts."

Late in the 1971–72 season the Detroit Red Wings eventually came calling. The seed that was planted by Mr. Cole with Mr. Abel was about to sprout. The Wings wanted to see what Doug Grant was made of. Doug was in school, he was married, but "I gave it a try." He played three games for Fort Worth in the Central League, and that was enough to impress the Wings. "They offered me $6,000 to sign and $7,600 to play. I told them I wouldn't take it. They said, 'What do you want?' I said, '$10,000 and $8,500.' They said, 'You got it.'"

Boom! Just like that, the kid from Newfoundland went from the mill to the local senior team to Canadian University to the pros. He spent his first professional season in the American League with Virginia. Then in 1973–74 he hit the big time. He spent the majority of the season in the NHL. He played in 37 games for the Wings. Newfoundland hockey history and this hockey card were born. "I do remember posing for that picture. It was after practice. I had no idea they were taking pictures. I was a rookie; the old vets knew what was going on. So they all went in and were getting their hair poofed up and everything else. I walked off the ice, and they said, 'Get back out there.' So I just went out and they took the picture."

Meantime, in Newfoundland, Grant's career was big news. With his first NHL game at MSG out of the way, he was getting down to business for the season. And the folks back home wanted to see Grant in action. As you know, back in the day, NHL games were not an almost-nightly TV feature like they are during the winter these days. On December 5, 1973, the Wings were taking on the Chicago Blackhawks. "The game was on *Wednesday Night Hockey* that they used to broadcast then."

That was the good news; the bad news: Grant was on the bench. But that night, before the game, he realized just what a big deal his NHL career meant to all his friends and fellow Newfoundlanders. "There was a telegram in the dressing room with I don't know how many thousands of signatures on it, asking Detroit to play me."

Grant didn't get the start. Instead, Detroit decided to start former Blackhawk Denis DeJordy against his old team. "As it happened, they scored four goals in the first period on poor old Denis, and I ended up finishing the game. We lost 8–2, or something like that."

The score aside, at least Doug got 40 minutes of playing and TV time that night. Doug Grant ended up playing in 77 career NHL games for Detroit and St. Louis. He retired from pro hockey after the 1981–82 season. He ended up with two NHL cards, this one with Detroit and another one with the Blues, but he had no idea that his card was stuffed into packs of O-Pee-Chee until years into his post-playing life. "I never saw the card itself until I was retired and back living in St. John's. My son Doug went to a card fair and came home and said, 'Dad, I got your hockey card.' I said, 'What hockey card?' He said, 'Your Detroit Red Wings rookie card.' He said he paid 10 bucks for it. It was $9.75 too much."

RICK VAIVE 1980–81 O-PEE-CHEE #242

"The first time I saw it, I was shocked," laughs Rick Vaive. "It was kind of weird-looking. I think they did a pretty decent job making it look like me, but it was just weird. I think I know why — it was in the middle of the trade from Vancouver to Toronto"

The trade Vaive is talking about happened on February

Chapter Seven   AIRBRUSH

18, 1980. Rick Vaive and Bill Derlago went to the Leafs; Tiger Williams and Jerry Butler went to the Canucks. A trade in the middle of February should have given the card makers plenty of time to get Vaive in a Toronto uniform, but it didn't happen. "They had to do something. I've seen some cards where they've just put a different sweater on the person, but mine was like a complete overhaul."

The overhaul can be defined by one thing: the hair. I get that the card makers had to airbrush a Leafs uniform onto Rick — in 1980, that was standard operating procedure. But can somebody explain why they decided to paint his hair? Maybe the artist got into the zone and just couldn't stop at the uniform.

"You think they would have put a helmet on me or something. I don't know. The first time I saw it, I went, 'What the hell is this?' Obviously I had no control over it. No one ever contacted me to say, 'What do you want us to do?' So it is what it is. It's kind of unique, though . . . it's probably one of the only cards like that."

The card was the first from Vaive's almost nine years

in Toronto. "It was quite disappointing at first. You get picked fifth overall — you expect you're going to be [in Vancouver] for a while."

When the hard-shooting Vaive showed up in Toronto, the message from Punch Imlach was simple: go play. "For him to come out and say go play, do your thing, that kind of gives you a little bit of peace of mind. They just want you to go play and do your best. It's kind of nice when you're told that."

And go play is exactly what Vaive did. With his notoriously stiff Titan, he went out and scored 33 goals. The following season he made Leafs history. "I was around 45 goals when the press started coming to me and saying, 'You're getting pretty close to 50 goals, which means you could become the first Leaf to ever do it.' I was shocked. With all the great players who have played there over the years — Keon, Sittler, and MacDonald and further back — I thought, *No one has ever done that in Toronto?* I was actually shocked."

Frank Mahovlich scored 48 goals in 1960–61. That record stood until March 22, 1982, when Vaive scored his 49th of the season in an 8–5 win over Chicago. "Frank Mahovlich came in our room and congratulated me and took a picture with me when I broke his record. Those are great moments, but at the time you're not completely appreciative. You're not thinking a whole lot about it. You're thinking about your next game."

In his next game, two nights later, Rick Vaive became the first Leaf to score 50 in a season. Typical of the Ballard years, nothing of note marked the occasion. "There was no ceremony. Harold didn't have a night for it or anything like that."

But at least one person knew history when she saw it. "My wife had a ring made for me, so that I'd have something to remember it by. At the time, I said, 'Why did you do that?' Because you're 22 years old and you just don't think of those things when you're 22."

Vaive followed up his 54-goal season with 52 the next year and 51 the year after that. He is the only Leaf to score 50 or more in three straight seasons. "Now, 35 years later, you sit back and you think a lot about it and you say, 'Wow, that was pretty good.' To be named in the same conversation as Gretzky and Bossy as the only guys who scored more over those three years, you start thinking about it the older you get. It becomes more of an accomplishment when you're retired. When you're 22, it's just like, 'Oh, wow, I got 50 goals. I was the first player to do it. Great. That means I'm going to make more money.' Which, in Toronto, really didn't mean that much.

"I heard a story about Mr. Ilitch when John Ogrodnick scored 50 goals. The Wings were on the road, maybe out in Alberta, and John scored his 50th. A couple of days later, there was a cheque for $50,000 in his stall.

"I'm sure for Auston Matthews it really hasn't sunk in that he broke the Leafs' rookie record [for goals in a season], and I'm sure it won't for some time — but 20 years from now, he'll probably really start thinking about it and say, 'Well, that was pretty damn good.'"

Perhaps Matthews will break Vaive's record one day. I can guarantee you that Matthews will never have a card like this, though: 1980s airbrushing will, fortunately or unfortunately, never surface again. It's history — just like Vaive's three straight 50-goal campaigns. And just like Vaive's appreciation for his 50-plus goal seasons has grown over time, so has his appreciation for his rookie card. It is, after all, a work of art. "I'm fine with it. It's almost like a painting. It's like a Picasso. That's the way I look at it . . . I'm a Picasso."

NORTH STARS — **KEN SOLHEIM**

LEFT WING
AILIER GAUCHE

Now with Minnesota

KEN SOLHEIM
LEFT WING/AILIER GAUCHE ● NORTH STARS

131

Minor league & NHL record Fiche dans les ligues mineures et la LNH

YEAR	TEAM	GP	G	A	PTS	PIM
80-81	Black Hawks	5	2	0	2	0
80-81	Medicine Hat	64	68	43	111	87
80-81	North Stars	5	3	0	3	0
81-82	Nashville	44	23	18	41	40
81-82	North Stars	29	4	5	9	4
82-83	North Stars	25	2	2	4	4
82-83	Red Wings	10	0	0	0	2
NHL TOTALS		74	10	10	20	10

Ken is single and enjoys playing baseball in the summer. He has two sisters and a brother.
Ken est célibataire et il joue au baseball pour se détendre en été. Il a deux soeurs et un frère.

Scored a goal on first shot in Stanley Cup play against Buffalo in deciding game of 1981 quarterfinals.
Il marqua un but à son premier lancer dans un match de la Coupe Stanley. Ce fut le but gagnant du match et du quart de finals contre Buffalo en 1981.

Ht: 6'3" Wt: 210 Shoots: L 1st Pro Season 80-81
Acquired: Trade with North Stars
Born: 3-27-61, Hythe, Alta. Home: Hythe, Alta.
©1983 O-Pee-Chee Ptd. in Canada Imprimé au Canada

©1983 NHLPA

KEN SOLHEIM   1983–84
O-PEE-CHEE #131

Once up a time, the NHL trade deadline wasn't the semi-official national holiday that it is now; it was just another day. Believe it or not, there was a time when network TV personalities weren't waiting, cellphones in hand, in front of a live audience for someone — anyone — to get traded.

Sure, a few players moved, but it was nothing like it is today. On March 8, 1983, there was one deal. Ken Solheim was sent from Minnesota to Detroit for future considerations. Thank all that is holy that Daren Millard and Nick Kypreos weren't working — that's all they'd have to discuss over the course of 10 hours of live television. The trade didn't create a lot of buzz, but it did create this airbrushed hockey card . . . kind of. "I played 10 games with the Wings that year, and then the next year I played for their farm team in Adirondack. The year after that, my rights went back to Minnesota. It was one of those future-consideration trades. That's why the card is the way it is, I think," says Ken Solheim.

Now, here's where things get a little tricky: on September 20, 1984, Solheim was sent back to Minnesota. He was the "futures" in his own deal — essentially, he was traded for himself. The card lists him as "Now with Minnesota." But this card came out in the fall of 1983. So how did the card makers know he would be traded back to the North Stars a year later? Either this is an error card or someone predicted the future or I have no understanding of the concept of time.

It could be all three.

"I'm not really sure why it's coloured in. I never got to the bottom of it. I've been asked so many times why it looks painted. I really have no explanation for it other than when I got traded they must have air-brushed over it. It looked like it was an original North Stars card. I wish I had an answer, but I don't know."

So if he was already in a North Stars uniform, why not just leave the dang thing alone? Deadlines, I would imagine. That and limited Photoshopping skills in 1983.

I'm still impressed that someone predicted the future.

Who knows? Maybe they had a flux capacitor at O-Pee-Chee back in the day. Bottom line: it gave us this airbrushed magic. After all, there's a magical number that really stands out on the back of Solheim's card: 68. He scored 68 goals in 64 games during his final year of junior with the Medicine Hat Tigers. "I don't know if you remember a guy by the name of Steve Tsujiura. He played for the Tigers too. He was a small kid, very talented, an extremely skilled playmaker. We just kind of hit it off. We had a really good chemistry and he was a great set-up man. I just found the opening, and he fed me the puck all the time. I was fortunate enough to have a couple good years, and then things kind of went south when I went pro."

South? Solheim made the NHL: how could things go south? Well, just like our friend Dean Kolstad, it has to do with some other numbers on the back of his card: six-foot-three, 210 pounds. In 1981, a coach could look at your height, your weight, or your goals and determine what type of player he wanted you to become. When Ken Solheim joined the Minnesota North Stars, his size meant a lot more to his coach than his 68 goals in his final year of junior. "I was a goal scorer all my life, and then I got to Minnesota. Glen Sonmor was the coach. He was one of those old-school coaches who loved the tough guys, and that's how he wanted me to play."

Sonmor *was* old-time hockey. In the WHA, he coached the likes of Frank Beaton, Gordie Gallant, Dave Hanson, and Steve Durbano. When he saw Solheim, he saw a very big kid. "I just wasn't willing to play that way. I didn't have a whole lot of ice time, and my style of play didn't suit him. I spent a lot of time going up and down, to and from the minors."

"Minnesota had guys like Jack Carlson, Willi Plett, and Paul Holmgren. And I've often wondered why he wanted me to play like that. He had all these other guys to do that.

"I just didn't have the personality, the mean," continues Solheim, who didn't take a single penalty in the five games he appeared with Sonmor's North Stars in 1980–81. "You either have it or you don't. I think

AIRBRUSH · KEN SOLHEIM

it's really hard to convert a passive person into a hard-nosed fighter. It probably had an effect on my career.

"I understand the reason why he wanted me to play like that — so I can create room out there and make room for myself. I understand all that — that's part of the game. You want to make a name for yourself so you can use your skills, but I just wasn't willing to play like that. I never did play like that. It's not that I couldn't. Looking back now, with all the concussions, I'm kind of glad I didn't play that way. Some of the guys are struggling now. It's sad."

Solheim says he got a "little taste" of his dream of making it to the NHL — and he ended up playing in 135 regular-season NHL games. His final six were with the Edmonton Oilers. It was almost full circle for Solheim, who played in the Alberta Junior League for Doug Messier's St. Albert Saints, just outside of Edmonton, before he went to Medicine Hat. "That was probably the highlight of my career, to play with the Oilers. I played on a line with Gretzky and Kurri for a couple of games, and then I played with Messier and Anderson for a couple of games. To play with Gretzky and those guys was the highlight of my career. It will go down as one of the best teams ever."

Just in case I ever end up on a line with 99, I ask Ken if he has any advice for playing with the Great One.

"Just play your game and relax. That was the toughest thing. I remember I was so nervous and uptight. It's tough to play that way. You've just got to relax and play your game. That's easy to say, but there was a lot of pressure. I was just a young guy coming to this team. I thought, *Do I belong here or not?*"

That's the thing. Even at the highest level of hockey, players question if they belong. It's like any other line of work. Remember your first few days at a new job? I know I've questioned if I belong over the years. Perhaps you have as well. Ken Solheim did too during his NHL career. "The mental part of the game is to understand that you're good enough to be there and to have the confidence to play with those guys. And I had

a hard time with that. I don't think I had the confidence to say to myself, 'You're good enough to be here.' It takes time. It really takes time to fit in."

Solheim called it quits after the 1986 season. He thought about heading to Europe but decided to return to Medicine Hat. He spent 30 years with Goodyear before he retired for a second time — no hockey cards mark the occasion this time around, though. "I'd give the airbrush maybe a seven out of 10," Solheim says of his only hockey card. "The helmet doesn't look bad."

Harold Snepsts

Ht: 6'3" Wt: 215 Shoots: L 1st Pro Season: 1974-75
Acquired: Trade with Vancouver, 6-21-84
Born: 10-24-54, Edmonton, Alberta
Home: Vancouver, British Columbia

108

NHL record / Fiche dans la LNH

YEAR	TEAM	GP	G	A	PTS	PIM
74-75	Canucks	27	1	2	3	30
75-76	Canucks	78	3	15	18	125
76-77	Canucks	79	4	18	22	149
77-78	Canucks	75	4	16	20	118
78-79	Canucks	76	7	24	31	130
79-80	Canucks	79	3	20	23	202
80-81	Canucks	76	3	16	19	212
81-82	Canucks	68	3	14	17	153
82-83	Canucks	46	2	8	10	80
83-84	Canucks	79	4	16	20	152
NHL TOTALS		683	34	149	183	1351

Became the Canucks All-time leader in games played,
83-84.
En 83-84, il devint le meneur chez les Canucks pour les
parties jouées.

Harold Snepsts

NORTH STARS

D

HAROLD SNEPSTS   1984–85
O-PEE-CHEE #108

This card made absolutely no sense to my 10-year-old self. To tell you the truth, it was unthinkable. How could Harold Snepsts — Mr. Vancouver Canuck — be in a Minnesota North Stars uniform?

I'll be honest, growing up in Nova Scotia, I was not overly exposed to the Vancouver Canucks. In fact, I only knew a few things about them: they made an incredible run to the Cup Final in 1982, where New York Islander Billy Smith slashed and saved everything in sight, their goalie was a guy named King Richard, and they had a really slick forward in Thomas Gradin and a defender with an awesome moustache named Harold Snepsts. In fact, for reasons I still don't fully comprehend, Harold Snepsts was a kind of cult hero to me and my grade-school buddies, even though we rarely saw him play.

So what in the hell was Harold Snepsts doing in a crudely drawn Minnesota North Stars sweater with, as Snepsts points out to me over 30 years later, "Vancouver socks on." It turns out, Harold was in Minnesota green and gold because he was no longer a Canuck. It's right there in the fine print on the back of the card: "Acquired: Trade with Vancouver, 6-21-84."

"I was out with the [Vancouver] office staff that evening, and I was with the general manager's secretary — the general manager was Harry Neale at the time — and she informed me that we had just made a trade."

That was all that the secretary knew. As of that moment, the Canucks had picked up Al MacAdam for future considerations. However, it didn't take long for Harold, who had played in 683 regular-season games for the Canucks at that point, to find out that he was the "future considerations."

"I came home late that night, and in the morning I got a phone call from Harry Neale saying I was part of the deal." The man I thought was Mr. Canuck was no longer a Canuck at all. Vancouver was the only team that Snepsts had ever known. He made his NHL debut with them a decade earlier, but now he was a North Star.

"It came as a surprise," says Snepsts. "The secretary phoned me after

Harry talked to me, and she was in tears. She said, 'I promise I didn't know anything about it.'"

Harry Neale's secretary wasn't the only one caught off guard. The Canucks without Snepsts? It was unthinkable for me as a kid. The feeling was mutual and much more heated in Vancouver. But this airbrush confirmed it, Snepsts was gone; he was now a crudely crayoned member of the North Stars. If there was crying and wails of *Haaarold* on the streets of Vancouver, Snepsts wasn't waiting around town to witness it. "I left the city that night to visit our trainer who lived in Phoenix. I don't know what the reaction was. I just packed my bags and left."

Looking back on that June 1984 trade, Harold Snepsts ended up with a lot more than just an airbrushed hockey card. He believes he got a new lease on his NHL career: "I thought I was going to finish my career with Vancouver. But, in hindsight, it probably extended my career. After I left, the Canucks had some lean years. So staying there probably would have shortened my career."

And he soon learned what playing in a real rivalry was like. Snepsts says the Oilers hated the Flames and vice versa, but the Canucks didn't have any real rivals back in the 1980s. That changed for Snepsts when he joined the North Stars in the Norris Division, or as he calls it, "the Black and Blue Division."

In 1984–85, when Snepsts and his Minny teammates lined up against Detroit or Chicago, it was game on. "I enjoyed it. They were intense games, and the teams hated each other. The fans hated each other and the players got to the point where they hated each other."

You may think leaving a division that featured guys like Dave Semenko and Tim Hunter would give a guy a break. It did not. In his one and only season in Minnesota, Snepsts piled up a career high 232 minutes in the penalty box. He dropped the gloves 15 times that year, another career high. Among those that Snepsts threw down with were Norris Division opponents Joey Kocur, Behn Wilson, and Gerard Gallant. Did

Snepsts have a special hate-on for anyone in particular? No. "Anybody who tried to score on us, I didn't like."

After one season in Minnesota, Snepsts ended up in Detroit for a few seasons where he was a teammate of a young Steve Yzerman. "He was probably the best player that I ever played with. He was just an unbelievable teammate, an unbelievable player. I can't say enough good things about him."

Snepsts and his Detroit teammates made it to the conference final in the spring of both 1987 and 1988. Unfortunately, they were up against a dynasty both times. "We became a pretty good team. We thought we were going to win the Stanley Cup, but we lost to Edmonton twice."

Snepsts returned to Vancouver for a second tour with the Canucks before ending his career with the Blues. It turns out this airbrushed hockey card was not the end of Mr. Canuck. There are some things a crude 1980s pre-Photoshop colouring job just can't take away from a man. This card didn't totally turn Snepsts into a North Star. Take a look at those socks again. The Vancouver colours remain. "When I say, 'Look at the socks,' they are all surprised." I know I was.

The fact is, as a 10-year-old, this card represented something that seemed impossible to me. But now I think the overlooked socks were actually quite telling. Snepsts was always going to be a Vancouver Canuck at heart, whether he was traded or his uniform was painted green and gold. And even today, Harold Snepsts is still a Vancouver Canuck; he is a scout for the team and a member of the team's Ring of Honour.

The hockey cards that mean the most to Harold are his early ones. The ones that show him in those classic old Vancouver uniforms. "In the early days, it meant something. You were pretty proud that you got a hockey card, but later on it didn't matter to me at all."

O-Pee-Chee

GARY NYLUND
D ◆ BLACKHAWKS

GARY NYLUND

243

HEIGHT: 6'3" WEIGHT: 210 SHOOTS: LEFT

Born: 10-28-63, Surrey, B.C.   Home: Vancouver, B.C.
Last Amateur Club: Portland Winter Hawks (1981-82)
Acquired: 1st Round Choice (3rd Overall) 1982 Draft

NHL RECORD
FICHE DANS LA LNH

Year Année	Team Équipe	GP	G	A	PTS	PIM
82-83	Maple Leafs	16	0	3	3	16
83-84	Maple Leafs	47	2	14	16	103
84-85	Maple Leafs	76	3	17	20	99
85-86	Maple Leafs	79	2	16	18	180
NHL Totals/Totaux dans la LNH		218	7	50	57	398

1985-86 Game Winning Goals: 0
Buts gagnants en 1985-86: 0

Played on Canadian National Team that
won World Championship in 1981. Was a 2-time
WHL All-Star.
Il joua pour l'équipe nationale canadienne qui
remporta le championnat mondial junior en 1981.
Deux fois membre de l'équipe d'étoiles de la W.H.L.

© 1986
NHLPA

Ptd. in Canada./Imprimé au Canada
©1986 O-Pee-Chee

NHL   NHLPA

GARY NYLUND

At first glance, this airbrushed portrait of Gary Nylund doesn't look all that different from any other primitively executed 1980s quick fix. "The Chief looks a little squished, doesn't it?" says Nylund, three decades after this card hit the market.

The story behind this card, though, separates it from any other airbrushed atrocity that was ever found in wax packs. Card makers had to do a quick fix because Gary Nylund became a Chicago Blackhawk in the summer of 1986. But it wasn't because of a trade. On August 27, 1986, Gary Nylund became the first NHLer to ever switch teams via free agency. The newest Chicago Blackhawk was big news in 1986. "Believe it or not, it's actually a question in Trivial Pursuit. I heard that anyway, I've never seen it. That's my claim to fame."

Three things kept players from switching teams via free agency back in the day. "Collusion back in those days was rampant," says Nylund. "Plus, you basically had to play forever to become a free agent. And once you did, compensation was massive, usually a player on your active roster."

Nylund, though, slipped through the cracks into free agency. And even just the *type* of free agent he was sounds like something out of a spy novel, not the kind of thing you'd think of when you look at an old hockey card: "I was Double Eagle free agent."

Huh?

"The owners didn't want anyone switching teams through free agency. They wanted to make it difficult for players to go from one team to another, so they put these restrictions on us, and you had to play so many years before you had that opportunity."

On Canada Day 1986, there wasn't a *Free Agency Special* on Sportsnet because there were essentially no free agents. And if you were a free agent, chances were you were in your mid to late 30s. And even if you were a coveted pro, with compensation so high, you probably weren't going anywhere. Nylund, though, the Double Eagle, was a different story. An obscure rule stated that if a player was under 23 and had four years in the league but under 220 games played, he would become a Double Eagle free agent. Gary Nylund qualified. "I started in the NHL when I was 18, so I'd played four seasons. I was injured for one season, but I'd played four seasons. It wasn't total free agency — it was free agency with compensation."

When Nylund signed with the Blackhawks, an arbitrator had to decide what the Leafs would get as compensation. The decision? Jerome Dupont and Ken Yaremchuk would immediately leave Chicago and join the Leafs, plus Toronto would get a fourth-round pick. These days, when a restricted free agent changes teams, only draft picks are part of the compensation, and when an unrestricted free agent leaves your team, you get no compensation at all. In 1986, you got compensatory bodies: actual NHL players had to switch addresses. "That's how it worked. I was the first one to move."

I'm trying to picture a 22-year-old facing Harold Ballard, the legendarily grumpy Leafs owner, and letting him know that his Toronto days were over. That he's the one to finally rock the NHL boat and switch teams. But it wasn't a problem for Nylund. "Mr. Ballard and I had a kind of special relationship. It was nothing to do with me, really; it was more to do with my dad. My dad was RCMP and Ballard loved the RCMP. So he let off me. He was always good to me."

The plan had never been for Nylund to leave Ballard's Leafs. Toronto had high hopes for the big defenceman when they took him third overall in the 1982 Draft. A top prospect, as the back of the card tells you, Nylund "was a 2-time WHL All-Star." The card also points out that Gary Nylund "played on the Canadian National Junior Team that won the World Championship in 1981." For the record, it was actually Nylund's 1982 team that won the World Juniors. Nine months later, he was a Leaf. (That 1982 Junior team was the first Canadian team to ever win the World Juniors.) "It was still a large-scale stage; it just wasn't televised. The Worlds just didn't have the media coverage that it has now. We were treated like gold. We had guys like Don Cherry come in between periods and wish us luck. We were on TV on Boxing Day. We played the Russians and beat them 7–0 in Winnipeg, and we went on to win the gold medal,

which no Canadian team had ever done before. It was a big deal, but it didn't get the coverage that it should have."

That 1982 team set the tone for what we see today. And when I say set the tone, I mean both on the ice and musically. When Nylund and his Canadian teammates won gold, they lined up for the national anthem. There was just one problem. No one had a copy of the Canadian anthem on January 2, 1982, in Rochester, Minnesota. "We lined up at the blue line and they gave away the medals, but because they didn't have the anthem, the Czechs started skating off the ice." That did not sit well with Team Canada.

"We sent a couple of our guys down to tell them, not that nicely, to basically get back on the blue line — they were going to listen to our anthem. We had no other recourse but to sing it. So we did. And that's kind of a tradition now, where the players are arm in arm singing the anthem. I think we started it and they even do it to this day."

Nylund and his teenage teammates were pioneers. A few years later, Nylund was a pioneer as far as NHL free agency goes, although he doesn't really see it that way. "I don't know if I was that much of a pioneer," Nylund, now a firefighter in British Columbia, says. "Everything was kind of stacked in the owners' advantage. If they wanted to put a stop to it, they could have, but it's pretty hard to take things back once you've set them in motion. Free agency has gotten a whole lot better over the years. That was a step in the right direction."

Nylund has something of a shocked look on his face on this card. Maybe he can't believe a call on the ice, but I like to think the look sums up the story behind his shocking move from Toronto to Chicago. It's a move that made the card makers jump into action and put Nylund in a crudely drawn Blackhawks jersey. They didn't even bother to colour his helmet or gloves. "I don't think they paid the nine-year-old enough money to colour the rest of the card. Maybe they didn't have any black crayons. They obviously had a red crayon. It's not a sought-after card. But I get a lot of guys wanting me to sign it because it is very strange."

O-PEE-CHEE

O-Pee-Chee

left wing
ailier gauche

63

RANDY CUNNEYWORTH

HEIGHT: 6' 0"   WEIGHT: 190   SHOOTS: LEFT
Last Amateur Club: Ottawa 67's (1979-80)
Acquired: Trade with Pittsburgh, 6-15-89
Born: 5-10-61, Etobicoke, Ontario   Home: Rochester, N.Y.

NHL RECORD / FICHE DANS LA LNH

Year Année	Team Équipe	GP	G	A	PTS	PIM
80-81	Sabres	1	0	0	0	2
81-82	Sabres	20	2	4	6	47
85-86	Penguins	75	15	30	45	74
86-87	Penguins	79	26	27	53	142
87-88	Penguins	71	35	39	74	141
88-89	Penguins	70	25	19	44	156
NHL Totals/Totaux dans la LNH		316	103	119	222	562

GAME WINNING GOALS / BUTS GAGNANTS 1988-89: 1

Randy was credited with 10 PPG during the 1988-89 season.
● Randy réussit 10 buts lors d'attaques à cinq durant la saison 1988-89.

NHL PLAYOFF RECORD/FICHE DURANT LES ÉLIMINATOIRES

		GP	G	A	PTS	PIM
1989		11	3	5	8	26
CAREER/CARRIÈRE		11	3	5	8	26

NATIONAL HOCKEY LEAGUE
LIGUE NATIONALE DE HOCKEY

OFFICIAL LICENSED PRODUCT
PRODUIT LICENCIE OFFICIEL

© 1989 NHLPA

© 1989 O-PEE-CHEE CO. LTD

PTD. IN CANADA
IMPRIME AU CANADA

O-Pee-Chee

RANDY CUNNEYWORTH
WINNIPEG JETS

Randy Cunneyworth

1989–90
O-Pee-Chee #63

"It might have been more special if they had put me on Dale Hawerchuk's body, or something like that," says a laughing Randy Cunneyworth. He didn't get the Ken Linseman/Mike Krushelnyski 1984–85 O-Pee-Chee treatment, where they stuck Linseman on Krushelnyski's body; no, instead, Randy Cunneyworth got a full-body airbrush. The only thing that's real on this card is Cunneyworth's head. The rest is vintage O-Pee-Chee paint magic.

The details are fantastic. We've got a nicely drawn Sherwood and the gloves are rendered in fine detail. The only thing that's a little off are the size of Cunneyworth's shoulders. His right one is extremely large. He looks more like a player from today, covered in giant shoulder pads, than a defenceman from 1989.

"At the time, I just thought they were too lazy to come out [and get a new picture]. I don't know what the procedure is for taking pictures and getting them on cards. It's one of those things where you're just proud to have a hockey card — it doesn't matter what's painted on it. But it wasn't the prettiest card.

"I can't even comment on the art other than the fact that it is totally Photoshopped. But I guess it gets the idea across that you're with a different organization."

A June 1989 trade from the Pittsburgh Penguins to the Winnipeg Jets necessitated this airbrush job. Cunneyworth left a Pens team that was just two years away from the first of two straight Cups. Mario Lemieux was in full stride, but by the time the Pens won the Cup in the spring of 1991, Cunneyworth was playing for the Hartford Whalers. "I was a few years removed when they won. I was happy for Pittsburgh but a little bit jealous that I wasn't there for it. But that's the way it goes."

Cunneyworth is what we call a hockey lifer. He played in 866 career NHL regular-season games and spent his last year as a player–assistant coach with the Rochester Americans. He went on to become a head coach in the AHL, an assistant in the NHL, and an interim head coach with the Montreal Canadiens. When we catch up on the phone, he's in Rochester, where he serves as player development coach in the Buffalo Sabres organization. This old Cunneyworth card has been in my collection for almost three decades. And we card geeks aren't the only ones who dig up relics from our childhood. So do hockey lifers like Randy Cunneyworth. He recently came across an autograph book from a minor hockey banquet at the Royal York Hotel in Toronto in 1973. Cunneyworth was 10 years old. His mom and dad took him to the banquet at the end of the year. He ended up with autographs from his heroes: names like Bobby Orr, Bobby Hull, Dave Keon, Norm Ullman, King Clancy, and more. "I think I ended up with a Bobby Orr stick and all those autographs and a couple of trophies. It was quite a big deal for me at 10. We literally just came across it in a box. The funny part is my dad signed page one. So it's kind of funny that it's got his autograph. He never played in the NHL at all. But he loved hockey. He played beer league."

Like pretty much everyone else, Cunneyworth didn't keep the cards he had as a kid; they are history now. "On our street, we had a lot of guys who loved hockey. It was a typical Canadian street. Everybody collected and everybody traded. The bubble gum was good too."

But he has kept most of his own cards from his playing days, including this one. "My favourite cards were the full-sized action shots. I've got a couple that were taken in warm-ups and a couple of game-action photos. I always jokingly tell people that in the game-action ones, 'I scored right after that shot was taken.'"

And then there's this beauty: part action, part crayon, maybe part paint . . . but all hockey card.

MAPLE LEAFS PAUL HARRISON

GOALIE

35

HEIGHT: 6'1" WEIGHT: 175 SHOOTS: LEFT
1st Pro Season: 1975-76 Acquired: Trade with North Stars, 6-14-78
Born: 2-11-55, Timmins, Ontario Home: Timmins, Ontario

123

PAUL HARRISON

Paul's talents include extremely quick reflexes that give him perhaps the fastest hands and feet in the business. He has a brother, Dave, at University of Windsor. Paul possède des réflexes extrêmement rapides qui lui donnent les mains et les pieds probablement les plus rapides dans la ligue. Son frère Dave joue pour l'Université de Windsor.

MINOR LEAGUE AND NHL RECORD
FICHE DANS LA LNH ET LES LIGUES MINEURES

YEAR	TEAM	GP	MIN	GA	AVG	SO
75-76	NORTH STARS	6	307	28	5.47	0
75-76	PROVIDENCE	3	145	13	5.38	0
76-77	NORTH STARS	2	120	11	5.50	0
76-77	NEW HAVEN	55	3265	172	3.16	2
77-78	NORTH STARS	27	1555	99	3.82	1
NHL TOTALS		35	1982	138	4.18	1

Special Autograph Series • Série signée spéciale

Paul Harrison

PAUL HARRISON   1978–79
O-PEE-CHEE #123

"That summer, Dave Hutchison joined the Leafs and Davey Burrows came in a trade. I think all of us had the cheesy blue paint jobs on our sweaters," says former Maple Leafs goalie Paul Harrison. "But I guess back in the day, that's the level of importance they put on those cards."

Yeah, it is a pretty cheesy paint job — it has an almost-watercolour quality. But like most airbrush jobs, I've fallen in love with it. Harrison, not so much. "You thought that was a decent job? I thought that was terrible!"

This is Harrison's rookie card, and it's kind of fitting that O-Pee-Chee did what appears to be a rush job. Harrison was traded to the Leafs from Minnesota on June 14, 1978. He spent as much of the summer in Timmins as he possibly could before he rushed off to Toronto that September. He had a good reason to hang around home in the summer of '78. "My daughter was born in Timmins around noon, and later on that afternoon I had to fly to Toronto for the start of Leafs training camp."

That's how Harrison kicked off his two-plus season adventure in the centre of the Hockey Universe. When I think *Paul Harrison*, I think of the duckbill mask. All the old footage of him with the Leafs show him in face protection that was becoming all the rage at the time. However, that mask is nowhere to be seen on this card. "That picture was from my first year in Minnesota. That would have been from a 1975 game. Of course, they're passing it off as a '78 Leafs rookie card. But I wore that mask coming out of junior hockey in Oshawa before I had a new one made. Right after that mask, I went to a mask better known as the Mike Liut mask, even though I think I wore it before Mike did."

Goalies first started to express themselves via their masks in the 1970s. Think of the great stuff we saw: Gary Simmons of the Kings had the cobra; Gilles Gratton had the lion for the New York Rangers. Harrison went with plain white. "Shortly after I wore the mask on that hockey card, [hockey mask painter] Greg Harrison made a new mask for me in Toronto. And when he sent it to Minnesota, it was fully painted up. I don't think anyone had ever seen a painted mask at that point; it might have been one of the first times he did a paint job. Our coach at the time was Ted Harris. He was an old-school, hard-nosed Montreal Canadiens player, and when I wore that mask in practice, he skated over and told me to get rid of it or get it painted white again. I had to send it off to our trainer Doc Rose, and it came back white. I wore a white mask the rest of my career because I didn't want to upset the coach. I think his exact words were 'Get that shit off that mask.'"

Harrison was used mainly as a backup during his time with the Leafs, but played in 25 games during his first year. Mike Palmateer started the rest. "He's a great guy. He's a student of the game. He used to break down goals and saves in between periods and work on things all the time. He was spectacular to watch but also very studious."

Palmateer wasn't the only one pulling off spectacular glove saves. Pretty much every goalie back in the day would pull off a miraculous save or two every night — it was just the way the position was played back then. "It was more spectacular," Harrison says of the style of yesteryear. As the back of the card states, "Paul's talents include extremely quick reflexes that give him perhaps the fastest hands and feet in the business."

That style helped make for Harrison's most famous save as a Leaf. It was in 1979. The Leafs were taking on the Canadiens, the last time the two teams met in the Stanley Cup playoffs. The Habs had a 3–0 series lead in the quarterfinals. With the game tied 4–4, the Canadiens were on the attack in the dying seconds of regulation. Larry Robinson cut in, Harrison went for the poke-check. The puck found Jacques Lemaire, who sent it blazing for the far corner of the net. It was humming along about a foot off the ice when Harrison got a glove on it to keep the Leafs alive. "It was probably the best timely save I ever made. It was probably the luckiest save I ever made too. He pretty much shot it in my glove because I was way out of position after the poke-check. It was nice to make the save at that time. I know I got a pretty good reaction from my teammates for it. They all came out on the ice and tapped my pads and stuff like that. It was a good way to keep us in the game. Unfortunately, Montreal scored on a power play in overtime and that was the end of that."

Paul Harrison moved back to Timmins when his career wrapped up in the spring of 1983. He had two young daughters, and he and his wife knew they wanted to raise them in Northern Ontario. He figured that maybe he would become a firefighter. "I went down to city hall to inquire. They said, 'We've got no spots at the fire hall, but we're looking for a policeman. Are you interested?' And that was basically how I became a police officer."

Harrison spent 30 years and a day as a police officer. "I didn't want them to think I was anxious to retire. So I did that extra day."

Harrison served on the municipal police force and then the OPP as a drug prevention officer. The guy he looks at on this card is from another era. "The hockey was so long ago. It's almost like it's somebody else.

"My career paths have been pretty incredible. My dream as a child was to be a hockey player, and having a chance to compete in the NHL was fantastic. I think I should have set my dreams a little higher. I should have set them to be the best goaltender that ever lived. But I was content to play in the league, and I played against all the great players: Gretzky was starting his career; Gordie Howe was ending his; I played against Bobby Hull in exhibition games when Minnesota played Winnipeg in the WHA; Trottier and the great Islander teams; the Montreal teams. Bobby Orr, to me, was the greatest hockey player and the greatest person that I ever met. He represents why young people want to be hockey players: humble skill and intensity. When there was a scrum in a Bruins game, Bobby was usually at the bottom, because he started it. I played in an era that was incredible; I was exposed to so much talent. There was a lot of fire there. To me, that's Canadian hockey.

"I've been incredibly fortunate. I think hockey kind of prepared me for the policing, and the policing prepared me for getting involved with drug prevention. I'm still heavily involved in First Nations equipment drives and presentations about making life choices in school. It's something I'll be doing for a long time."

SCORE™

NHL Prospect '90

404

NHL Prospect '90

WINNIPEG JETS

KRIS DRAPER • C

Ht: 5'11" Wt: 190 Shoots: Left Born: May 24, 1971 Toronto, Ontario
Acquired: 3rd Choice (61st Overall, 1989)

Kris was one of five non-Major A players on the Canadian team that won the 1990 World Junior Championship in Helsinki. A strong defensive player, he won key faceoffs in the last minute of the final game against Czechoslovakia. Kris, a product of Toronto's Don Mills Flyers, whose graduates include the NHL's Peter Zezel and Scott Mellanby, has spent the last two years with Canada's National Team and has played in the Izvestia Tournament in Moscow.

His father, Michael, played at Michigan Tech and later in the minors. Kris is likely to play with the Ottawa 67's of the Ontario Hockey League in 1990-91.

© 1990 SCORE. PRINTED IN U.S.A.

NHLPA

KRIS DRAPER
Winnipeg Jets

KRIS DRAPER   1990–91
SCORE #404

While I was watching the greatest hockey moment of my young life on TV, Kris Draper watched it live in person. Gretzky to Lemieux, September 15, 1987: Canada wins Game 3 of the best of three Canada Cup Final, 6–5. Kris Draper saw the game from his seats at Copps Coliseum.

"Just watching that game and seeing the passion and

Chapter Eight ROOKIE CARDS

how the NHL players just came together to represent their country — you could see how bad they wanted to beat the Russians, and especially how bad they wanted to beat them at home in Canada — that made an impression on me for sure. To be there for those two games, Game 2 and Game 3 of the Final, you felt not only proud to be Canadian, but you also felt proud to play the game of hockey. Proud that we do it the right way over here. And that was something that made a lasting impact on me," Draper says.

Three years later, the kid who was in the crowd at Hamilton's Copps Coliseum, cheering on Team Canada, was on his very own hockey card with a red Maple Leaf on his chest. "I remember the first time I saw my hockey card and the first time that someone asked me to autograph my card. I pretty much lit up the rink. I thought it was the absolute coolest thing to have my own hockey card."

Draper was just a kid on this card, and I was just a kid at the time too. He's just three years older than me, but in my mind, if he was playing on our national team he must have been an old man. *Why in the hell*, I thought at the time,

does a guy on the Canadian national team have an NHL prospect card?
Actually, this was the first time I ever saw a national team member on
a hockey card. The national team was usually loaded with older guys.
Sure, there was the odd up-and-comer during an Olympic year, but in
between Olympics, not so much. Kris Draper, though, was an exception.
"My uncle Dave Draper was involved in Hockey Canada, and they were
starting a program out in Calgary after the '88 Olympics. They wanted
to start a program to build towards the '92 Olympics in Albertville."

Kris Draper was invited to an evaluation camp in Calgary straight
out of midget hockey. While his buddies were going off to junior camps,
he headed west for a tryout with the national team. "I was 17 years old,
and I figured I'd just go out. I was playing hockey, I was in Calgary, I
had a Team Canada practice jersey on, and I thought this was great —
just getting an opportunity, some exposure. I went out there with no
expectations. And from the practices to the scrimmages, things went
well. There was another 17-year-old there: Brandy Semchuk, and he was
a local kid from Calgary. There was a 19-year-old, Adrien Plavsic, who
was from Montreal. Craig Fisher was a Toronto kid. There were four
or five of us who were under 20. But for the most part, the team was
made up of American League or International League guys or players
who were playing over in Europe. I just felt a little more comfortable
with every skate and every practice. I had a good five or six days. Paul
Henry was one of the scouts who invited me out there. He said, 'You've
opened some eyes this week.' I was obviously very proud of that. That's
the reason I went out. So I got on a plane and went home."

Soon enough, Paul Henry was calling the Draper family. He wanted
Kris on the team. Kris's uncle Dave was on board, and his dad was cool
with the idea, but there was one hurdle left: *Mom.* A mother sending her
kid to a Major Junior locale is one thing, but sending your 17-year-old away
to travel the world is another. "My mom was totally against it. I might have
just turned 17 and she did not want me a four-and-a-half-hour plane ride
away. But at the time, I wasn't sure if I was even going to play Major Junior.

The Windsor Spitfires owned my rights, but both my dad and uncle Dave played at Michigan Tech, so I wasn't sure if I was going to go to school. And playing with the Olympic program let me keep my eligibility for both. It was an amateur program. If I wanted to go for a year and it didn't work, I could go play Major Junior or I could go play college hockey. That was really the biggest reason why I went out there. And what a great opportunity as a 17-year-old to go out and travel the world."

So while most kids his age were in high school geography class, trying to figure out where in the hell places like Norway and Czechoslovakia were on a map, Draper was actually visiting those countries. And this is my favourite part of his story: a little over a year after he was cheering against the Russians at the Canada Cup, Draper was playing against them at the Izvestia Tournament. He had watched the Soviet's famous KLM Line and the Russian 5 from the stands; now he was on the ice against Krutov, Larionov, Makarov, Fetisov, and Kasatonov. "They were exactly as advertised. Some of the greatest hockey players to play the game. I think the final score may have ended up being 8–1 for them, and at one point I just remember chasing the puck around. Dave King came to me and said, 'Drapes, you gotta sit down and watch the rest of this game.' I wanted to play, but these guys were *so* good. Just imagine them on an international ice surface that gave them a little bit more room and time and space. It was amazing just watching their play, especially on the big ice and in their hometown."

For 17-year-old Draper, there was a benefit to playing against the top players in the world. He was clearly not like most guys on an NHL prospect card. He was not setting the Major Junior leagues on fire; he was learning a different aspect of the game. "The one thing that I had to do differently than every other 16-, 17-, and 18-year-old was learn how to play hockey without the puck. For the most part, whenever a future NHLer is playing Major Junior, he's the star on his team. They are the guys who play on the power play, they're scoring points — 50, 60 goals — but that wasn't me. Because we were playing against superior teams, I had to learn to play the game without the puck. And in the end, when you look at my career, that was a big reason why I got opportunities I did."

As the back of the card states, Draper took a brief time away from the national team to win the 1990 World Junior title. Then, in 1991, he won another, in Saskatoon. To me, at least, this was the tournament's official coming out party. Every game was televised nationally in Canada and played in front of a packed house in Saskatoon. John Slaney of Canada scored the tournament winner in dramatic fashion, and the tourney put players like Slaney, Steven Rice, Mike Craig, and Kris Draper in front of Canadian hockey minds. "That was really when they started televising the World Juniors. The year before, we had won in Finland, and then we went back to back. We beat Russia. There were just so many things that were tied to that goal and to that Word Junior Championship that made it so special and so memorable. It was a coming out party for Eric Lindros. There was a lot of hype and a lot of media around that team."

After finally spending some time with the Ottawa 67's, Draper turned pro. Initially, he hit a little rut and bounced around the Winnipeg Jets system. While he was going up and down between Moncton and Winnipeg, you could easily snag this card for a buck. And that's what the Detroit Red Wings got him for. Doug MacLean, who was the Detroit Red Wings assistant GM at the time, was also in charge of the Wings AHL affiliate in Adirondack. He traded "futures" to the Jets for Kris Draper on June 30, 1993, with the intention of stacking Detroit's AHL team. Those future considerations ended up being one dollar. Draper had a solid season in the AHL and got the call-up to Detroit in January '94. That spring in San Jose he found out that he was traded for a dollar. "I was doing an interview during the first round of the Stanley Cup playoffs, and a reporter from San Jose told me that I was traded for a dollar."

Draper was wrapping up a post-game media scrum when the comment caught his attention. "I had a goal and an assist. I ended up doing an interview or a little scrum and one of the reporters came to me and said, 'That's not bad for a kid who was traded for a dollar.' And then he walked away. I was left just sitting there — you know when someone says something and you don't really comprehend what was said? That was me right there. The guy started walking away, and I said, 'Excuse me, I don't understand what you're talking about.' He said, 'You don't know?' I said, 'I don't know what?' I was actually getting a little mad. And he repeats himself, 'You were traded for a dollar.' And then he said, 'But you're doing pretty good.' That was the way that I found out."

Kris Draper . . . for a dollar. This is just one of many reasons I like to call my buddy Doug MacLean "Legend." It is easily one of the most lopsided trades in hockey history. The Wings got a guy who played in 1,157 games over 17 seasons and won four Stanley Cups and a Selke Trophy for the price of a couple of common hockey cards. "I think it's a great story. There is never a set path to fulfill your dream. There are very few Wayne Gretzkys, Mario Lemieuxs, Sidney Crosbys, Connor McDavids — those guys are generational talents. But in the end, there are 750 jobs available in the National Hockey League, and there are different ways to get one. And I did it very differently. I went from midget hockey to the Olympic program. I went back and played a year in the OHL. There were a lot of things that went on. Things didn't go well for me in Winnipeg. Basically one team gave up on me and another team gave me an opportunity, and here you and I are talking about my career. Who would have thought, when I got picked up for a dollar by the Detroit Red Wings, that this was going to happen?"

There's another kicker. The kid who was cheering on Gretzky at the '87 Canada Cup kept wearing the Maple Leaf. He even had his very own "where were you" moment when he scored the winning goal for Canada in the 2004 World Cup of Hockey. I, for one, remember where I was: watching the game at a Hooters. And Draper remembers exactly where he was when he got the call to join the team for the tournament. "We were on vacation, and I got the invite for the 2004 World Cup. It was Wayne Gretzky who invited me. It was on my voicemail. I bet you I listened to that message a hundred times. I called Wayne back just like I called you back."

I, for one, am glad he did.

CLAUDE VILGRAIN 1990–91
UPPER DECK #250

"I had finished the season with the Devils, in the playoffs the year before. I had a good camp the next year, but they still sent me down to the minors. When I got to Utica, I looked in my stall and there was an envelope. I opened it and someone wanted me to sign this card, and that made my day. I didn't care anymore [about being sent down]. I saw that card and I thought I had made it. I got my hockey card; I can retire now," says Claude Vilgrain, who now coaches the Midget AAA Calgary Buffaloes.

Vilgrain was 27 years old when he got his first hockey card. His birthplace, listed on the back of this card, Port-au-Prince, Haiti, gives you just the slightest hint as to his unusual path to getting his very own rookie card. These days, Vilgrain likes to tell his young players, "You never know who's watching. Every shift counts. Every shift can change a career." In the 1960s, a phone call changed the Vilgrains' lives and put Claude's career and life into motion.

"My dad studied for about seven years at Universite de Laval and then went back to Haiti. He eventually got a job offer to work for the government in Quebec. Prior to that, he was trying to go to Africa. He thought he had a job there. But there was a misunderstanding. So I could have been a little kid playing soccer in Africa instead of hockey in Canada."

The phone call that sent the Vilgrains to Quebec eventually led to the moment when hockey came knocking. "Some of our friends gave us a table-hockey game for my eighth birthday. That was the first time I was really introduced to hockey. After everyone left, there was a game on TV. It was Montreal against Chicago."

Vilgrain fell in love. He watched the Habs and rookie Ken Dryden win a shocking Cup in 1971. "That's how old I am," he says, laughing. He began collecting hockey cards and signed up to play. "My parents didn't know much about the sport. The neighbours tried to walk them through it. I showed up with Sears catalogues as shin pads and couldn't skate well, but by the second year I was able to play."

His parents may not have known a thing about the game, but young Claude took to it. "My dad was a good soccer player. I remember him telling us stories about him playing against Pele in a tournament or a friendly. I think my family is pretty athletic, and I was pretty good in all the sports."

His introduction to hockey was very innocent. He didn't even have his own hockey bag, but he managed. Vilgrain played on a lot of outdoor rinks. One day, though, he made an all-star team that got to play at a brand new rink in Charlesbourg. "As usual, I was getting dressed at home. My buddy showed up with a hockey bag and his equipment was in there. He said, 'There's a dressing room at the rink. There's no need to dress at home.' So I told my mom, 'Hey, I don't need to dress at home. Do we have any bags?' She started to pull out a garbage bag, but I thought, *I can't go with that.* Finally, she got two straw bags from Haiti. Basically I put one skate in one bag, a skate in the other, a shin pad. I had my stick around my neck with these two bags and I went to the all-star game. I still ended up being named the MVP."

Less than a decade later, Vilgrain was playing Major Junior hockey for the Laval Titan. He made the team out of AA. After his first year, the Titan drafted a 15-year-old kid named Mario Lemieux. "I was kind of the number one centre, and the day he got drafted I became number two.

"The first practice he undressed our best defenceman one-on-one. We said, 'Ooohhh.' He was doing stuff at 15 that you'd see guys like Pavel Datsyuk do. He could kill a penalty on his own. Our team averaged about 800 to 1,000 fans a game in a 3,000-seat arena before he got there. After Mario got there, the place was packed, and I swear about 2,000 of them were scouts."

Vilgrain was drafted by the Detroit Red Wings in 1982. His journey to the NHL and the story of his first hockey card took a few more twists and turns. A few weeks after the draft, Mike Ilitch bought the Wings and Detroit went through a major overhaul. Vilgrain never even attended a training camp. When his junior career came to an end, he turned down an offer to play pro in Kalamazoo. Instead, he chose to play in the relative obscurity of Canadian university hockey. He took a spot at the Universite de Moncton with the defending national champion Blue Eagles. "I thought if I played well there, you never know . . ."

Vilgrain stayed in Moncton for three seasons. He then attended a camp with the Calgary Flames. Eventually, he landed with Dave King's Canadian national team. On February 13, 1988, Claude Vilgrain and the rest of Canada's Olympic team marched into Calgary's McMahon Stadium for the Opening Ceremonies of the 1988 Olympic Games. The first thing Vilgrain did when he entered the stadium was scan the crowd for his parents. He spotted them. "I couldn't believe I found them. They were very proud. They never thought we'd go that far. My parents thought I was too nice of a kid to make it that far, but I did it.

"I thought of the sacrifices they had made. My poor dad, standing on the snowbanks with his three toques and his five jackets — he didn't understand the game but he was always there to encourage me. My mom: when she could, she would be there. She didn't understand much either, but they were there to watch me play."

Following the Olympics, Vilgrain finally made it to the NHL. He played his first NHL game for the Vancouver Canucks on March 1, 1988, against Philly, and played in another five games with the Canucks that year. That was followed by a season in the minors. Vilgrain managed to get into another six games with New Jersey in 1989–90. Those six games were enough to get him a hockey card. "It's like a stamp. I can put my name in history. I worked so hard. I was a late bloomer in every league I went to. In minor hockey, I could have played AAA, but I played AA instead because my friends didn't make the AAA team. You work so hard. Making the NHL is one thing that validates you; for some people it would be the Hall of Fame. But for me, it was just to get that card."

For a kid who didn't even know what hockey was when he got to Canada, this rookie card is a reminder of the sacrifices, of the Sears-catalogue shin pads, the makeshift hockey bags, the three years in Moncton, the 1988 Olympics, and all the ups and downs of pro hockey.

"I grew up collecting cards. Then all of a sudden I was on my own card. That was very sweet. I always remember where I was and how I felt when I walked into the changing room in Utica and saw that card. It was special, that's for sure."

BRAD MAY

1990-91
SCORE #427

Sometime in the late spring of 1992, I posed for my high school graduation photo. My hair was freshly cut and, following the photographer's suggestion, I tilted my head to the side. Thinking back on the moment, even then I knew I did not look cool. All these years later, I still don't look cool. The same cannot be said, however, for another 18-year-old who posed for a photograph just a couple of years earlier.

On June 16, 1990, the NHL Draft was held in Vancouver, B.C. The Buffalo Sabres took Brad May 14th overall. That day, he posed for the picture that ended up on his Score rookie card. "Dude, I went to Moores, the Suit People. I bought a plaid, grey-checkered suit. It was really, really sweet. I actually had a pair of snakeskin cowboy boots that matched the colour of the suit. And I'm telling you, the boots were money. The biggest day of my life, being drafted into the NHL, and I show up in a pair of snakeskin cowboy boots," Brad May tells me and laughs.

Unfortunately, we don't get to see the boots or the suit on the card. We do, however, get to see the hair. Believe it or not, that mane trickling down the back of Brad May's neck is a tamed version of what he was wearing in 1990. "I had the sweetest haircut ever. I went to the barber in Markham before I went out to Vancouver. I had about three inches of hair cut off the back of my mullet, and it was still sweet. Tight above the ears."

Tight above the ears was key at the start of the '90s. Even the slightest hint of a sideburn would get you shunned by most members of the teenage and hockey communities. Sideburns were out, mullets were in, and few rocked a better one than Brad May. "I got it high and tight above the ears. I'm telling you, in 1990, that was the look. Look at MacGyver back then."

It's tough to argue with a man when he brings up the Richard Dean Anderson/MacGyver look, and I won't even bother. The one thing I will point out, though, is the Sabres lid. In the early '90s the protocol at the time was to put a nice curve in the beak of your hat and pull it down.

Why, then, was the closest thing the hockey world had to an 18-year-old MacGyver sporting the "hat sitting atop a mullet" look?

"I think it was a straight brim, which is actually in style today, but you have to pull it down to the eyebrows. I just kind of put it on there because I didn't want to mess up the flow. So my hat basically just sat there. It was on a 45-degree angle — the wrong, wrong way, at the top of my head. If they told me that this was the picture they were going for, I think I would have worked the hat a little more."

At this point, I suggest to "Mayday" that he could have done anything that night in Vancouver. The man could have crashed a wedding with this look. Plaid suit: check. Snakeskin boots: check. Tie: check. Mullet: check. Hat: check. "For a wedding, I'd take the hat off, obviously. There are ladies in the room." (That's an excellent point.) "And I want to say, I had just learned about hair gel and all that stuff, so I actually had gel in my hair. I don't know if I got into that in the late '80s or whenever, but I'm telling you I took a lot of time getting myself ready for the draft.

"I even had my eyebrows plucked at the barber shop in Markham. When I say plucked, he probably used a little trimmer — but that barber got me going."

Draft day was just the beginning of Brad May's NHL journey. And as we talk, we get a little serious. If a guy makes it all the way to the draft, he obviously has a lot of people to thank for his success. I ask him, "If the photographer would have asked you who you would have liked to join you in this picture, who would you choose? Who helped you get to that point in your career?"

"That's a great question. It's too hard for me to really answer because I don't want to leave anybody out." Brad pauses and gives the question more thought. "I have a brother, I have a sister. If I said my mom and dad . . . you know what? Bill LaForge. I'm going to say Bill LaForge."

LaForge coached May with the Niagara Falls Thunder. He was there when May was a rookie who put up 22 points and 304 PIMs. He turned him into a second-year player who had 91 points and 223 PIMs.

"Unfortunately, Bill has passed away, so I'll never have the chance to talk to him again. He was influential and instrumental in me getting to that point. He certainly drew out the player in me *and* the tough guy, kind of melding the two. He was the architect, the one who instilled the confidence and belief in me. And without confidence and belief, you're never going to be successful."

Two months after this picture was taken, May was at his first Buffalo Sabres camp: "My first practice, I fought Rob Ray." A year after that, May and Ray were teammates. May became a cult hero in Buffalo — rewatch Rick Jenneret's "MAYDAY" call when the Sabres beat the Boston Bruins in overtime in Game 4 of the first round of the 1993 playoffs — won a Cup with Anaheim, and played over 1,000 regular-season games the hard way. "I had a great time. I had some injuries, some big ones: shoulder surgeries and stuff, broken hands. That's all a part of it. I never looked at it as a grind. I actually enjoyed it. I loved playing. I loved everything about the game: the locker room, the travel, the camaraderie. All that stuff was great. Maybe that's why I played a little longer than others, because I did thoroughly enjoy the experience. Now there were a lot of shitty days in there . . . but you gotta love what you do."

And to love the role you play, you gotta look the part. And you gotta love the look. "No kidding, I felt like I owned Vancouver," says May. "I felt so good."

Lou Franceschetti

Left Wing

396

Lou Franceschetti   Left Wing

Toronto Maple Leafs

Height:	6'0"	YEAR	TEAM	GP	G	A	PTS	PIM	+/-
Weight:	190 lbs.	85-86	Capitals	76	7	14	21	131	-4
Born:	Mar. 28, 1958	86-87	Capitals	75	12	9	21	127	-9
	Toronto,	87-88	Capitals	59	4	8	12	113	+2
	Ontario	88-89	Capitals	63	7	10	17	123	+2
Shoots:	Left	89-90	Leafs	80	21	15	36	127	-4
			NHL TOTALS	407	57	73	130	689	-12

LOU FRANCESCHETTI
1990–91
UPPER DECK #396

There are certain names that simply sound right when Bob Cole says them on a Saturday night. Close your eyes and in your best Bob Cole voice, try it yourself: "Darcy Tucker . . . SCORES . . . TUCKER!" You know what I'm talking about. Another name that works? Franceschetti — as in Lou. For one full season, Lou Franceschetti was a Leaf, and Bob Cole calling out his name was magical.

"It was just unbelievable. I've got a lot of the games taped from those days," says Franceschetti, one of the most likeable guys you'll ever bump into anywhere around Toronto. And, of course, after Lou scored for the Leafs, legendary Leafs public address announcer Paul Morris would take over.

"The announcement of my name by Paul Morris at the Gardens still gives me shivers."

If you go looking for cardboard evidence of Lou Franceschetti's NHL career, you can't find anything before 1990. Franceschetti, a Toronto kid, was selected 71st overall by Washington in the 1978 Draft. He spent over a decade in the Washington organization. When the spring of 1989 arrived, Franceschetti was a free agent, with 327 NHL games on his resume and still no hockey card. "Not having a card was the furthest thing from my mind. But the ones that came out with the Leafs came out pretty nice."

In June 1989, Franceschetti's life changed: the Toronto Maple Leafs traded for the rights to negotiate with him. "[Leafs GM] Gordie Stellick called me on June 29 and told me I'd just been traded. They gave up a fifth-round pick at the time. They told me the terms, and I called my agent to more or less confirm everything." Technically he was still a free agent, and suddenly he was hot commodity. Before Franceschetti put pen to paper with the Leafs, he got a call from the Pittsburgh Penguins. They wanted to sign him as well. "I knew from playing against Pittsburgh all those years in the Patrick Division that the Pens would have been great for me. Not necessarily playing on a line with Mario, but just being in that atmosphere, knowing that the franchise was going to turn around sooner or later. But I told them that I had given my word to the Leafs, that I had agreed to a contract. If it had been another team I may have reneged, but I was coming home. My family and friends were here."

Franceschetti stuck to his word. He was going to play for the team he watched win the Stanley Cup on a black-and-white TV in 1967. He was a Toronto Maple Leaf. And soon enough he would become a full-time NHLer — no more splitting seasons between the American and National Leagues. His new head coach, Doug Carpenter, gave him the game plan: "Doug said, 'Lou, this is your job. This is what we are going to do with you. We are going to put you on the wing on the third or fourth line, and you go out and take it whichever way you want.' He knew what I had to offer. I was a pain in the ass to play against when he was the coach in New Jersey the four previous years. It was comforting knowing that I didn't have to go to training camp and beat somebody out for a job or worry about if a rookie came up and played really well that I'd be the first guy sent to the minors, like I was in Washington."

Franceschetti played in all 80 games for the Leafs that year. It was a career season, with 21 goals, 15 assists, and 127 penalty minutes. "Having the 21 goals was a great bonus. I never thought I was going to score 20. I thought maybe I'd pitch in and get between 10 and 15, with the style of play that I could offer the Leafs, which they didn't have at the time. Everything about that year was a bonus to me. I guess the only downside was getting knocked out in the first round by St. Louis."

When you score 21 in Toronto, you're going to get a hockey card. The next winter, the 32-year-old finally got his "rookie" card. In fact, he got six of them. The Upper Deck one where he is wearing the "A" is his favourite. "Getting the 'A' more or less happened by default. It was right after Wendel blew his knee out when Viacheslav Fetisov hit him in New Jersey. They needed somebody to fill in part-time. Me being the next elder statesman on the team, next to Brad Marsh and Rob Ramage, I guess Dougie Carpenter felt it was right to put it on my jersey."

Franceschetti spent only one season and 16 games of another one with the Leafs before he was shipped to Buffalo in a trade for Mike

Foligno. He says it seems like he was in Toronto for a lot longer. "I was here for only one year, but because of what I accomplished, everybody thinks I was here for three or four or five years. That makes me feel good. It was 25 years ago and people still remember what I did for the Leafs, and they enjoyed what I contributed and my style of play."

And if you ever bump into Lou Franceschetti at the Air Canada Centre, he might just hand you something that looks a lot like this rookie card. "I'm probably going to use the Upper Deck photo as my business card."

LOWELL MacDONALD

1968–69
O-Pee-Chee #42

It's his rookie card, and Lowell MacDonald looks like he's laughing. And why not? He's playing in a place he never imagined hockey would take him. "There's no question: for a kid from a coal mining town of 1,000 people to end up in L.A. is unbelievable."

That coal mining town was Thorburn, Nova Scotia. It's about 20 minutes from my hometown of Pictou. In minor hockey, we played against Thorburn all the time. When I was a teenager, Moose River Sports Corner, the local card shop in New Glasgow, had a former NHLer into the store to sign cards. The store owner, Lorne, told me the guy was from Thorburn. His name was Lowell MacDonald.

I could not believe that a guy from Pictou County played in the NHL in the '60s and '70s. To me, it might as well have been 1492. But when we showed up at Moose River Sports Corner on the scheduled day, there was Lowell MacDonald, smiling and signing cards. Turns out, he had a bunch of cards. My brother and I thought if a guy from Thorburn can make to the NHL, why can't a guy from Pictou? "And Pictou is a much bigger city than Thorburn," Lowell says and laughs as I tell him my teenage tale.

Okay, my brother and I didn't make the NHL. I'm a sportscaster and he's a comedian. But three guys from my brother's rep hockey team did make it to the show. Lowell MacDonald was the first, however. "There's no question, when you're playing you're saying to yourself, *Hopefully there will be more players*. There was Parker MacDonald, there was Forbes Kennedy, but there wasn't anybody else from Pictou County. But then you had Jon Sim, Colin White, Joey MacDonald, and Derrick Walser, so all of a sudden you're thinking, *Well, maybe I did break ground so that those guys didn't get lost in the shuffle*. As you know, in the old days, that OHA was strictly Ontario and some kids from Quebec."

The path that led Lowell MacDonald to this card was long. He led his high school team to a Nova Scotia title and then he was off to Hamilton to play junior for the Hamilton Red Wings, where he won a Memorial Cup in 1961–62. He snuck into his first NHL game with Detroit that year too.

He spent the next few seasons playing briefly in the NHL but mostly in Detroit's minor-league system. He was traded to the Leafs in the summer of 1965. The Kings took him in the expansion draft ahead of their first season in the NHL. Then the circus began: "My wife came out to L.A. and she is from the same area in Nova Scotia. Our kids were both very young. We'd go over to the Fabulous Forum when it finally opened. Our locker room and the Lakers locker room were interconnected, with the training facilities in between. You'd say to yourself, 'Holy jumping Moses.'"

And just like that, the kid from small-town Nova Scotia was rubbing shoulders with the brightest stars of the Hollywood sports scene. "My kids were two and three, I took them over to see Elgin Baylor and Wilt the Stilt — one of the best players to ever play in the NBA. The kids would go over and skate early in the morning; they were just learning to skate. And we would go down to Disneyland, which was, holy mackerel, a treat and a half."

Sharing space with the Lakers wasn't perfect, though. As Lowell and I chat a little bit more about the laughter captured on the card, he bursts into a story about the first time the new Kings got to check out their dressing room. "We had Howie Hughes and Howie Menard. Both of them were pretty short. They sat in their stalls and their feet were six inches off the ground. They had to bring in something they could sit on so they could tie their skates. The people that built the stalls thought it was for the Lakers, so everything was made for Wilt the Stilt. Howie Menard didn't quite fit."

It wasn't just the dressing rooms that were a bit off-kilter. The L.A. pro-sports circus often revolved around owner Jack Kent Cooke, who kept a close eye on his players and head coach Red Kelly. "He had a phone hooked down to the bench. Poor Red. That was early in the going. You're saying, 'Now is he telling Red to bench me or play that guy more?' It was a different situation."

So here's the thing about the kid on the hockey card. Suddenly, he left it all behind. His cards were no longer in wax packs because Lowell MacDonald was no longer a player. It seemed like he had disappeared. He was just 29, but he was finished. Lowell MacDonald could handle life in the NHL; he just couldn't handle flying. And so he retired. "I couldn't fly. I went back to St. Mary's University and finished up my bachelor's degree."

But then an old friend called. It was old Detroit teammate and former Kings coach Red Kelly, who was then coaching in Pittsburgh. "Red Kelly called and said, 'Look Lowell, we want you to give it a try. It's 100,000 miles of flying playing for the Kings versus 40,000 miles here in Pittsburgh.'"

Kelly convinced MacDonald to try Pittsburgh. His comeback lasted all of about a week. "I got hit at training camp, and for two years I never played a game. I had more surgeries on my left knee than Heinz has pickles."

But Red Kelly stuck with MacDonald. "Let me tell you, if it hadn't have been for Red, Baz Bastien would have sent me to Siberia on the first boat that was leaving. But Red stuck with me, and I gave him four-and-a-half good years with the Penguins before I got hurt again."

MacDonald's first full season with Pens was in 1972–73. He scored 34 goals and won the Masterson. The next year he led the Penguins with 43 goals and was second on the team with 82 points. "If it weren't for Red, I wouldn't have gotten any of that. Nobody else would have hung in there and said, 'Geez, I think you can still play.' I'm beholden to Red for the rest of my life."

Lowell MacDonald talks about Kelly more than about himself. And he talks about other old teammates too, like legendary junior coach Brian Kilrea. When I caught up with Lowell, he had just returned from the Kings' 50th anniversary celebrations. "I was just out in L.A. in the middle of October. I've never been treated that well in all my life . . . they treated us better than kings."

When MacDonald was on the flight to L.A., the pilot made a point of announcing that two very special people were on-board. Lowell looked around for movie stars, only to discover that the pilot was talking about him and former Kings' play-by-play man Jiggs McDonald. Lowell had made it to the bright lights of L.A., he just doesn't act like it. "Except for the bubble gum cards arriving in the mail, you say to yourself, *I don't think I even played there.* It was so long ago."

I'm thrilled to have this card in my collection. It's a reminder that no matter where you come from, you can make it.

The other thing Lowell loves to talk about is golf. Flip the card over and you'll know why. There's a cartoon of Lowell golfing, his favourite summer activity. "I had back surgery last year, and I didn't play a round. This summer I got back on the course in New Glasgow. I was riding in a cart because I knew I couldn't pull a cart up the hill. But now I'm back here in Florida, walking nine holes. It's lucky you caught me, because normally I'd be out there at three o'clock."

I sometimes see Lowell at the Abercrombie Golf Club when I'm back home in the summer, and he tells me that it was a golf legend who gave him one of his biggest sport thrills. "I got a chance to play with Arnold Palmer in Latrobe." MacDonald was even invited into Palmer's home after the round and before that night's dinner: "I've never had anybody that I thought was a god be so ordinary and accommodating as Palmer. He let us go through his home. When the golf ended, he invited all the celebrities over before dinner. He was just the most gracious host. You thought, *Geez, the guy may have grown up in Thorburn.*"

No. That's where Lowell MacDonald's from. That's something I found out a long time ago.

Don Nachbaur 1981–82
O-Pee-Chee #138

"Of all the games . . . they had to use that picture? That was the only time I wore that mask. It was kind of disappointing because I wanted a real hockey card, not a picture with a big bubble on it," says Don Nachbaur.

Such is life. Nachbaur didn't like the picture on his hockey card, but at least they spelled his name right. Oh,

Chapter Nine   ERRORS

wait. No, they didn't. "It's like snack bar. They spelled my name wrong on that card. It's not b-a-u-e-r. It's b-a-u-r."

Nachbaur got the double whammy: a misspelled name and a not-so-flattering picture for a tough guy. "I remember exactly where that card was taken. It was in Washington because that's the only game that I wore that mask. I had been in a fight with Chicago's Al Secord the night before, and I got my lip all split up. I had a problem with my cheekbone. I wore the mask one game and I took it off the next. When the hockey card came out, I went, 'You gotta be kidding me?' I was really, really disappointed that was the picture. But that's life.

"My son says, 'Dad, you were a tough guy, and you're wearing a mask?' I had no choice in the matter. My trainer had already slapped it on my helmet. I had played with a broken nose many times before, and I never wore a mask. But in that particular instance, I had a cut that they wanted to protect for a night, so that's why I wore it."

So thanks to the mask, we can pinpoint the exact date this picture was taken. It was January 18, 1981, in

Washington, D.C. The Caps beat the Whalers 3–2. Now, how about a few more details on that scrap with Secord. "The fight was at centre ice. We both threw punches and landed punches, and we both hit the ice. As I was getting up Mark Howe looked at me and went, 'Oh, Snack. You gotta get off. You need stitches — you're leaking bad.' I could feel my lip burning and then I tasted the blood. You know, just before he said that, I looked over at Secord and his nose was bleeding, so I thought I got him good. Then I got in the locker room and went, 'Oh my God.' My lip was split in half. My cheek was all swollen. He had hit me with a pretty big punch — a big left on the right side of my face. I thought I had done really well in the fight until I looked in the mirror. Apparently, I didn't do so well. Mark Howe made me aware of that right on the ice."

Nachbaur was 12 days shy of his 21st birthday the night the photo for his only hockey card was taken. He was a B.C. kid playing on the other side of the continent with his hockey hero. "I grew up in Prince George, B.C., and back in the '60s there were two channels: CTV and CBC. My buddies and I would be on the outdoor rink all day Saturday but we'd race home for *Hockey Night in Canada*. This was before the Vancouver Canucks came into the league and I was a big Leafs fan. Dave Keon was my guy. I tried to be just like him. The way he hunched over at faceoffs. He always put his stick across his shin pads. He was an effortless skater and a really tenacious checker. I loved Dave Keon."

When Nachbaur showed up for his first-ever Whalers camp, he was in for the thrill of his life. He survived rookie camp and was invited to the main camp. The Whalers brass called all the rookies into a room, and then, "[Whalers GM] Jack Kelley read out the rules of camp and what the expectations were. Then he said, 'I'm going to read out the rooming list. I want all the rookies to take the stuff out of their rooms and move to new rooms. We'll get your keys. Here's who you're rooming with.' They went down the order. They said Gordie Howe with Ray Allison. And it hit me right there. I said, 'Oh my God. How good is that?' They are putting the right-winger they drafted with the top right-winger, the oldest guy, Gordie Howe. So the next guy was Stu Smith. He was a second-rounder. They said, 'Stewie Smith with Rick Ley.' Both defencemen. And then they went, 'Don Nachbaur with Dave Keon' and my heart damn near exploded. It was beating so fast. So I went up to my room, grabbed my bag, walked into the new room, and Dave was already in bed watching TV, getting ready for the next day. I walked over to him. I shook his hand and introduced myself. I said, 'Hi, Davey,' because that's what they used to call him on *Hockey Night in Canada*: Davey Keon. He looked at me and he goes, 'It's not Davey. It's David.'"

Nachbaur and his hockey hero were roommates for his first two seasons in the NHL. "It was a dream come true, to be honest with you. He drove me to all the scrimmages in the morning. He is a really good person. During practice, he'd spend time with me. I still consider him a good friend today.

"There was no such thing as taking a day off in practice. He was highly conditioned. He was 42 years old, but when you looked at him, you wouldn't know it. You'd have thought he was in his 20s. He still had a muscular frame to him. He was in very, very good condition and took good care of himself. I think he was the ultimate professional. Everything he did at practice meant something. I watched him in practice and tried to emulate what he did on faceoffs."

Okay, hold on. So far, the kid from B.C. had made the NHL, he was on the same team with his hockey hero, and he was rooming with him. Now what could make this better? Well, it wasn't long before Nachbaur got to play on a line with his hero as well. "I played on his left wing for a game. At one point, he went down the right wing against Montreal. This was in Hartford. He beat a defencemen wide and I drove to the net. I got between the two hash marks. He was on the right side, on his backhand. Now, remember, his stick was flat. He sent a rocket backhand towards the middle, right on my tape. All I did was open up my blade and redirect it top shelf. I got two goals that night. It was the only time I ever scored two goals in a National Hockey League game. When he

came over to congratulate me, I looked at him and said, 'Oh my God. What a pass, right on the tape.' And his comment was 'Where did you want it? In your feet?'"

That's tough to beat. I'd be more than happy to have my name spelled wrong and to be in a mask on my one and only hockey card for the chance to play alongside my idol. Nachbaur's name was misspelled on his sticks for most of his career too. Once, he even got a tour of the Sherwood factory and threw away the rubber stamp that they used to burn his misspelled name onto his sticks. He got a new batch of sticks two weeks later. His name was spelled wrong again. At the end of his career in Philly, they just started putting "Snack," his nickname, on his sticks. The misspelling happened all the time, the mask only happened once, even though he probably should have worn one on at least one more occasion: "Chris Nilan had broken my nose and had pushed it underneath my eye. The doctors straightened it out in the locker room, and I'd be damned if I was wearing a mask at the Boston Garden the next night. We played the game, and the following day I had surgery. The season was over."

Nachbaur pauses for a second. Then he adds, "I probably thought they were going to take another hockey card picture that night."

O-Pee-Chee

JOEL OTTO
C ♦ FLAMES

JOEL OTTO

247

HEIGHT: 6'4" WEIGHT: 220 SHOOTS: RIGHT

Born: 10-29-61, St. Cloud, Minn.   Home: St. Cloud, Minn.
Last Amateur Club: Bemidji State (1983-84)
Acquired: Signed As Free Agent, 9-11-84

NHL RECORD
FICHE DANS LA LNH

Year Team Année Équipe	GP	G	A	PTS	PIM
84-85 Flames	17	4	8	12	30
85-86 Flames	79	25	34	59	188
NHL Totals/Totaux dans la LNH	96	29	42	71	218

1985-86 Game Winning Goal: 2
Buts gagnants en 1985-86: 2

Was a finalist for Hobey Baker Award at Bemidji State in 1983-84. He scored his first NHL Goal vs. LA Kings, March 3, 1985.
Finaliste dans la course au Trophée Hobey Baker alors qu'il fréquentait l'Université d'État Bemidji en 1983-84. C'est le 3 mars 1985, contre les Kings, qu'il marqua son premier but dans la LNH.

NHL
NHLPA
©1986 O-Pee-Chee
Ptd. in Canada/Imprimé au Canada

JOEL OTTO   **1986–87**
O-PEE-CHEE #247

Moe Lemay on a Joel Otto rookie card? If you told Bemidji State freshman Joel Otto that Lemay would end up on his rookie card he would have been okay with that. "I would have taken that — absolutely," says the assistant coach of the WHL's Calgary Hitmen. The simple fact of having his own NHL card would have blown his young mind. "I would have been quite flabbergasted."

The same is true for the rest of the hockey world. When Joel Otto was a teenager, he was not on any NHL scout's radar. No wonder the card makers got him mixed up with Lemay in 1986. Otto pretty much came out of nowhere. "I do remember back then thinking it was kind of a novelty. I was going, 'Wait a minute. Maybe this is worth something!' I can't remember who I asked about it. But they said, 'Don't get excited. It happens quite often.' Maybe if it was a Gretzky error it would be something different, but with this one, there's nothing to it. It just kind of happened."

The error was not corrected. So if you were a kid not all that familiar with Joel Otto and the Flames, you were probably left wondering why the player on the front of the card was wearing a Vancouver Canucks uniform. You also probably wondered why the player shot left when he was listed as right-handed. Plus, this guy in the Canucks uniform didn't look six-foot-four, 220 pounds. He and Otto were swapped — so the same questions were likely being asked when people came across a Lemay card with Joel Otto in his Flames uniform. "I was kind of excited just to have a card at that point. I wasn't too worried about anything." Mistakes happen.

"I sit here reading the paper in Calgary, and every now and then you'll say, 'That ain't so and so in that picture.' Somebody makes a mistake. I don't know who was proofing the cards."

Otto ended up with countless cards as the career he never imagined possible progressed. He wasn't recruited heavily coming out of high school hockey in Minnesota. He got a bit of interest from a few Division II colleges and wound up going to Division III Bemidji State in

Minnesota. Otto didn't have a scholarship. He was just a kid looking to play a little hockey. The NHL wasn't even a distant dream. "I blossomed more in my years up there than I did in high school. When I was 18, I needed to mature. Getting away from home was a big step."

Unlike a lot of Canadian kids who play Major Junior and leave home at 15 or 16, there wasn't a lot of pressure on Otto. He was just a kid playing college hockey. His freshman year was nothing spectacular. He walked on the team and put up five goals and 11 assists in 23 games. But here's the thing: he kept getting better. By the time he was a senior, the kid who didn't get a single Division 1 scholarship offer was nominated for the Hobey Baker Award as the top player in NCAA hockey. "I was the beneficiary of a pretty good year. We went undefeated and won the national championship. That was quite an accomplishment. We had some really good players on that squad, and I was the recipient of those opportunities."

Otto is being modest here. By his senior year, Bemidji State was a Division II program. He led the team with 75 points in 31 games. The Calgary Flames, who were establishing a great pipeline into U.S. college hockey, took notice. Flames GM Cliff Fletcher and his head coach Bob Johnson, a legend at the University of Wisconsin, were making the most of an untapped market. "Obviously, the Flames had the foresight. You could probably list a bunch of guys from my era who came from the college route."

The Flames were the masters of finding late bloomers and signing NCAA free agents: guys like Neil Sheehy, Colin Patterson, and Otto himself. Joel won a Cup with the Flames in 1989 and played 943 NHL regular-season games. As far as late bloomers go, he is the poster boy: "I can only speak from my standpoint. By the time I turned pro, I was turning 23 — it's a little different. I was more mature, and I could handle quite a bit of things that I certainly couldn't have handled when I was 18 or 19."

Today, Otto deals with kids looking to bloom as soon as possible. As an assistant coach in the WHL, he deals with teenagers who are chasing

the dream. There are players on the Hitmen who are only 16. "They have a lot going on in their lives: being away from home for the first time, going to school, and then coming to practice. It's a rigid schedule. There is travel that can be unbearable. We are okay in Calgary, but obviously there are other Western League teams with a lot of bus rides. The players have to deal with a lot in their first year, but they mature quickly."

As a college walk-on, you can see why getting an NHL rookie card was such a far-off thought. Joel Otto was never supposed to get a regular shift. He was never supposed to win a national championship. He was never supposed to be nominated for the Hobey Baker. He was never supposed to sign a pro contract. He was never supposed to play in the NHL. He was never supposed to win a Stanley Cup. He was never supposed to get his own hockey card. Who cares if Moe Lemay is pictured on his first card?

"I wasn't too bent out of shape," he says. And, besides, when you play 943 regular-season games, you're going to end up with quite a few cards. A ton, actually, that will have *your* picture on them. "When I retired, different card companies kept sending them to me. I have a closet full of hockey cards that I can't get rid of."

O-Pee-Chee

HIGHLIGHTS
FAITS SAILLANTS

'89

LEETCH SETS ROOKIE RECORD

New York Ranger Brian Leetch set an NHL record for goals by a rookie defenseman with 23 in 1988-89. The old mark was held by Barry Beck who had 22 goals in 1977-78. Leetch went on to win the NHL Rookie of the Year Award.

LEETCH ÉTABLIT UN RECORD COMME RECRUE

Brian Leetch des Rangers de New-York a établi un record pour les buts marqués par une recrue à la défensive, avec 23 en 1988-89. L'ancien record était détenu par Barry Beck, qui en avait réussi 22 en 1977-78. Leetch remporta aussi la distinction de "Recrue de l'Année" dans la LNH.

326

HIGHLIGHTS '89

1989–90
O-PEE-CHEE #326

Mistakes happen. Players make them all the time, and, ultimately, that's what leads to goals. When someone makes a mistake, someone scores. Believe it or not, there may even be an error or two in this book. As much as I've tried to write the perfect book, chances are I have not and, gasp, there may be a typo or two . . . I hope not, but again, mistakes happen.

Think about how tough the gig must have been for card makers before the internet. There was no quick and ready way to double-check what a guy looked like. If a picture was filed away as, say, Brian Leetch, it may have been printed on a Brian Leetch card even if it wasn't a picture of Brian Leetch. And perhaps that's what happened with card number 326 in the 1989–90 O-Pee-Chee set. "I don't know how it happened," says David Shaw. "Brian and I were defence partners. I'm not sure how I was mistaken for him. I don't know. Did they do it on purpose?"

Likely not. But once upon a time, David Shaw, a steady, reliable presence on the New York Rangers blue line who played in 769 regular-season NHL games, was mistaken for Brian Leetch. Shaw ended up on a card that commemorated a rookie record. As the back of the card states, "New York Ranger Brian Leetch set an NHL record for goals by a defenceman with 23 in 1988–89." "Brian came up after the Calgary Olympics in '88," says David. "He was very creative. He saw the ice really well. Offensively, he was always good. You could see he was going to be an eventual Norris Trophy winner. He was the best offensive defenceman I ever saw. I played with Ray Bourque, who was honestly a lot better all around than Brian was, but Brian was like a [Paul] Coffey. He saw the ice really well."

Leetch won the Norris Trophy two times and was inducted into the Hall of Fame in 2009. But on at least one occasion he was mistaken for David Shaw. Shaw wasn't all that troubled by the mistake; he was more impressed with the fact that he ended up with Leetch's stats. "The first I saw of it? It was probably after a game the following year, from the people who stay and try to collect autographs. Some people actually had both of us sign it after games. Brian would sign it and then I'd come out later and they'd say, 'Can you sign this card too?' I'd say, 'Yeah, sure.' So there are copies of this card out there with both of our signatures on it."

Mistakes happen, but sometimes they can be a little baffling. Like how do you mistake a right-handed shooting, brown-haired defenceman for a left-handed shooting, red-haired defenceman? Shaw points out one other important detail, at least according to him: "And I'm good-looking and he's not, right?"

RICHARD BRODEUR

1987–88
O-PEE-CHEE #257

When is an error card not an error card? Richard Brodeur's final card, number 257 in the 1987–88 O-Pee-Chee set, has always been considered an error card. The card has been said to feature a picture of Frank Caprice, not Richard Brodeur. But here's the thing: "That's Richard," Frank Caprice says. "I wore the SK600 helmet. That's Richard."

Caprice should know, right? So let's consider this an error card that is not actually erroneous. And here's some more evidence: Caprice is never officially listed as having worn No. 35 for the Canucks, nor can he ever remember wearing No. 35. Frank Caprice says he only wore the No. 30 for the Canucks. The Richard Brodeur error card, at least according to the guy who is supposedly the error on the error card, is not an error at all.

Even though he played in 102 NHL regular-season games, Frank Caprice never got an official NHL card. Yes, he was featured in a few local sets, but his cards were never in packs from coast to coast. "Back then, O-Pee-Chee didn't tend to do the whole team. They did the stars of the teams, typically. And I had to battle to get my time in net. There were times that I was a starter, but most of the time I was the backup. But I was always on the Shell cards and things like that. But now my kids say, 'How come you never had an O-Pee-Chee card, Dad?' Well, I just wasn't one of the premier players on the team, so ending up on an error is better than not ending up on any card at all."

Notice that Caprice says he did end up on an error card. That's because he did. Caprice snuck into packs of O-Pee-Chee Premier in 1990–91. He's shown on the back of Kirk McLean's card. "Somebody sent the McLean card to me, probably four or five years back, and they asked me to sign it. I sent it back, but they gave me a copy of it so I could have it for the record."

The card game can be almost as strange as the one on ice. Caprice hadn't played a game for the Canucks since the 1987–88 season, but here he was on a Kirk McLean card a couple of years later. It's no wonder the error slipped in there. Numerous goalies found themselves in the

Canucks crease for the latter part of the 1980s, as Vancouver searched for a number one goalie. Brodeur was the "King" of the Canucks crease for quite a few years before a number of 'tenders eventually dethroned him. "When I first got there, Richard had just come off the '82 Cup run, and that's when the fans started calling him 'King Richard.' He had that spectacular playoffs. I came in after winning the gold medal at the World Juniors, so I knew my chances of making the team were pretty much slim to none after Richard's playoff run."

Caprice started his apprenticeship in the Canucks organization in 1982, with the Fredericton Express. He played 20 minutes for the Canucks that year. The following season, he made his first NHL start. In the early to mid 1980s, there were a number of Western NHL teams that had their affiliates in the Maritimes. As a kid, I got to see future Edmonton Oilers, Calgary Flames, and Vancouver Canucks play in my neck of the woods. It may have been great for me, but it didn't make for the quickest commute for a minor-leaguer if he got called up to the big club. "I loved the people in Fredericton. They were friendly, friendly people. The winters were a little cold and a little snowy. I got called up from Fredericton a couple times. You flew from Fredericton to Toronto. Then Toronto to Vancouver. But I never ran into any trouble."

The only problem Caprice had to overcome on one of his first call-ups was shock. He'd spent a day making his way to Vancouver in 1983, when he took to the ice on December 10 for the morning skate. "I got there, practiced that morning, and Roger Neilson [Vancouver's head coach] comes to me and says, 'So, are you ready to go?'"

Caprice, maybe a little dreary from a long travel day, was not quite sure what his coach was talking about. "I'm like, 'Go for what?' He says, 'You're playing tonight.' I said, 'I'm playing tonight? We're playing against Edmonton.'"

Surely the coach was playing a joke on the kid. Why would he throw a 21-year-old to the wolves like that? Caprice couldn't believe his coach would just throw him in against Wayne Gretzky and the high-flying

Edmonton Oilers, who had already poured in 20 goals in their three games against Vancouver that season. "He's like, 'Yep. I want to see if you can play as good here as you've been playing down in Fredericton.' It was quite a shock to get off the plane, practice that morning, and find out I'm playing against the Oilers that night."

Perhaps Caprice was still in a state of shock when he let in the first goal of the game just 54 seconds into the first period. "The very first shot went in. I'm sitting there thinking, *Well, it was nice while I was here. I'm never going to play in the NHL again.* Our team was nervous after I let in the first goal. The crowd was nervous. The coaches were nervous. The team, I think, tightened up. Edmonton just played their game. I made a couple of saves. The confidence level grew and we scored a couple of goals. They had a late barrage in the third, and we held them off."

The Canucks won 3–2. Caprice made 26 saves. "I never beat them again for the rest of my career," says Caprice with a laugh.

He stayed with the Canucks for a while, but with three goalies in the picture — Brodeur, John Garrett, and himself — he eventually was sent back to Fredericton. He spent the better part of the next five years fighting for a spot on the Canucks. "I wouldn't say there was competitiveness with me and Richard, but he wanted to stay and I wanted to stay. There was one point where I was playing so well that they sent Richard down and kept me up. Then I tore my hamstring about five or six games in, and they called Richard back up. It was more competitive with Richard and me than it was with Troy Gamble and me. And then when Kirk McLean came in, the coach at the time was Bob McCammon. He pretty much said, 'Kirk's my guy. He's going to be my guy.' So I knew right there where I stood. I had a great training camp, started off the season really well, and Bob didn't seem to care. But that's the way it was; I've got no bitterness or complaints. I had a great time in Vancouver. I played with some great people and played with some great goalies. Kirk is going to be a Hall of Famer."

Caprice played his final NHL game in March 1988. And, yes, he

actually ended up on a big-league card a couple of years later when he graced the back of Kirk McLean's O-Pee-Chee Premier. Caprice had to fight for his spot in the Canucks crease, and I guess he had to fight for a hockey card as well. He snuck into packs with that cameo on the McLean — not on the Brodeur — but still, Caprice says, "I wish I had my own card."

Who doesn't?

OLAF KÖLZIG
1995–96
PINNACLE #134

"It's the most embarrassing card ever," says Olie the Goalie.

This Olaf Kölzig card is more than familiar to card aficionados. It's from the post-boom era, a product from card makers trying to differentiate themselves from the competition. By the time it hit the market in the mid 1990s, we had already seen cards of players pictured with golf clubs,

GOALIES

in expensive cars, and in leather jackets, so, sure, why the hell not? Let's have a card of an NHL goalie holding a hot dog with his name etched in mustard.

"It was a game in Tampa," Kölzig explains. "We were playing in the old Thunderdome, which is Tropicana Field now. I was backing up. In Tampa, you sat out in the runway; you didn't sit with the team. There was always a bunch of camera guys there, and I got to talking with one of them. I asked him what was the most unusual picture he had taken. He told me one time, he caught a guy eating popcorn. I said, 'Did you ever catch a guy eating a hot dog or wings or anything like that?'"

After the first period, Kölzig returned to the Capitals' room. When he returned to his backup post for the second period, his new photographer friend had a gift for him: a hot dog. And it came with a personal touch. OLAF was written in mustard on the dog. "He said, 'Here, I'll take a picture of you.'"

Kölzig didn't think much of posing at the time. Remember, this is well before smart phones, and posing for a picture was almost a treat. So Kölzig grabbed the dog and struck a pose. He thought that would pretty much be the end of it. "The photographer said, 'I doubt that anything is going to happen. The league doesn't really approve of this stuff.' I said, 'Yeah, no big deal. Just send me a copy when you get it developed.'"

The memory of the dog soon faded away, lost in time, it seemed. The next season, the dog came calling, in a major way. "The next year, I was coming out of the USAir Arena, the old Capital Centre, and there was a group of fans, like there always is, asking for autographs. There were a couple of them who were just howling. And I asked them what was so funny, and they handed me a card and it was the picture of me holding the hot dog with the mustard."

The goalie and the dog were there for everyone's enjoyment. They still are — this card will live on forever. In *Hockey Card Stories*, John Garrett revealed how he had stuffed a half-eaten hot dog into his goalie pads one night at the old Colisee in Quebec, when he took to the ice. No one knew about *that* dog. But this one is different. Here's Kölzig, professional athlete, getting set to chow down. And as Kölzig points out, there's an added bonus. "I mean, the hot dog was bad enough, but the guy used a fish-eye lens on his camera, so it made me look like I was 350 pounds."

And there's one more thing: it turns out, this is also an error card. "To add insult to injury, the guy in the action shot on the back is Rick Tabaracci. I was mortified when I saw it."

Now it's time for the serious question. Yeah, Kölzig has a hot dog in his hand, but did he, like his fellow goalie John Garrett actually eat the hot dog? "I handed it back. I was in plain view of everybody. I was right across from our bench. I was still trying to break in at that point. I didn't reach the comfort level yet of eating a hot dog in front of head coach Jim Schoenfeld."

That's a pro move for a young guy. This picture was taken long before Kölzig became an NHL All-Star and Washington mainstay.

When he was posing here, Kölzig was just a young kid, trying to break in with a team that seemed to have its goaltending under wraps. The year this picture was taken, Kölzig only appeared in 14 games; it was a shortened lock-out season. And in 1995–96, he played in only 18 games behind Vezina Trophy winner Jim Carey. If it took a lot of discipline to not bite into that delicious-looking snack that night at the Trop, Kölzig's patience was really tested as he spent his first six pro seasons bouncing back and forth between the minors and the NHL, before finally making the Caps full-time in 1996–97. "My patience was tested, but I still believed in myself. I still felt that if I worked as hard as I could in practice and the right circumstance or situation presented itself, I'd be ready to take it. I don't know if that would happen nowadays. I don't know if teams have that patience, especially in the salary-cap era. If you haven't made progress or established yourself in three or four years, I don't think you'll get that shot."

Kölzig was named AHL playoff MVP when he led the Portland Pirates to a Calder Cup title in the spring of 1994. It took him another two seasons before he was finally a full-time NHLer. "I was teasing management with my play down in the minors as far as the playoffs went. So they were just waiting for me, I guess, to get my act together and do it in the NHL. When Dave Prior got hired on as goalie coach in '97, that's when my career finally took off."

The Caps drafted Kölzig in the first round in 1989. Eight years later, in the 1997–98 season, Kölzig was firmly established as the Caps' number one man in net. Over the next decade, he appeared in 640 games and helped the Caps reach a Cup Final in 1998.

So, yes, Kölzig was a survivor in the dog-eat-dog world of the NHL. Part of his success was no doubt due to his persistence. Each trip back to the minors meant another opportunity to give up, but he never did. As he pointed out, teams nowadays likely wouldn't have the patience, or the luxury, to put up with such a long minor-league apprenticeship from one of their prospects. In that way, the game has changed.

And compared to over 20 years ago, the business of the game has changed too. But maybe not as much as we think. After all, Kölzig is no longer the only NHLer to appear on a hockey card with a hot dog. Thanks to Upper Deck's 2018 Phil Kessel hot-dog card, Kölzig now has company. Fact is, Olie and Phil aren't the only ones eating hot dogs. "I've come across a few backup goalies who are pounding back a few chien-chauds in the dressing rooms."

It's too bad Kölzig thinks this card is the worst card ever. I think it's one of the best. "I'd probably think so too if it was a card of you with your name written in mustard," he says.

Good point.

DARREN PANG 1988–89
O-PEE-CHEE #51

Darren Pang is transfixed on his 1988–89 rookie card. He's staring at something, or is it someone? Whatever, or whomever, it is, they have the full attention of the Chicago Blackhawks rookie. "That picture took place in New Jersey. They didn't have a Jumbotron, but they had screens at each end. So I was watching a replay of Bob Mason. He was our goalie. I was watching a play that just went inside the post, and the puck was hanging on the goal line. It was no goal. The guy beside me is Wayne Presley and that's why we're both looking up," says Panger.

I love that answer. Darren Pang knows the exact second the picture was snapped. His long-ago hockey card photo is not a mystery to him. Most guys have no idea when their picture was taken, but the man who is an excellent commentator today can take you to the exact second. When Pang headed out onto the ice at the Meadowlands that night, he immediately noticed hockey photographer Bruce Bennett. Bennett, Pang says, was a familiar face for most NHLers. He took photos at the All-Star Game and at the Stanley Cup Final. "I saw him in the warm-up and I never really thought anything of it. He was right beside our bench almost the entire game. I didn't know that he was taking pictures for hockey cards. I remember the exact play, and afterwards he said that he got a couple of good shots of me that could be used for my hockey card. And I said, 'Bruce, not of me on the bench.'"

But it worked for the photographer, and a few months later it was the photo used for Darren Pang's first hockey card. "So that's why I have a recollection of the moment. People will bug me, saying you got your first O-Pee-Chee card and you're on the bench! So everybody assumed that I backed up that year. The reality is I played nearly 50 games. But the photo they used just happened to be one where I was on the bench."

If you've ever had the chance to chat with Darren Pang, it is a true treat. The guy you see on TV is the same guy you will meet off the air. On TV, his passion for the game jumps through the screen. He was no different when he played the game. On a night like this at the Meadowlands, I can only imagine that he was a pretty vocal guy on the bench. "Oh, goodness, yeah. I really felt most times I was more like an assistant coach to the forwards. They trusted my analysis of players and goalies. They'd ask, 'What did you see on that chance?' I had to be sharp. My nickname was Spank. Denis Savard used to say, 'Spank, what did you see there? Did he cheat glove? Is he giving me the short side?' I was constantly watching and analyzing the play so I had an answer for them. I think that's one of the things that you want from an assistant coach. The players want answers and they don't want them tomorrow. They want them then and there. So I found that really challenging and really fun. I did talk a lot."

With such a sharp eye for detail, it is no wonder that Pang ended up in the broadcast booth. When this picture was taken, though, broadcasting was nowhere on the 23-year-old's mind: "No chance did I think that in a couple of years I would be done and would have a microphone in my hand."

Things changed for Pang near the end of the 1989 season. The Blackhawks were playing the Flames in the Campbell Conference Final. At a practice before Game 4, Wayne Van Dorp fell on his goalie's leg and Pang tore his ACL. He just didn't know it yet. "I went through the summer rehabbing it only to find late in the summer that I had a torn ACL instead of a sprained knee."

Pang spent the first half of the season rehabbing. And while he was injured, he also got his feet wet in the broadcasting business. He started doing colour commentary on college hockey games. Here's a neat little tidbit: all three of the broadcasters Pang worked with in the 1989–90 season — Mike Christie, Randy Hahn, and Mike Goldberg — went on to work in the NHL. "I was still a player in the NHL but [Chicago GM] Bob Pulford allowed me to go out and do that. He was really worried that my career was done. He was a nice man and he really cared about me. He said, 'This would be a nice way for you to start your next career.' At the time I'm thinking, *Yeah, in 10 years I'll do this*. It ended up that I didn't come back and play in the NHL, so it was great advice from Bob Pulford."

Pang joined the Blackhawks IHL affiliate, the Indianapolis Ice, in late February. "I went down there, and me and Jimmy Waite were the goalies. We ended up winning the Turner Cup that year. I thought that I was on my way to recovery. I felt pretty good, at that level anyway. I was actually training a month before camp the next year, and I hurt my knee again."

That's when Pang learned his pro hockey career was over. His doctor told him his ligament was done. It wouldn't be able to hold up on a nightly basis in the NHL. Bob Pulford, Pang's agent Larry Kelly, and a TV producer named Lisa Selser met with Pang, talked about retirement, and suggested a career in broadcasting. Pang took up their offer. His first couple of years in the business, he made $38,500 a year working on Chicago broadcasts. He wasn't getting rich, but he was hooked. It was different than playing but still a jolt to the system. "I didn't throw up before broadcasting, but I did before hockey games. I love broadcasting. The first time I put a live IFB [broadcast monitor] in my ear and I was able to talk to a producer and talk about what I thought, about what I was seeing — it was exhilarating. It was more exhilarating than the stress of being a goalie."

If there's one thing broadcasters get asked a lot, it is "How do you not swear on air?" We all have our little tricks. Mine is simple: I don't swear because I like to pay my mortgage. Some of us will use a replacement word or two. Darren Pang's most famous two words are *holy jumpin'!* He'll give the viewing audience his signature phrase after a great goal or a big save. I have to ask: is jumpin' a substitute for something else? And when did he utter his famous two words for the first time? "That picture on my rookie card was in the Meadowlands. My first *holy jumpin'* was in New Jersey at the Meadowlands on ESPN."

Pang was in the booth alongside Steve Levy. Before the game, the Devils had recalled Steve Sullivan from Albany of the AHL. Sullivan was a smaller guy and Pang was a smaller guy. Pang caught up with Sullivan before the game and was impressed. Sullivan had an immediate supporter in the broadcast booth. "I'm pumping Sullivan up during the game, but he's not doing anything. He's had a rough start and I'm getting a little disappointed, thinking this guy's supposed to be this neat little player."

That is when Steve Sullivan stepped up and went on a one-man mission against the Philadelphia Flyers. "He got the puck and he danced and put it through a defenceman's legs. He went in on the goalie, Ron Hextall, and he went forehand, backhand, top shelf under the bar and in. And before Steve Levy could say anything, I went, 'Holy jumpin'! What a play!' I must have gone on for 30 seconds. And Levy said, 'Wow. Where did that come from?' I said, 'It was bottled up.' I was so excited for the kid because I was pumping him up and he hadn't done anything. I was going to say *holy shit*, that's how excited I was, and *holy jumpin'* came out."

Holy jumpin' sounds a lot better than *holy shit*. It makes for a longer career as well. Pang had a couple of *holy jumpin'* moments during his career. If you dig a little into the bio on the back of this card, you can unearth one. "Credited with 6 Assists in 87–88," it says. Six assists are pretty impressive for a stay-at-home defenceman these days, let alone a goaltender. So how does a 'tender rack up six helpers? Pang gives a modest answer: "You have a great defenceman like Doug Wilson and an unbelievable Hall of Famer like Denis Savard."

However, one of Pang's six assists came about from more than just handing the puck off to Doug Wilson. "It is with my buddy Wayne Presley who is on the card with me. He and I are still really good friends to this day. He was a really good penalty killer. Hartford was on a power play, and they kept dumping the puck in the same corner. At a stoppage of play, I said to Wayne, 'Elvis, if they dump it in again, just kind of linger around in the neutral zone, and I'm going to get the puck to you.' It was a 1–1 game in the third period. And, sure enough, the Whalers dumped it in the corner. I backhanded it over everybody. Wayne had a breakaway on Mike Liut, and he scored the game-winning goal. So at least one of the six assists was an important one — a distinct play. I think it's still a Blackhawks record actually."

Pang got his revenge on photographer Bruce Bennett during his second year in the NHL. Well, maybe not revenge . . . but he did get a better hockey card in 1989–90. During Pang's second full season in Chicago, his Blackhawks were back in the Meadowlands. Pang spotted Bennett again and came up with a plan. There was no way he was going to be shown on the bench for a second straight season. He skated over to Bennett. "Sure enough he's taking pictures again, and sure enough I'm not playing. So I look at him on the bench and I say, 'Hey, Bruce, would you mind if I put my mask on, so you at least get one of me that looks like I'm playing?' He said, 'Sure thing.'"

Darren Pang put on his Blackhawks mask and struck his best pose. It worked. "My next hockey card, I have a mask on and it's almost in the same spot, but I'm not on the bench. I was on the ice just next to the bench.

"I always thought, *Wow, wouldn't it be something if I had a hockey card,*" Pang says, "and here we are talking about one."

And at least one card turned out just the way Darren Pang wanted it to.

TIM BERNHARDT 1985–86 O-PEE-CHEE #166

"When I look at that card, what do I see?" asks Tim Bernhardt. "I see skinny goaltending equipment, that's for sure. I see about a quarter of the protection they have now, at about a quarter of the size they have now. You had to play a different style of goaltending back then with the equipment we used."

It seems I have met a kindred spirit over a hockey card. This is the lone hockey card of Tim Bernhardt's career and while looking at it, we talk about the biggest pet peeve I have with hockey today: the size of goaltending equipment. To me, it's a total joke. Bernhardt hit on the issue when he said the style he played back in the mid '80s was different. I follow up with something I say far too often, "Goalies don't make saves anymore; they block shots." And the Arizona Coyotes scout and I are on the same wavelength.

"That's exactly right, you just nailed it. I've been scouting for 20 years. On the weekend, I was watching a goalie, and I said, 'He's blocking the puck. There are no saves.' It's kind of sad. They've taken a lot of the excitement out of the game. The way Mike Palmateer had to play was exciting. Now I'm watching some of the saves and I'm watching some of the highlights, and I think, *He just stood there*. He got himself into position and the puck didn't hit him, so it's a goal. It's not very exciting. I really think that they have to get the equipment back under control. It's taken a bit out of the game."

Take another look. What's that strange thing behind Bernhardt in this photograph? Recognize it? That's what they call a net. Yes, there was once a time when you could see the net behind an NHL goaltender. A player actually had a target to shoot at, and when a player had a big target, it meant that a goalie had to move. Goalies had to cross their crease — it was beautiful athleticism. Now, sure, the goalies are tremendous athletes, but that huge equipment has changed the style and the game in the process. "For me, personally, the way they play doesn't look like it would be as fun," Bernhardt says.

When Tim Bernhardt played for the Toronto Maple Leafs, he had many chances to have "fun." To say the 1984–85 Toronto Maple Leafs were a loose defensive club is being generous. They finished 21st overall in a 21-team league, giving up an average of 32.52 shots per game. If by fun Tim Bernhardt meant jumping all around the crease, he had plenty of good times during his 37 games with Toronto that year. "I think the busiest night I had was against the Edmonton Oilers. They were in their prime or just getting towards their prime. It was in Edmonton and I think the shots were something like 48–20, and we got a 3–3 tie. Back then, three goals was as low as it got, especially with the Leafs."

Bernhardt signed with Toronto as a free agent in 1984, and he began the season in the AHL. But after the Leafs' two young goalies, Allan Bester and Ken Wregget, just couldn't take any more, the veteran pro got the call. As the back of his card says, "By season's end he was Toronto's #1 goaltender by a wide margin." His main job? Try to keep the Leafs in as many games as possible. "You try to survive. We had a game against the Oilers the following year where we beat them 11–9 in Maple Leaf Gardens. I mean 11–9! Both Moog and Fuhr were in that game. I played the whole game. I let in nine goals and got the win. On one of the goals, I think Gretzky had a breakaway and I stopped him. He picked up the rebound and threw it out front to Coffey who scored. It was one of those nights."

If you thought life in the crease was chaotic, it was just as wild around Maple Leaf Gardens. Remember, Harold Ballard owned this Leafs team and John Brophy was the coach.

"With Ballard, it was always a zoo. There was always talk about coaches getting fired. I remember at one practice, Broph was sweeping the snow behind my net, and he looked up in the stands at Harold. He said, 'Hey, Harold, how's this? Can I at least sweep the ice after you fire me?' He didn't say it loud, he said it so only I could hear him.

"There are lots of John Brophy stories. I really liked Broph. He was good to me. As long as you came to play, he was good with you. We had a player named Cam Plante. He was a very talented kid. He came off one shift, and he said, 'My ankle!' And Broph said, 'Get back out there.'

Cam said, 'My ankle's killing me, I can't.' So he started to walk down towards the dressing room. Broph leaned around and yelled, 'That thing better be effing broken!' That's John Brophy."

Bernhardt wound up getting injured in the 1985–86 season. He played in only 23 games with the Leafs that year, and just one more in 1986–87. He was part of a Toronto goalie group that was in full-blown turmoil. I remember tuning in to *Hockey Night in Canada* on a Saturday night as a kid; you never knew who would be in the net for the Leafs. "It was a bad team, and whenever you have a bad team, they're just going to keep rolling somebody out there. There wasn't a lot that the goaltenders could do. That's why the Leafs were a last place team that year."

I can guarantee that, as a scout with Arizona, Tim Bernhardt has seen more hockey than either you or me. As a former 'tender, he has a passion for the nets. When we spoke, we couldn't stop talking about just how different a 'tender looked in 1985. When you look at this card, it truly is baffling just how huge the equipment is today. "It's funny for kids to see, because of the equipment — the way that the equipment looked and the size of the equipment. Even when you were there, you forget how vast the difference is between the equipment now and what it was back then.

"I was never injured by a shot. I was definitely bruised, a lot. It's the width of the pads today that kills me. The goalies claim that they can get hurt. Your forearm is maybe, unless you're Popeye, three or four inches, so why the equipment is seven or eight inches wide, I have no idea. It makes no sense.

"It's a farce. The goalies really do want to just protect the net. They claim that they can get hurt, but I think it's a bit of a farce."

Patrick Roy was one of the first goalies to popularize the butterfly position at the NHL level. When he led the Habs to a Cup in 1986, he was in his butterfly all the time. And he was doing it with what I'll call normal equipment. And he was acrobatic as well — there were glove saves galore. But over time, just like every other 'tender in the game,

things on Roy got bigger. "If you ever get Patrick Roy's hockey cards, study them. I think you'll see from the time he came into the league until the time he left the league, his goals against average continually dropped. When you look at the pictures on the cards, you can see that his equipment continually gets bigger and bigger and bigger. It's staggering how the two things coincide."

It's then that Bernhardt makes another great observation. I remember playing road-hockey goalie as a kid. You'd always leave a little extra room on the glove side, just so you could stick out your baseball glove and make a spectacular save. All the kids in the driveway would hoot and holler. Making a big glove save was a blast. Now, though, that's not how the position is played. "Being acrobatic was part of the fun of being a goalie. That's why most kids get into it in road hockey, because it's kind of fun to be a little acrobatic. But that's gone by the wayside. Now it's just get in position and block. And that could be the reason why the quality of goaltending has suffered. In Canada, we are struggling to find goalies right now. I think that a lot of the kids have gotten away from the position, because when you're young you get into it because it is fun. But, nowadays, you get coaches who right away start teaching them to block. I think a lot of kids lose interest in it."

So, I ask Tim: how would a modern goalie do in the old equipment? "From what I hear, they wouldn't try it, because they might get hurt," Bernhardt says and laughs. "I think they'd be similar to the old goalies. The position has been revolutionized because of the equipment more than anything. It's not because of the athlete. I think it is more about the equipment.

"I'll be proud of my card forever," he says before we wrap up. "It will always mean a lot to me. Only those of us who were there know what it was like and what we went through. Kids look at that card now and they see the goals against average, they see the size of the goalie, and they laugh and stuff, but it was all relevant at the time."

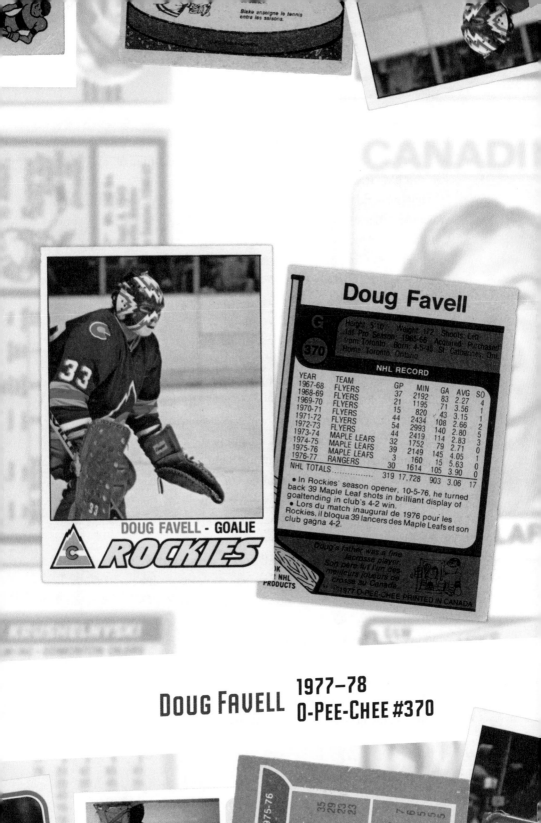

Doug Favell

G 370

Height: 5'10" Weight: 172 Shoots: Left
1st Pro Season: 1965-66 Acquired: Purchased
from Toronto. Born: 4-5-45, St. Catharines, Ont.
Home: Toronto, Ontario

NHL RECORD

YEAR	TEAM	GP	MIN	GA	AVG	SO
1967-68	FLYERS	37	2192	83	2.27	4
1968-69	FLYERS	21	1195	71	3.56	1
1969-70	FLYERS	15	820	43	3.15	1
1970-71	FLYERS	44	2434	108	2.66	2
1971-72	FLYERS	54	2993	140	2.80	5
1972-73	MAPLE LEAFS	44	2419	114	2.83	3
1973-74	MAPLE LEAFS	32	1752	79	2.71	0
1974-75	MAPLE LEAFS	39	2149	145	4.05	1
1975-76	RANGERS	3	160	15	5.63	0
1976-77		30	1614	105	3.90	0
NHL TOTALS		319	17,728	903	3.06	17

● In Rockies' season opener, 10-5-76, he turned
back 39 Maple Leaf shots in brilliant display of
goaltending in club's 4-2 win.
● Lors du match inaugural de 1976 pour les
Rockies, il bloqua 39 lancers des Maple Leafs et son
club gagna 4-2.

Doug's father was a fine
lacrosse player.
Son père fut l'un des
meilleurs joueurs de
crosse au Canada.

© 1977 O-PEE-CHEE PRINTED IN CANADA

DOUG FAVELL - GOALIE

ROCKIES

DOUG FAVELL 1977-78
O-PEE-CHEE #370

In the crease, Doug Favell always looked cool. The man had style, and the colours still jump off this 1977–78 O-Pee-Chee. It's Favell's first card with the Colorado Rockies. I love the old Rockies uniform, and when you combine it with one of Favell's famous masks, you've got one fine-looking goaltender. "That was my Leafs mask when I got traded in '76 to Colorado. That was a Greg Harrison mask," Favell tells me at the Sport Card and Memorabilia Expo in Toronto. "I got traded at training camp in September. Greg came to me and said, 'Give me your mask and I'll have it ready for you when you're ready to go in Colorado.' That design was just from his imagination. He put the mountains on there. I had nothing to do with that one."

Favell was one of the first goalies in the game to make the mask more than just a practical piece of equipment; he turned it into a fashion accessory. Favell wore the first fully painted mask in NHL history on Halloween night in 1971, for the Philadelphia Flyers. "I said to the trainer Frank Lewis, 'Frank, why don't you paint that like a big pumpkin for Halloween night? Can you do that?' Frank took the mask home in the afternoon and painted it. I wore it that night and we beat the L.A. Kings 4–1. Goalies are superstitious, so I kept it going and it worked until the end of the year. I let in a goal in the last game with four seconds to go, which cost us the playoffs. So I had to get rid of the orange, and I went to the stripes the next year."

Over the years, just how Favell's mask went from white to pumpkin orange has been the subject of much conjecture and storytelling. It was once reported that the Flyers trainer pulled a prank and painted Favell's mask as a joke. "That story doesn't make sense, because trainers wouldn't just take your equipment and do something like that with it. They wouldn't paint your mask without your permission. They wouldn't go, 'If the goalie shows up for a game, he'll really like that.' I actually asked Frank to paint it because I thought it would be fun on Halloween.

"You know how things can get turned around over the years. I said I did it as a joke but it came that the trainer did it as a joke. Then the story evolved until it became that the trainer took it home to play a joke."

By the time Favell landed in Colorado, he was one of a legion of NHL goalies with painted headgear. For some unknown reason, the back of this card lists Favell as a New York Ranger for the 1976–77 season, but he never suited up for the team. Let's call this an error card then — he was definitely all Rockie in 1976–77. The bio is right, though, when it says, "In Rockies season opener, 10-5-76, he turned back 39 Maple Leaf shots in a brilliant display of goaltending in club's 4–2 win." "At least 39 shots," says Favell. "When I got traded from the Leafs to Colorado, it was strange that the first game was Toronto in Colorado, so I was a little pumped after the Leafs let me go. I guess I played pretty well that night."

The best save of the night? "Lanny McDonald. When you made a glove save back then, they were all pretty good." I take a glance down at Favell's card and look at his glove. I'm amazed that guys could actually catch a puck in one of those things. Favell's Cooper glove is just dangling in front of him. Notice the curve on the thumb piece? That was Favell's work. "I used to cut into my glove. The thumb had a piece of fibreglass in it, and I used to take the fibre out. I'd cut it and take the fibre out so I could bend my thumb to turn the glove over. I was taking stuff off equipment. We weren't putting it on — we were taking stuff off back then."

I'm guilty of making an assumption at this point. When I ask Doug about life off the ice in the mile-high city, I say that it must have been a bit of a bummer going from a hockey hotbed like Toronto to a place where the NHL wasn't all that popular in the late 1970s. A lot of people, myself included, look at the Rockies as a failed experiment.

"I think our opening night crowd was maybe 8,000 or 9,000. It took a while but by the second year we made the playoffs, we were sold out. Our playoff game against Philly was sold out. They were scalping tickets and it was taking off.

"And then the next year . . . I think we've all heard Don Cherry's story about what went on with the general manager Ray Miron. We had

a pretty good thing going, but then Ray sent me down to the minors. They traded Barry Beck. It just all fell apart the next year, and it never recovered. Grapes came in and tried to put it back together. He had seen what Miron had done, and it wasn't pretty. But Colorado was a great hockey town, and obviously they've gone back and they've been successful. It was just a matter of getting winning teams in there."

This is a '70s card so I have to mention the great cartoon on the back: there's a hockey player holding a picture of a lacrosse player. "Doug's father was a fine lacrosse player," it says. That would be Doug Favell Sr. "He won three Mann Cups. Two most valuable player awards in the Mann Cup. He's in the Canadian and the Ontario lacrosse halls of fame. I'm very proud of my dad."

"This card won't cost you much," Favell says. "This is probably one of my least expensive cards. I think this one is a nickel. My big ones are at least a quarter." But, regardless, it does give you a fine look at one of the game's innovators. Doug Favell didn't just stop pucks, he brought a little flair to the game. I ask Favell where you can find his masks these days.

"Don't look in the Hall of Fame," he kids. "I've got most of my masks. I've kept them. It's just a personal collection, and that's the way I like to keep it."

I get the impression that Doug Favell didn't mean to be a trendsetter when he first painted his mask orange, and he didn't mean to be a trendsetter when he rocked this Rockies mask. But you know what? The man knows how to dress to this day. He's still styling now, I tell him. "You caught me off guard with that one, Ken. I didn't know I was styling. I just get up in the morning and try to get through the day."

ERIC LINDROS

Lindrustrum — not Lindros, but *Lindrustrum*. That's the word that I always think of when I look at this card.

It was a dream job, and I had it. At the height of the hockey-card boom, you could find me every Saturday in downtown Pictou, Nova Scotia, working in a shop that sold hockey and baseball cards along with Heaton goalie

HALL OF FAMERS
Chapter Eleven

equipment. I also made change for the arcade that our store was located in.

A posse of kids would hang out, and I'd sell cards by the dozen, plus the latest goaltending equipment. I remember selling a Heaton glove that had webbing, which is now illegal, as well as a goalie mask for around $1,200. Big bucks for a lid back then. It was the kind of mask most goalies wear now. But back in 1991, you couldn't find those masks anywhere, until my good friend Sandy, the shop owner, brought them to Pictou.

The masks didn't fly off the shelves. But one thing we kept selling over and over and over and over was the 1990–91 Score Eric Lindros rookie card. Why wouldn't we? It was the hottest card at the time. Lindros wasn't even in the NHL, but he was a slam-dunk to go number one overall in the 1991 Draft. He was the perfect combination of size and skill, and everyone was thinking the same thing: *when this kid hits the NHL, he is going to tear it apart, so I better get his rookie card now.* Kids wanted it, casual fans wanted it, and in the winter of 1990–91, bandwagon-jumping investors looking to cash in wanted the Score Eric Lindros rookie as well.

I'll never forget one day, when this guy rolled into the shop. He approached me at the counter, looked me right in the eye, and said, "Do you have any Eric *Lindrustrum* rookies?" Clearly the dude knew nothing about hockey. I could tell he was looking to "invest" in Lindros. It was my job to help him out and point him in the right direction.

"*Lindrustrum?*" I said. "Do you mean Eric Lindros?"

"No" was the curt reply. "Lindrustrum. The big guy playing junior in Ontario."

I looked down and pointed at the two or three Lindros rookies we had for sale. "You mean Eric Lindros."

"No, Lindrustrum!" he barked.

Looking down at the cards and then right at this bandwagoner, there was only one response. I looked him right in the eye and said, "Sorry, we don't have any Lindrustrum rookies."

The dude left the shop. I laughed. That "investor" was one of thousands who jumped into the hobby. He was more than willing to shell out $15 for what he thought was a *Lindrustrum* rookie. He figured he'd cash in one day once Lindrustrum became the greatest superstar in the game. But, hey, the least the "investor" could have done was get the name of his cardboard meal-ticket right.

While all this Lindros madness was going on, the guy in the centre of it all wasn't paying any attention to it. He was just playing hockey. "I lived in a bit of a bubble," says Lindros all these years later.

The year this card came out, the future Hall of Famer tore up the OHL. Even though he played in only 57 games, he led the OHL with 149 points. And if you wanted an Eric Lindros hockey card, Score was the only option. "I didn't sign an NHL contract. Score had exclusive rights to me," says Lindros. Sure enough, he did go number one overall in the 1991 Draft. But as we all know, he didn't sign with the Nordiques. Score had won big time. They had the Big E locked up. If you wanted his card, Score was your only option. "While the Quebec trade was getting worked out, I was solely with Score."

And Score got as much out of Lindros as they possibly could. Since no one else could produce a card of hockey's hottest prospect, Score went to the max both before and after the draft. Aside from his true rookie card, this one, Score cranked out cards of Lindros pictured with his Junior B team, the St. Michael's Buzzers; Lindros posing; even Lindros in a baseball card set taking batting practice in a Toronto Blue Jays uniform. "They had some real beauty shots in there," Lindros says and laughs. His favourite, though, was a Score card from 1991–92. "They did one where I was a really young kid in a red snowsuit, skating in London, Ontario. I had the double blades on. I thought that was pretty funny."

So while at least one wheeler-dealer was looking for a *Lindrustrum* card and teenagers like me were scrambling to get our hands on as many Lindros cards as possible, the teenager on the cards was paying little, if any, attention to the fact that he was the biggest name on hockey cards from about 1990 until 1992. "I had joined the Olympic program, and we spent some time in Europe and we were all over the map. We were based in Calgary, and other than going to the rink and heading out to the movie theatre, I didn't do much. There weren't any other 18-year-olds on that Olympic team. Most of those guys were older. I think Joey Juneau was 23. There weren't many young players. I was with a bunch of older guys, and I'll be honest with you, they weren't collecting cards."

Lindros put up some monster points with the Generals before he joined the Olympic program. In his rookie year, he had 18 goals and 18 assists in just 17 playoff games. Lindros and the Generals won the OHL Championship and the Memorial Cup that year. "I played with some really good players. I ended up playing with Mike Craig and Iain Fraser. Craiger was a second-rounder who went to Minnesota and Iain Fraser was our overage captain who was also an excellent player. He was part of the Islander organization."

But it's not so much the games and goals we focus on when we chat about this old card. Instead, we talk a bit about why Lindros wore No. 88 once he got to Oshawa. He'd always worn eight until that point. "When I went to Oshawa, Fraser wore eight so they gave me the option of 24 and something else, and the third option was 88. So I said let's go 88."

When we go down memory lane, Lindros mostly ends up chatting about the guys he played with, not the points he put up. The kid on this card did have a little fun from time to time. If you were in an Oshawa mall in the late 1980s, you may have caught a glimpse of him. "Freddie Brathwaite and I got the rookie initiation. I don't know if you've ever been to the Oshawa Centre, but we got dropped off in our underwear with brown paper bags. And we had to run through the mall."

The goal was to make it from one end of the mall to the other; an idling car would be waiting at the other exit to make the getaway. They put the paper bags on their heads, opened the door, and started running. "So here's this tall skinny white guy," Lindros says, laughing again. "And Freddie, who is five-foot-eight. Everyone in the whole place knew who we were. There was no secret. We had these stupid eye holes in those brown paper bags.

"Security was chasing us. And as we were running, people were saying, 'Hi, Eric. Hey, Freddie. How's it going?'"

The friendly mall-goers weren't just sending their greetings to Lindros and Brathwaite, they were helping them too. As the security guards engaged in hot pursuit, shoppers came to their aid. "'We'll block them,' they said. And, of course, you get to the other end of the mall and the car that was supposed to be there to take you away isn't there. It's the middle of January and you're freezing your kahunas off in your underwear. We had lots of fun there." As far as I can tell, he and Brathwaite got away.

And if you were a kid around 1990, you wanted to look exactly like the guy on the card. Not the underwear and paper-bag version, but the hulking "Future Superstar" hockey player. I was around six-foot-one and 145 pounds at the time. There was no way I could fill out a uniform like

Lindros, but I could at least rock a quality lid. Everyone in my high school hockey league wore the Cooper SK2000 helmet that Lindros sported on the front of this card, me included. "That was the CHL helmet of the year." It sure as hell was. But if you were really cool, you had a multi-coloured SK2000, just like Lindros and the Generals. "I always wondered," says Lindros, "if the Generals were wearing red at the front and blue in the back, if the Junior B team had the opposite."

This card represented so much to so many people. For some, it was a chance to become a millionaire. For others, it was a chance to have a piece of hockey's next big thing in your collection. But that's not what this card is about all these years later. Lindros was a superstar. He was inducted into the Hockey Hall of Fame. He had a lot of fun and made a lot of money playing the game he loved. This card, however, didn't make anyone rich. Why? Well, Score likely printed eight billion of these things. One thing we've learned about the card makers of the boom era is they put the *mass* in mass production. There is no shortage of Lindros rookies lying around in card albums and plastic protectors.

Maybe I did that would-be investor looking to cash in on a few *Lindrustrum* rookies a favour and saved him a few bucks. But whoever did end up shelling out $15 for those Lindros rookies in our store's display case still ended up with a pretty cool card. And I'm sure they knew exactly who Eric Lindros, not *Lindrustrum*, was.

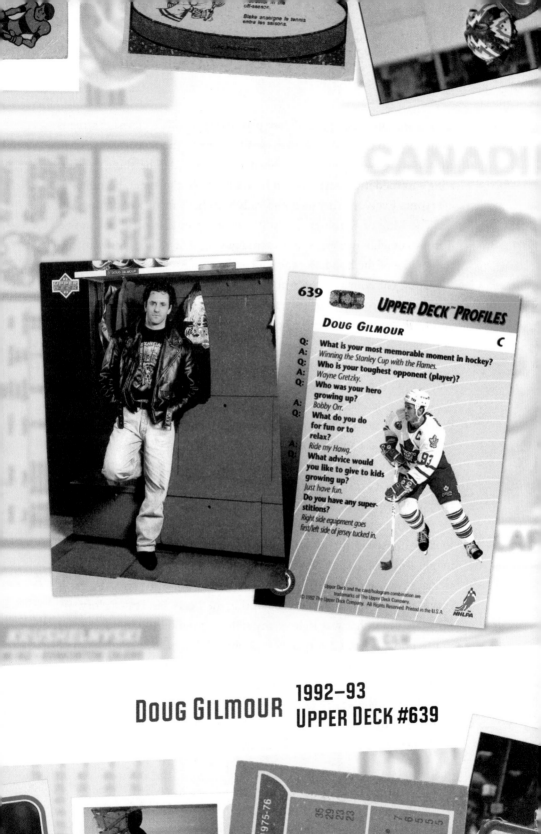

639 **UPPER DECK™ PROFILES**

DOUG GILMOUR C

Q: **What is your most memorable moment in hockey?**
A: *Winning the Stanley Cup with the Flames.*
Q: **Who is your toughest opponent (player)?**
A: *Wayne Gretzky.*
Q: **Who was your hero growing up?**
A: *Bobby Orr.*
Q: **What do you do for fun or to relax?**
A: *Ride my Hawg.*
Q: **What advice would you like to give to kids growing up?**
Just have fun.
Do you have any super-stitions?
Right side equipment goes first/left side of jersey tucked in.

DOUG GILMOUR **1992–93 UPPER DECK #639**

Back in the late '70s, a great sitcom played on Canadian television screens from coast to coast. Al Waxman was the star of the *King of Kensington*. Al, the King, was the king of his neighbourhood. The show's theme song summed it up best: "When he walks down the street, he smiles at everyone. Everyone that he meets calls him the King of Kensington."

The King of Kensington is still a presence in that small downtown Toronto neighbourhood: there's actually a King of Kensington statue in the middle of the hood. But the King of Kensington was pure fiction.

Doug Gilmour was the real deal. And he was not only the King of Kensington. From 1992 to 1997, Doug Gilmour was the King of Toronto and Leafs Nation at a time when the Maple Leafs were anything but a punchline.

The Leafs had a solid team in the early 1990s. Gilmour and his teammates took the L.A. Kings to a seventh and deciding game in the 1993 Western Conference Final. It's a series that still evokes severe emotions in thousands, if not millions, of Leafs fans. Just ask referee Kerry Fraser — but that's not just a whole other story, it's a whole other book.

"I see the boys on Leafs TV, and when the '93 playoff game against L.A. is on — it's just remarkable how long ago it was now, and it brings a couple of memories back. It was a different time," says Gilmour.

The time when Doug Gilmour ruled the city brings us one cool-looking hockey card: the 1992–93 Gilmour from Upper Deck. Killer is not in uniform, instead he's decked out in his best Harley wear. Black leather jacket, black belt, blue jeans, black shoes, slicked back hair. Kids, this is cool. This is how Gilmour rocked during the Leafs' last era of glory.

"Oh, yeah, that was right at my stall," remembers Gilmour. Earlier in this book, I showed you Gilbert Dionne doing his best impression of a baseball player for his Upper Deck "Profiles" card. Other "Profiles" cards had Denis Savard with a few racehorses, Ray Bourque with his golf clubs, Adam Oates with a baseball bat. None, however, looked as slick as No. 93.

"They were all trying to figure out what kind of passions you had off the ice, and, at the time, I was very much into motorcycles. Well, it started in Calgary, that's where I started riding. They said, 'You still ride Harleys?' And when I said, 'Yeah,' they said, 'Well, get dressed up and come on over here.' So I took the picture and it was good."

Good as in stylin'. Actually, life in Toronto in the early '90s was more than good for Gilmour.

The Leafs played at the historic Maple Leaf Gardens. In his first full year with the Buds, Gilmour had an apartment right around the corner, on Wood Street. "It took us 20 seconds to get to the rink in the morning. All your focus was there, so it was a nice time."

That focus worked. Gilmour put up massive numbers during his first full season in Toronto in 1992–93. In 83 games, Gilmour scored 32 goals and added a staggering 95 assists for 127 points. Then came that magical playoff ride where he put up 35 points in 21 playoff games before the Leafs eventually lost out to Wayne Gretzky's Kings.

Gilmour was the man. There are stories of how he had to sneak past his adoring fans to get into the rink. But he did manage to find some peace, once in a while. "You find your restaurants and places that you want to go to, and you kind of continue just going back to the same place. Most of my time eating and stuff I was down at Lower Jarvis Street."

But, of course, the ultimate freedom came on a motorcycle. What better way to enjoy a little "me" time — to get away from the insanity — than on a Harley? But that was 20 years ago. "I don't ride now. No. Have I thought about it? Yes. I contemplate it all the time. If I was going to ride, I'd ride here in Kingston. I'm not a highway rider on a bike."

The bike may be gone, but the cards are still around. Hundreds of them. Gilmour's best years coincided with the hockey card boom of the early '90s, so there's no shortage of cardboard in the Gilmour house-hold. Do his kids see the cards? The answer is yes.

"They laugh," says Gilmour. "Anytime the hockey card companies would come out with a new card, they always gave you 500 of them. So

I've got a crap load of cards from different teams, and they're all pretty much downstairs in boxes and hockey bags that the kids go through every once in a while."

So the Gilmour kids have seen the 1992–93 Upper Deck when Gilmour was the King of Toronto. But here's the best part, they've seen the real getup too. Gilmour still has his old Harley jackets around the house.

"I probably have about four or five different leather coats with Harley Davidson logos on them. They're still all there, you know. I think my boys wear them more than I do."

And amongst those coats is *the* coat. The jacket from the 1992–93 Upper Deck card is the ultimate Doug Gilmour collectible.

"It's in my closet."

BRETT HULL
1991–92 UPPER DECK #464

The shot — that's what Brett Hull was all about (to me, at least) in 1991. Years later, Hull's partner-in-crime during the Hull and Oates days, Adam Oates, would tell me that Hull was also a great playmaker, but to me, in the early 1990s, Brett Hull was all about the big shot. "My dad, Bobby, kind of started the shot, and Boom Boom Geoffrion," Hull tells me backstage at the National Sports Collectors convention in Chicago, Illinois.

This Upper Deck offering sums up Hull for me perfectly. He was coming off an incredible 86-goal season (the third highest single-season total ever) when he posed for this card. "They asked me to pose for it, and I had no idea how cool it was going to look, but it turned out. It's a really nice card."

These days, fans marvel at snipers like Alexander Ovechkin, Steve Stamkos, and Patrik Laine lining up on the off wing on a power play and one-timing a puck into the back of the net. Hull pretty much patented that play when he was seemingly scoring at will with the St. Louis Blues. It wasn't anything that took a lot of planning, though; Hull played on instinct. "I just played. I didn't worry about anything. I didn't care what people thought. I just went out and tried to have fun and score goals."

Hull scored a lot of goals: 741 in the regular season and another 103 in the playoffs. And he scored most of them using what kids these days would call an antique: his Easton aluminum stick. It's as closely associated with him during his St. Louis days as his No. 16 or his flowing blond locks. It took a man to use it, because it took a man to lift it. It was thick, and it was heavy. It was unlike anything players use today. "I think the first guy ever to use it was Brad Park. I saw him using it way before I ever played. I started using aluminum in college. In junior, I used wood. And then in college, I used aluminum with the wooden blade."

The thing about the stick on this card was that the thing didn't bend, at least compared to today's sticks. You watch a player with a composite stick rip a one-timer now, or even a wrist shot, and the stick bends so much, it ends up looking like a boomerang. Brett Hull's Easton still put

86 pucks into the back of the net in 1990–91. "With the aluminum, there was no stiff or extra stiff or senior men's or women's shaft. They wrote numbers on them, but they were all the same."

Like the game, the sticks have changed since Hull posed for this beauty over a quarter of a century ago. Towards the end of his career, Hull gave in and went to a composite stick. The one he was using during his final days in the NHL was pretty much the polar opposite of the stick he used to score 86 goals. "I was composite as soon as a good shaft came out. I used a 62 flex. I wanted it as whippy as I could."

As for the game now, compared to 1991 at least, it is pretty much a track meet. Speed is the name of the game. There's hardly any time to wind up for the big slapshot anymore and rarely enough room. Hull says he just went out and had fun, and I wonder if that would be allowed today, with constant video analysis and all the coaches who talk about playing a system. "It's a joke. To me, the game's terrible now. When you watch the Stanley Cup Final and the best play is flip it to centre and hope for a good bounce? That's not hockey.

"I don't know if I could play today. I'm not big enough or fast enough." I think Hull is being a bit coy here. After all, goal scoring works in any era, and I like to think this card does too.

IN ACTION
PAUL COFFEY
Oilers Defense/Défenseur

102 IN ACTION

EDMONTON, Feb. 7 — Defenseman Paul Coffey scored two goals and two assists tonight as the Edmonton Oilers routed the New York Rangers, 8-4. Coffey scored his 25th goal of the season at 14:23 of the first period, added number 26 at 7:00 of the second, and contributed two assists in the third period.

Edmonton, le 7 février — Le défenseur Paul Coffey marqua deux buts et produisit deux assistances ce soir, alors que les Oilers d'Edmonton écrasèrent les Rangers de New York 8 à 4. Coffey marqua son 25ème but de la saison après 14 minutes 23 secondes de jeu dans la première période; il ajouta le numéro 26 après 7 minutes de jeu durant la deuxième période. Il contribua ses deux assistances pendant la troisième période.

©1982 O-Pee-Chee Ptd. in Canada•Imprimé au Canada

PAUL COFFEY 1982–83 O-Pee-Chee In Action #102

Not every O-Pee-Chee In Action card from 1982–83 actually captured "action." Lanny McDonald was shown bent over like he was waiting for the play to begin, and Bernie Federko was just waiting around as well. But O-Pee-Chee truly nailed the spirit of the thing with this Paul Coffey card. When I think of Coffey, I think of speed. I think of him picking up the puck behind his own net as he gets set to tear up ice. That is exactly what this card shows: the speed and the pending rush of one of the best defenceman of all time. "What's going through my mind? Probably 'Who am I going to move the puck to? And then if there's no pass, is there a lane I can take?'" says Coffey.

"The thing I always tried to do was get back and get the puck in a hurry and then come out with half to three-quarters speed . . . and if you have your head up, it's easier to make a play."

Speed is what the game is all about now, but that wasn't the case in 1982. The game was fast, but it was also tough, and if you had speed, like Coffey, you often paid the price if you decided to lug the puck up ice. "Back then, you couldn't go by a guy without getting a two-hander. That's just the way it was. You had to know who you were playing against. You had to know how much room you were going to get. Truth is, today everybody can skate. Back then, some guys couldn't. I always say that as a defenceman, you'd be going back to get the puck, and you'd give a guy a little head fake and you'd hear a splat. A lot of guys would basically hit the boards. Nowadays, a guy puts a move on someone and beats him, all you hear is heavy breathing. They're still coming."

As a kid, I was a Montreal Canadiens fan, but I was smart enough to know a great player when I saw one. I considered Paul Coffey the best skater in the game. But no matter how hard I tried, I could never skate like he did. There are several things to blame for that: my lack of athletic ability, my genetic makeup (sorry, Mom and Dad), and a lack of God-given talent are just a few of them.

"I do remember my dad always saying to me when I went to the outdoor rinks, 'Don't bother coming home unless your groins are sore.'

I used to always say, 'What do you mean?' He just wanted me to stretch out and stride as long as I could. Now did that make my stride as fluid and as long as it was? I don't know," says Coffey.

Just a few years before this card came out, Paul landed in Alberta for his first training camp with the Oilers. He showed up with speed, but he was raw. "I was offensive in junior, but I wasn't smart with the give-and-gos. I didn't know any of that stuff in junior. In junior, you'd just pick the puck up and make it up as you went along. I learned from Donnie Murdoch at our first training camp in Jasper, Alberta. He said to me, 'You gotta start the give-and-go with the puck a little bit.' I said, 'What do you mean?' He said, 'Well, when you come around the net, I'll be on the hash marks on the right wing. Give me a pass and just keep going and I'll give it back to you.' I thought, *This sounds easy*. I gave him the puck, and I got it back."

Like most great plans, it was simple and effective. Coffey gave and then went. The Oilers matched him up on the point with Garry Lariviere. "He said, quote unquote, 'Kid, I hear you got pretty good wheels. You got the green light when you're playing with me.' You don't do it every shift or every time you get the puck, but it helps to build confidence."

And Coffey also got the green light from head coach Glen Sather. Soon enough, he was showing off the speed and skill that this card portrays. He was a perfect fit for the most offensively gifted team in NHL history. "Playing with Wayne, I still remember: if I didn't get my ass up on the play, which made his job a little bit easier because it opened things up, he would get mad. He'd say, 'Get your butt up here.' He used to always say, 'This is not tabletop hockey. Don't stay back. You gotta get up.'"

In 1982–83, the year this card came out, Coffey amassed 96 points. The next year he had 126. Seasons of 121 and 138 followed. Coffey's 138-point total is just one point shy of Bobby Orr's record for most points by a defenceman in a single season. And Paul Coffey did it all using one of the most legendary sticks of all time. It's in his hands as he burns around the back of the net on this card: the Sherwood 5030.

"Sherwood makes a great stick," says Coffey.

They sure as hell do. But let's be more specific, I'm not just talking about a Sherwood 5030. I'm talking about the Sherwood 5030 with the Coffey curve. I grew up using either the Sherwood 5030 with the Coffey curve or the Gretzky Titan. To this day, I still use a 5030 with the Coffey pattern. And I'm not alone. "That's the highest selling curve ever made. Sherwood had the best of the best back then. They had Flower [Guy Lafleur] and Ray Bourque. That curve, for whatever reason, has lasted a lifetime and it's every beer leaguer's dream.

"To this day, when I coach kids, there will be a men's league playing before us and guys are bumping and hammering on the glass, pointing to their sticks."

I've never considered myself to be an investigative reporter. I don't break news on a regular basis. I'm a sports anchor. I deliver the news and highlights. I'm a storyteller. But right now, I'm a news breaker. This is the biggest scoop of my life.

Beer leaguers refer to the stick as the Coffey curve. But I've got something to tell you, or, rather, Paul does. "That's not the curve I played with. If I had a curve that big, I would have been in the penalty box all game."

When Paul told me this, I was almost speechless. You mean to tell me the Coffey curve was not used by Paul Coffey? "Not that big. My curve wasn't small, but it definitely wasn't that big. The curve is not far off. But it's not bang on. But that's what they started selling. Maybe the curve was that way early on in my career but it wasn't that way at the end."

You never know what you're going to find out when you talk to someone about an old hockey card. Either way, I'll still continue to use the Coffey curve. Paul sums up the success of the curve like this: "If you're an average player, that puck will go to the top corner for you. That's what the people like."

"So you're telling me that's why I can pick the top corners?" I quickly respond.

Paul says, "Well, I'm not sure if you're an average player or you just like the top corner. I'm staying away from that."

For the record, I am a below-average player who does love the top corner. And thanks to the Coffey curve, I can hit it once in a while.

Coffey picked the corner a lot. And the second-highest scoring defenceman of all time still occasionally takes a gander at his old cards, trying to pinpoint just what moment in time was captured. "You know what I love doing? I love looking at a card and knowing what rink it's in. I just did a signing last weekend at the International Centre; there were a bunch of us there. Every time someone would come up with an item I'd show the security guy I was sitting beside and say, 'That's my first year.' He'd say, 'How do you know?' I'd say, 'Look at the blades. The blades of the skates were the first Tuuk blades they came out with, and they were see-through. They were a silver-grey Tuuk blade.' He goes, 'Man, you notice all that stuff?' I said, 'I notice everything.'

"All the cards definitely mean something to you. They mean a lot to the card holder, so it's gotta mean something to you."

THE FRANCHISE™

MIKE MODANO
North Stars™

Mike should be the cornerstone of the North Stars for years to come. A complete player with tremendous offensive skills, he's collected 57 goals and 139 points over his first two NHL seasons. "Playing with Mike gets me excited," said teammate Dave Gagner. "When we're going down the ice, it seems like I'm skating a little faster and the plays come a little faster."

SCORE

313

SCORE 91

THE FRANCHISE™
MIKE MODANO • North Stars™

MIKE MODANO

1990–91
SCORE #313

When the Minnesota North Stars drafted Mike Modano first overall in 1988, the hype machine started almost immediately. The tall, blond-haired, smooth-skating centre was going to carry this team on his back. "I think it probably started the day after the draft," says Modano over the phone from his home in Arizona.

Credit to the North Stars, though: they weren't a powerful team, but they didn't rush the kid. Modano returned to Prince Albert of the WHL for the season before he made his NHL debut in the '89 playoffs. In the fall of 1989, he made the NHL for good. The expectations seemed to come as quickly as his cards were produced back in the day. "At the time, the cards were very cool. We all thought it was kind of neat to see which cards were out there. The market just got pumped with a ton of them in the early '90s." Modano rookies flooded collectible stores. And in the boom years it seemed the goal of a lot of companies was to load their sets with as many versions of a Gretzky, Messier, or a guy like Modano as they could produce. In the Score set of 1991–92, 21 separate cards were labelled "The Franchise." Modano got the tag for Minny. It made sense: the team was staking its future on the 21-year-old.

Did he feel pressure?

"It was an exciting pressure. It made me focus. It made me get prepared. It made me work out. It made me train and do all these things that I needed to do in order to fulfill the expectations the organization had and hopefully solidify what kind a player I was."

I point out that Modano didn't even have any stubble on his face when the photo for this card was taken — he really was a kid. So many people were betting on him to deliver, however, as the back of the card clearly puts into context: "Mike should be the cornerstone of the North Stars for years to come."

"I think one of the benefits of being young is you don't really fully grasp the magnitude of the situation. The way sports were covered back then was really localized. You really didn't see too much outside of the town you played in. And, obviously, you didn't have all the games on TV.

You didn't have computers. You didn't have access to everything, at every minute of the day, so you really didn't have all that outside information about you. You just didn't have the ability to read or see what people were saying about you around the league. At that time, it was probably a good thing. I was just enjoying the game, having fun travelling around, hanging out with the older guys, enjoying the game, and still feeling like I was in Prince Albert playing with some kids. It really helped that I didn't have a ton of outside pressure."

I guess that's why guys say they don't read the papers or watch TV, but I don't really believe most modern players when they say they don't follow the media. Information is everywhere. But in Modano's case, there was a newspaper or two, and that was it. Information wasn't everywhere, and the kid just played hockey. The North Stars even moved "The Franchise" in with a local family. "That situation couldn't have worked out better, having all that stuff away from the rink taken care of for you . . . all you had to focus on was hockey."

On the ice, Modano responded. He averaged almost a point per game in his first four years in the league. He was thriving — though perhaps a better word is surviving — in the Norris Division. "It was a lot like Prince Albert. The WHL was about as tough of a league as I'd ever seen. But then, going to the Norris Division, you had Wendel Clark in Toronto: Tony Twist, Kelly Chase in St. Louis. You had Dave Manson and all these other animals in Chicago. It was really just a tough division. Every night you felt like you were skating for your life. You had to learn how to become a good skater and play the game with your head up. Otherwise they were going to take you out."

And you didn't have to just keep your head up during the game. You even had to be on your toes during the warm-up. Case in point? December 28, 1989, when the North Stars and Blackhawks had an all-out brawl during the warm-up. "Shane Churla went ballistic on Wayne Van Dorp. It was ugly — a whole melee. It was probably the ugliest thing I've seen."

Modano may have been just a rookie at the time, but he made a veteran move. When a brawl breaks out, you basically hold on to another guy. The idea is to make sure the opponent doesn't step out of line and join the fracas. Modano and a fellow young American on the Blackhawks found each other and embraced peacefully. "I had Jeremy Roenick at the time. We were both 18 or 19, so we were just wide-eyed. We could not believe what we were seeing. We just stayed away from the pile."

It was speed that separated Mike Modano from most of the players in the NHL. One of the things that I love about this card is, just like the Coffey card, it captures Modano in full flight. He's making a turn, a little bit of his hair swept up in the wind. The card, really, is a perfect picture of his game in 1991 and, for that matter, the rest of his career. "Speed was something I really prided myself in and worked on. At the end of my teenage years, I wanted to get really fast. I was always an advocate of trying to do everything at high speed with the puck. I knew there were guys who skated well without the puck, but there was only a handful of guys whose speed didn't alter what they did when they got the puck. Some guys get the puck and slow down. In practice, I tried to do everything with a puck. It drove Bob Gainey and Ken Hitchcock nuts that I would always have a puck to do everything, but there was a reason. For me that's something I tried to do because trying to make plays at a high speed with the puck, that's when you were really able to separate yourself from the defender and have a little more time to make a play."

Score may have put "The Franchise" tag on Modano early in his career, but he's the first to point out that he wasn't alone in Minny. He had a great supporting cast that set him on his way early in his career. "I was pretty lucky. I had some really great older guys. I had Neal Broten and Brian Bellows. My second year, Bobby Smith came in. Mike Gartner was there my first year, and Larry Murphy. I was around some pretty good guys who had at that point already had some great years and some consistent years. Basil McRae, Shane Churla — some guys who were really hard workers, who practiced hard, doing all the extra work that needed to be done that I probably didn't understand at the time. They made me really become disciplined."

You would think a young American superstar would be enough to make hockey thrive in Minnesota, but that wasn't the case. There is only so much a player can control, and just two years after the North Stars made the Cup Final in '91, Norm Green moved his team to Texas for the 1993–94 season. "It was just a business move. We were told that for the longest period of time. Sometimes you just have no control over what happens and you're just told where to go. We all thought, *How is this going to work down there?* We couldn't believe that they were plucking hockey out of Minnesota to move to Texas. We thought, *This is going to be a really tough sell.*"

But the Stars were an immediate hit in Dallas. And eventually, in 1999, Mike Modano validated "The Franchise" tag that everyone had placed on him when he helped the Dallas Stars win the Stanley Cup. "I think the pressure got a little bit more as you got older. We hadn't had any really good playoff runs since 1991, and time was of the essence. There are only these short windows that you have with these great teams and great players. From '97 until about 2002–03, we had a great group of guys and the kinds of great players that don't come around too often or get a chance to play on the same team. We knew it was kind of Cup or bust in 1999–2000. It was a total relief being able to pay back what the organization thought about me as a teenager. Gainey was there for quite a long time, so he saw the culmination of things. He had a lot of patience with me. Once the Cup was delivered, there was tons of relief."

"The Franchise" stayed in the Stars organization for 20 seasons. He is the Stars all-time leader in games played, goals, assists, and points.

Dino Ciccarelli
1998–99
UD Choice #93

I'll be honest, I didn't own this card in my younger days. By the time it came out, I was in my mid 20s and I didn't spend my time opening packs in card shops. I do have dozens of Dino Ciccarelli cards from my younger collecting days, but when you write a book like this and you talk to Dino Ciccarelli about one of his cards, I am pretty sure that you are required by law to discuss his 1998–99 Upper Deck Choice card. After all, as far as I can tell, it is the only hockey card in history to feature a rhinoceros beside a Hall of Famer.

The card was a result of an innocent little photoshoot at Busch Gardens while Ciccarelli was a member of the Tampa Bay Lightning. "The shoot was for the Lightning and for Busch Gardens. I thought it was going to be for internal use or advertising. I had no idea it was going to be turned into a hockey card," Ciccarelli says, laughing.

Can you blame Dino for thinking he and the rhino would never end up on cardboard together? That seems like a pretty safe assumption to me, especially when you consider that he was traded from Tampa Bay just a few days after he posed with his new 4,000-pound friend. On January 15, 1998, Ciccarelli was sent to the Florida Panthers in a four-player deal. The photo, one would assume, was history. Not so. Someone got their hands on this beauty and decided it was going to end up on a card. "They just superimposed the Panthers logo over the Lightning logo, and that's what they came up with."

A few short months later, the card hit the market. A guy who scored 608 regular-season goals and made his living in front of a net wasn't shown sniping or celebrating one of his hundreds of goals. Instead, he was shown feeding an animal that is described as "rather ill-tempered and have become more so in areas where they have been constantly disturbed."

"You don't want to piss off a rhino, or you get the horns," says Dino.

This comment, of course, demands an immediate follow-up question. Few players in the history of the NHL took more abuse in front of the net than Dino Ciccarelli. The guy lived on the edge of the blue paint.

Dino Ciccarelli paid the price to score goals and he was hacked and cross-checked nightly. So I have to ask: who was tougher — the rhino or Chris Pronger in front of the net?

"Chris Pronger," Ciccarelli says without hesitation. "But I was tougher after I got cross-checked. Then the horns would come out."

This card follows Ciccarelli everywhere; it's kind of tough for him to avoid the subject.

But, as Ciccarelli says, there's not much he can do about it. He and the rhino are out there, and they're not going away. He scored over 600 goals, is a Hall of Famer, and this is the card most collectors want to have in their collections. "The card with me tipping in a shot in front of the net and trying to score on Patrick Roy doesn't sell, but the card with me feeding a rhino does."

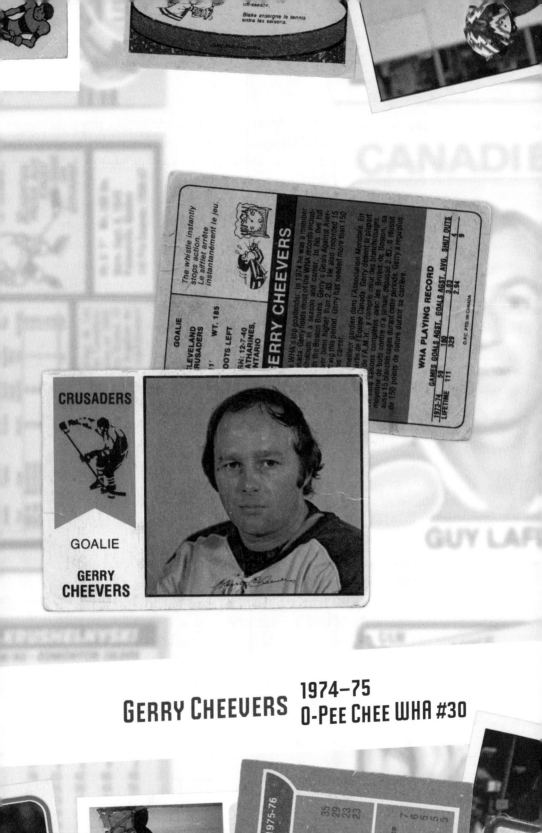

GERRY CHEEVERS

1974–75
O-Pee Chee WHA #30

Fittingly, I ran into Gerry Cheevers at a sports card show in Toronto, and that's where we started talking about this beauty. Gerry and I were doing an interview on his iconic stitches mask when I decided to do a little digging.

"That was with the Cleveland Crusaders. You can tell by the purple and white. There's no mask in this picture, but I definitely was using the mask there. I guess there aren't many masks on any of the card pictures."

That is true. This is a shot of Gerry in all of his glory, sans his famous lid. Cheevers talks about his mask all the time. What he doesn't talk about often are his days with the Crusaders. Likely because not a lot of people ask. He offers me this little tidbit: "You know the logo of the Cleveland Crusaders that was the lancer on a horse? Well, that was sort of my idea with [team owner] Nick Mileti. The idea was to make sure we had a horse on the logo. I loved the sweater.

"It's a unique card. The guy who took the picture was a novice, and he had no idea about hockey." The photog wanted Cheevers to strike a few poses. Cheevers complied. Luckily the standard hockey shot ended up on the card. "We had one picture holding the stick upside down. We were lucky to get this one, that's for sure."

Cheevers likely ended up with a novice photographer because big-league hockey was a new thing in Cleveland. Yes, the Barons were the AHL team that played in Cleveland from 1937 to 1973, but the WHA Crusaders were the big time. The WHA was set up to challenge the NHL. Bobby Hull was the first superstar to jump ship when he got his famous million-dollar deal, but other stars soon followed him to the rebel league for the inaugural season. Players like Derek Sanderson, Bernie Parent, and Cheevers made the switch. Many players likely wrestled with the decision to leave the NHL, but the then-32-year-old Cheevers wasn't one of them. "The deal I made didn't take guts. There was money involved, way more money than I would have ever made in five years in Boston. Some of the money was up front, and that's really what sealed the deal."

But Cheevers's move came at a cost — and it wasn't just that he would have to settle for novice hockey-card photographers for the next four seasons before returning to the NHL with the Bruins in January 1976. When Cheevers signed with the WHA, it cost him his spot on Team Canada in the 1972 Summit Series against the USSR. If you were in the WHA, you were not welcome on Team Canada. "In 1972, for the original Summit Series, Bobby Hull, J.C. Tremblay, and myself were picked to play on Team Canada, and they didn't allow us to play. And I know that hurt Bobby more than anything. I was glad I didn't play. And J.C. Tremblay was a tremendous hockey player who died too early, obviously. [Tremblay died of cancer in 1994 at the age of 55.] But I felt bad for Bobby Hull more than anyone. If anyone should have played in that series, it was him. It should not have been called Team Canada. It should have been called Team NHL."

But why didn't Cheevers want to suit up for the Summit Series? "I'll tell you a story that no one knows. When the '72 team was picked, head coach Harry Sinden told me that I was going to play the first game. And I said, 'Harry, I'm never in shape, let alone in September.' I'd likely be in shape by April. He said I had three months to get in shape. He said, 'I know I'll convince you, and you're going to play the first game.' It never happened."

While the Summit Series was going on, Gerry Cheevers was getting ready for his first season in the WHA. And by getting ready, I mean enjoying the summer. As you can see by the look of Cheevers on the front of this card, and he's the first to admit it, he wasn't exactly a fitness freak. The extent of Cheevers's off-season conditioning program would take place the night before the first day of training camp, and it went as follows: "I'd have to lose five pounds before I checked into camp. I'd jump into my car and put a garbage bag on, turn the heat up, and drive around for a couple hours. I'd be in the best shape of my life."

Cheevers has a theory as to why he looks so glum in this picture. It was taken at camp. "There was a reason I look that way: the workout the night before . . ."

Hall of Famer Cheevers is known for his years in Boston, his famous stitches mask, and his two Stanley Cup wins with the Bruins. But he wants you to know his time in Cleveland, though often overlooked, was a huge part of his career and his life. "Every year in the fall, we go to different spots in the country to play golf. Four of us get together: Gerry Pinder, Skippy Krake, Bobby Whidden the other goaltender, and myself. And we're still friends. If guys come through St. Catherines and I'm there in the summer, they'll stop in and we'll have a beer. It was a really close-knit team. I loved that team."

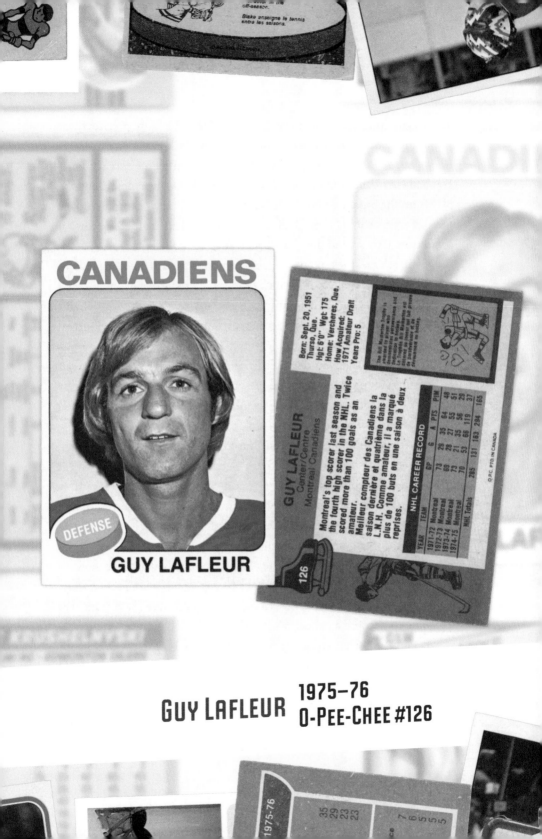

GUY LAFLEUR
1975–76
O-PEE-CHEE #126

There is nothing better than live television. Or, to be more precise, there is nothing better than live sports on television. Back in the 1970s, *Hockey Night in Canada* from the Montreal Forum offered the perfect scenario. You had Guy Lafleur flying on the ice and Danny Gallivan describing the play from the broadcast booth. It was magic, and dozens of times during the 1974–75 season, Danny Gallivan and Guy Lafleur teamed up for TV perfection. Guy scored the goals, and Danny described them.

If you ask me, the Lafleur-Gallivan combo peaked in the 1979 playoffs, when Guy blasted one past Bruins tender Gilles Gilbert. Don Cherry's Bruins were serving their infamous too-many-men-on-the-ice penalty, and the goal tied Game 7 of the Stanley Cup semifinal at 4. Montreal went on to win the series in OT.

This is how Gallivan described the goal: "Lafleur . . . coming out rather gingerly on the right side. He gives it in to Lemaire . . . back to Lafleur . . . he scores!" The perfect shot, low blocker side, accompanied by the perfect call made for perfect live television.

But trust me when I tell you, mistakes happen on live television. Sometimes you, the viewer, see them — sometimes we just roll with it and you don't even notice. So when it comes to mistakes, I'm rather forgiving. And so is a chuckling Guy Lafleur, when he sets his eyes on this old 1975–76 O-Pee-Chee that lists him, one of the greatest goal-scorers in the history of the game, as a defenceman.

"The first time I saw it, I said, 'What the hell's that?'" he says. "I thought, *The guys that are making the cards don't know much about hockey, or they don't follow the players.* I was laughing, and I'm sure I said, 'One day it's going to become a collector's item.' But I don't have one."

As Guy and I chat at the National in Chicago, I try to come up with a reason why the card makers might list him as a defenceman. Maybe they saw him on the point on the power play one night on *Hockey Night in Canada*? Scotty Bowman would use him on the blue line with the man-advantage. "I used to play a lot on the power play on the point. I loved it. We had such a great team at that time, and it was easy to play on the point."

What a terrifying thought: Guy Lafleur with his ripper of a slapshot, on the power play, with all that time and all that space. He says he had all that time and space not only because the other team was shorthanded, but also because of who the Habs had playing forward when they were on the power play. "[Jacques] Lemaire, [Steve] Shutt, [Yvan] Cournoyer. We had such a great offence that the two wingers on the other team didn't really check us on the point, because they were more worried about the three guys up front. It was not a tight game. It was more wide open at the point."

I'm smiling as I write this, just thinking of Guy Lafleur going unchecked with the man advantage. It must have been fun for No. 10.

"Yeah, it was," he says.

What's especially fitting, or unfitting, about this error card is the timing. Lafleur was listed as a defenceman after his breakout offensive season. After going number one in the 1971 NHL Draft, Lafleur jumped right into the Montreal Canadiens lineup from the Quebec Remparts. In his first three NHL seasons, he scored 29, 28, and 21 goals. Those numbers were considered somewhat underwhelming at the time. In his fourth season, 1974–75, he sniped 53, and he says it felt liberating. "Because people were expecting so much when I first came up, especially after Jean Beliveau's retirement. Everybody thought I would replace Jean Beliveau, but you don't replace a guy like that. But I had more ice time too. It was just a question of time. The first three years, I was not playing regularly, and I knew that if I got more ice time I would score more goals."

No one ever mistook Lafleur for a defenceman again. That 1974–75 season was his first of six straight with at least 50 goals or more. He and the Canadiens won four Cups in a row, starting in the spring of 1976. Lafleur led the way up front and, for the record, the Big Three of Larry Robinson, Serge Savard, and Guy Lapointe led the way on the blue line. "Those guys were competing so much together. It didn't matter who

they played with: Lapointe with Savard, Savard with Robinson, or vice versa. They were unbelievable."

It kind of makes me wonder, though: what if O-Pee-Chee was right, and Lafleur was a defenceman? Maybe it would have been the Big 4 instead of the Big 3. After all, if O-Pee-Chee was right and Guy was a defenceman, his 53 goals would be the most ever by a blue liner in a single season.

"No . . . I don't think I would have been a good defenceman." But he was a hell of a winger. And O-Pee-Chee never made that mistake again.

WAYNE GRETZKY

1979–80
O-Pee-Chee #18

In case you haven't realized, these little pieces of cardboard mean a lot to me. They are a connection to my childhood and to a game that I love. And no card epitomizes that more than Wayne Gretzky's rookie card.

As I stated before, as a kid in the 1980s I was a Montreal Canadiens fan, but I was smart enough to know that I was witnessing greatness every time No. 99 showed up on my television set. I knew, even through my youthful eyes, that my childhood was coinciding with the rise and prime of the greatest player to ever play the game.

And as a card-mad kid, I loved my Wayne Gretzky cards. He was the one guy I always wanted. I'd rip through pack after pack, just looking for that one guy. "Me too," says Gretzky. "I think as kids, we all wanted to get our favourite player. In my day, the best cards to get, so to speak, were always Gordie Howe, Bobby Orr, Jean Beliveau, and Gilbert Perreault. And it just seemed like you had to go through packs and packs before you could get that one card that you really wanted. Not to be critical, but I got a thousand Larry Hillmans," Gretzky laughs.

By the time I was around 13 or 14, my brother and I had collected every Gretzky card we wanted, except for one: the Gretzky rookie. No matter how hard we tried, no matter where we looked, we just couldn't find one. It seemed like no one could. When you'd attend a card show, you'd be lucky if you spotted one or two of them. If collectors had them, they weren't showing them off, they were likely stashing them away. The Gretzky rookie, my holy grail, seemed unattainable. Even if I saw one, I couldn't afford it anyway.

However, everything changed when my mom came home from an auction one day, with a box of cards. She told my brother Peter and I that the box cost her 10 bucks. Mom was always bringing home boxes of cards for us, hoping there would be a treasure inside. This time, we struck cardboard gold. My brother and I opened up the box, and we could not believe our eyes. Mom had gotten a box of *blue cards*. Gretzky's rookie was a *blue card*. We knew that maybe there was a chance our holy grail was stashed somewhere in that little treasure chest. We started going through the box. About halfway through, we came across it: a Gretzky rookie. It didn't matter to us that it had a crease or two. It didn't matter to us that someone had taken a marker to the bottom right corner of the card. We had a Gretzky rookie. We screamed. We jumped. We hugged. The second the buzz of discovering the blue Gretzky wore off, my brother and I dropped the gloves. There was only one Gretzky in the pile, and we both wanted it. We'd have to fight it out. The winner would own the Gretzky rookie.

With every body blow (Peter and I had an unwritten rule that we would not punch each other in the face), the thought of owning that blue Gretzky got closer and closer. Suddenly, Mom played the role of NHL referee Bruce Hood and put an end to the scrap. "Just share the card!" It was a great idea. We shared a bedroom, so why not share the Gretzky rookie. We both loved 99. We both loved the card. To this day, my brother and I joke that we share custody of our Gretzky rookie.

And now, three decades later, I'm talking about my Wayne Gretzky rookie card with Wayne Gretzky. And I want to know: when this card came out in 1979 did it mean anything to him? I mean, after all, he was already a household name by the final year of the 70s. He'd been in the spotlight since before he was a teenager. "Oh, yeah," says the NHL's all-time scoring leader. "The first time you see your first hockey card, it's a pretty nice feeling. I think that for anybody who becomes a professional athlete, to get a card, it's always a good feeling. So, for me, yes, it was exciting when I saw my first hockey card."

I just love this card. It's classic Gretzky. He's got the Titan, the tongues of his skates are sticking out and, of course, he has the JOFA lid. I, believe it or not, still wear the Gretzky JOFA helmet. I have to ask about it. I mean, the thing is a non–CSA approved piece of plastic with a piece of cork in the top. That's about it. I got mine in 1990. Gretzky got his when he joined the Oilers after a little trial and error at the start of his pro career with the WHA's Indianapolis Racers. "When I turned pro in '78, they really encouraged the young guys to take their helmets off. So when I went to my first training camp in Indianapolis I wasn't wearing a helmet."

Pause. Just think about that for a second. Wayne Gretzky flying down the ice, his hair flowing in the wind à la Guy Lafleur. That would have looked pretty cool, but his dad put the brakes on that quickly. "We were playing an intrasquad game in Indianapolis, and my dad happened to come to the game. During the warm-up, my dad came running down and said, 'Put your helmet on.' So I went into the locker room, and I was a little bit embarrassed, but I said to one of the guys, 'My dad says I should wear a helmet.' So I put one on."

It was a CCM bucket. It lasted only eight games. Gretzky was "sold or traded," as he says, to the Edmonton Oilers on November 2, 1978. Enter Wayne's new Edmonton teammate Dennis Sobchuk. "Dennis said, 'Kid. Wear this helmet; it's lighter. It's like not wearing a helmet.' So I put it on and I never took it off. That became my weapon of choice, so to speak, and that's how I got the JOFA helmet."

Man, I love talking about this card, but I'll let Wayne take it from here. "My card, the original first card, is a WHA picture. That's what's so crazy about it. If you look at it closely, it's a different emblem. We wore a different emblem in the WHA. It was orange lettering on the Oiler, which they changed the following year to the blue. If you look at the crest, it's a different colour."

I love that old orange logo; I also loved when the Oilers switched their uniforms back to the old WHA orange a few years ago. Now here's another detail about this card that I never knew: "In the WHA days, we wore white tape on our socks, and then when we went to the NHL, you had to use dark tape — either black or blue. It's very noticeable it's not an NHL picture."

And where this photo was taken was not even a regular WHA stop, at least not until 10 days of snow caused the roof of the Hartford Civic Center to collapse on January 8, 1978. The collapse forced the Whalers to play their home games in Springfield, Massachusetts. "[The photo] was taken at Springfield Arena. The roof had caved in at the Hartford Arena. So my first rookie card wasn't in the NHL, and it wasn't in an NHL arena."

This card means different things to different people. For me it's a time machine back to my childhood. It's the memory of the end of my most cherished childhood treasure hunt. For others, of course, it is an investment. In August 2016, a PSA 10 Gretzky rookie sold for $465,000 U.S. Mine won't get me that much. Not even close. That's not what this card-collecting nonsense is about for me, though. That's not to say that if I came across a stash of these, I wouldn't consider setting up a college fund for my kids. I think I'm a little too late for that, though. I should have gotten out of the gate early, like a friend of Wayne's did back in the day.

"I knew a guy from my hometown; he came to my door one day in about 1981, and he had 100 of my rookie cards in a box. I said, 'What are you doing?' And he goes, 'This is going to be my house one day.' And he ended up selling every card for about a thousand dollars. He made $100,000, and he bought a house. All I kept thinking was, *How dumb am I not to be collecting like he did?*"

A thought immediately pops into my head. "Why don't you look in Walter's basement! He's gotta have some of your rookie cards down there."

"Trust me, he doesn't," laughs 99. "Because I've looked."

Seems my brother and I weren't the only ones who went hunting for Gretzky rookies a long time ago.

Enjoy your cards. Enjoy the treasure hunt.

ACKNOWLEDGEMENTS

First off, a huge thank you to the players who I interviewed for this book. I know you've heard it before but it is the truth, hockey players are the best. Some of the men in this book didn't even make it to the NHL, others are the best of all time, but they all conducted themselves like Hall of Famers when they got a phone call from a stranger wanting to talk about an old hockey card. So I thank each and every one of you for your time and for sharing your stories.

A book like this does not happen without a very understanding family. A huge thank you to my wife and our two boys for their patience and understanding. Maybe one day I will pass my cards on to my boys; perhaps they will find them as fascinating as I do, but if they don't, at least they will know their old man got enough out of them to write a couple of books.

Massive thanks to my lit agent, Brian Wood, and to everyone at ECW, including Michael Holmes and Laura Pastore, for making this happen. Michael and Laura edited this book, so you can only imagine how patient they are.

I would like to say thank you to Sidney Crosby and Chris Carlin for taking the time to write the forewords for this book. It's always comforting to know that the best player in the game was a hockey card collector at one time as well. Both are Hall of Famers — on and off the ice and in and out of the sportscard world. Congrats to Chris for having his name included in the same sentence as Sid.

So many people helped bring this book together in a number of different ways. Google only goes so far in its power to locate people. I owe the following people huge thanks for helping me get in touch with some of the folks in this book. Thanks to James Dodds, Peter MacKay, Paul Coffey, Drew Mills (who will soon become an honouary Canadian along with Chris Carlin), Andrew Jackson and everyone at Jackson Events, the Legend Doug MacLean, Ken Whitmell, the Sports Card Expo, the National Sports Card Collectors Convention, Brian Ehrenworth, Colby Armstrong, Dennis Maruk, Jeff Azzopardi, and Hersh Borenstein.

Support is a huge thing when undertaking a project like this. Thank you to my co-workers at Sportsnet for listening to me go on and on about this book. That includes Evanka Osmak and Ryan Moynes. My big bosses seem to be cool with this whole writing thing as well, so thanks Steve Cassar, Rob Corte, and Scott Moore.

To Mom and Dad for buying me a ton of cards when I was a kid, to my brother Peter for collecting them with me, and to my sister Katie for not ripping all of them up (just some).

Hey, thank you, internet. Sites like hockeydb.com, hockey reference, and NHL trade tracker are big-time resources.

Additional thanks to Steve Fellin, Stephen Brunt, Jeff Marek, Don Cherry, Ron MacLean, The Bob, Daren Millard, Steve Dangle and *The Steve Dangle Podcast*, Joey Jerimiah, Terry Ryan, Terry Ryan Sr. for showing me his basement, Tim and Sid, the Calgary Hitmen, Nick Adonadis, Craig Clarke, Scott Landry, Troy Shanks, Robbie Forbes, Sandy MacKay, the Road Crew of Brian, Charlie, Ronnie, Russell, and

Dean. Plus, shoutouts to Barry, Carolyn, the Pictou Mariners, my hometown of Pictou, Hammer, and to everyone who bought this book, and the first one, too, of course.